BAMBOO LOTUS AND PALM

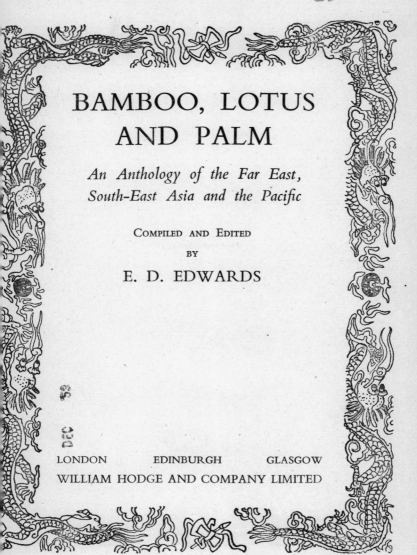

BAMBOO, LOTUS AND PALM

*An Anthology of the Far East,
South-East Asia and the Pacific*

COMPILED AND EDITED

BY

E. D. EDWARDS

LONDON   EDINBURGH   GLASGOW

WILLIAM HODGE AND COMPANY LIMITED

First Published 1948

MADE AND PRINTED IN GREAT BRITAIN BY
MORRISON AND GIBB LTD., LONDON AND EDINBURGH

*T*HE illustrations throughout the book are copied from old Chinese and Japanese art manuals and artists' note-books, many of the lively little Japanese figures being sketches by Hokusai.

CONTENTS

PREFACE

After more than five and a half years of armed conflict, during which one's outlook became so narrowed that the conditions of war came almost to be accepted as normal and unavoidable, it was a relief to turn, on the sudden cessation of hostilities, to view the East as it appeared to travellers who visited it in more inquiring if no less acquisitive times. It was a delight to discover how vividly they recorded their impressions, and with what confidence in themselves they took what they could wherever they went. ' What have these people to gain from civilization ? ' asked one. ' Pondering on the fate of other aboriginal tribes brought into contact with the white, I was ready to wish they had never been seen by us. But considerations of this kind cannot be entertained by those who see a simple duty before them and have the means to execute it. We were not responsible for the issues, and Providence may surely be trusted to work out its own ends.'

Bamboo, Lotus and Palm symbolize South-East Asia, the Far East and the Pacific, and out of a year's reading about these areas this anthology materialized. I hope it may interest some of the many thousands of men and women whose duties took them there during the war years, as well as others to whom the peoples of the East are no longer dwellers in a separate world. How different from ourselves and yet how like they are may at least be guessed from the glimpses into their lives and their minds allowed by the limitations of a small anthology.

E. E.

ACKNOWLEDGMENTS

THE Editor desires to express personal thanks to Miss F. R. Andrews, for permission to quote from the writings of the late Venerable Archdeacon Dr. John Batchelor; Lady Arnold, for the use of an extract from *Japonica*, by the late Sir Edwin Arnold; Dr. E. Hadfield, for allowing her to quote from *Among the Natives of the Loyalty Group*; Lady G. E. Scott, for a quotation from *The Burman, his Life and Notions*, by the late Sir J. G. Scott, who wrote under the pen-name Shway Yoe; Professor Kochi Doi, who long ago granted permission to include an extract from *Diaries of Court Ladies of Old Japan*, by Anne S. Omori and Kochi Doi; Mrs. Percival Lowell, for allowing the use of two passages from *Occult Japan*, by the late Percival Lowell, and Mr. K. M. Yamaguchi for extracts from *We Japanese*.

For permission to quote from the books named in the list that follows the Editor also extends her thanks to the following Authors (or their representatives) and Publishers:

J. J. Abraham, M.D., for *The Surgeon's Log* (Chapman & Hall); N. Allen, M.D., for *Korean Tales* (G. P. Putnam's Sons); Sir Edwin Arnold, for *Adzuma, or The Japanese Wife* (Longmans, Green); J. Dyer Ball, for *Things Chinese* (Sampson Low); T. F. Bevan, for *Toil, Travel and Discovery in British New Guinea* (Kegan Paul, Trench, & Trübner); Mrs. I. Bishop, for *Korea and her Neighbours* (John Murray); Carl Bock, for *Temples and Elephants* and *The Headhunters of Borneo* (Sampson Low); J. Ingram Bryan, M.D., for *Japanese All* (Methuen); F. W. Burbidge, for *The Gardens of the Sun* (John Murray); W. R. Carles, for *Life in Korea* (Macmillan); B. H. Chamberlain, for *The Classical Poetry of the Japanese* (Trübner); R. H. Codrington, D.D., for *The Melanesians* (Clarendon Press); C. F. Gordon Cumming, for *At Home in Fiji* and *Wanderings in China* (Blackwood); G. Dumoutier, for *Les Chants et les Traditions Populaires des Annamites* (Presses Universitaires de France); Sir John Foster-Fraser, for *Round the World on a Wheel* (Methuen); W. E. Griffis, for *Corea, the Hermit Nation* (W. H. Allen) and *The Mikado's Empire* (Harper Bros.); F. H. H. Guillemard, M.D., for *The Cruise of the Marechesa* (John Murray); H. H. Guppy for *The Solomon Islands* (Kegan Paul); Lafcadio Hearn, for *Glimpses of Unfamiliar Japan*, *Kokoro* and *Out of the East* (Osgood; McIlvaine); *In Ghostly Japan* (Sampson Low); *Kottō* (The Macmillan Co.); and *Kwaidan* (Jonathan Cape); Raden Adjeng Kartini, for *Letters of a Javanese Princess* (Duckworth); P. Lowell, for *Chosön, the Land of Morning Calm* (Trübner); Charles Lyne, for *New Guinea* (Sampson Low); E. H. Man, for *On the Aboriginal Inhabitants of the Andaman Islands* (Trübner); A. B. Mitford, for *Tales of Old Japan* (Macmillan); A. E. Moule, for *New China and Old* (Seeley & Co.); K. Okakura, for *The Book of Tea* (G. P. Putnam's Sons); Y. Okakura, for *The Japanese Spirit* (Constable); C. D. Paske, for *Life and Travel in Lower Burma* (W. H. Allen); G. Pratt (Translator), for *Some Folk Songs and Myths from Samoa* (The Royal Society of New South Wales); Sir. E. J. Reed, K.C.B., for *Japan, its History . . . and Religions* (John Murray); Sir E. M. Satow, K.C.M.G., for *The Voyage of Capt. John Saris to Japan* (The Hakluyt Society); D. M. Smeaton, for *The*

Acknowledgments

Loyal Karens of Burma (Kegan Paul, Trench, & Trübner) ; H. Warrington Smyth, for *Five Years in Siam* (John Murray) ; K. Suyematsu, for *Genji Monogatori* (Trübner) ; Sir F. A. Swettenham, for *About Perak* (Straits Times) ; W. R. Winston, for *Four Years in Upper Burma* (Epworth Press) ; F. Younghusband, for *Among the Celestials* (John Murray).

The Editor has endeavoured to trace all copyrights and to make correct acknowledgment of the sources of all extracts in this Anthology.

INTRODUCTION TO THE EAST

How describe an Eastern dawn? Sight alone will give a true impression of its strange beauty. Out of darkness and stillness, the transition to light—intense, brilliant light—and the sounds of awakened life, is rapid and complete, a short half-hour or less turning night into tropical day. The first indication of dawn is a grey haze, then the clouds clothing the western hills are shot with pale yellow and in a few minutes turn to gold, while eastern ranges are still in darkness. The light spreads to the western slopes, moves rapidly across the valleys and suddenly the sun, a great ball of fire, appears above the eastern hills. The fogs, which have risen from the rivers and marshes and covered the land as with a pall, rise like smoke and disappear, and the whole face of the land is flooded with light, the valleys and slopes of the eastern ranges being the last to feel the influence of the risen sun.

That grey half-light which preceded dawn is the signal for the Malays to be stirring. The doors are opened and, only half awake and shivering in the slight breeze made by the rising fog, they leave their houses and make for the nearest stream, there to bathe and fetch fresh water for the day's use.

SWETTENHAM

February 13, 1877.

I must tell you about a wonderful effect of phosphorescence which I have seen on the last two nights when looking down from my window on the lovely little bay. On Sunday the 11th there had been violent thunderstorms, with vivid lightning and downpours of rain, leaden skies, and a bright green sea. So heavy were the rainstorms that the whole bay was discoloured by the red mud washed down by the streamlets—a strange contrast to its usually faultless crystalline green. I chanced to look out about 11 p.m., and saw the whole bay glowing with pale white light ; and fiery wavelets rippled right up beneath the trees and round the rocks, which stood out sharp and black. The effect was of a sea of living light, and as I beheld it, framed by dark trees, with tall flowering aloes cutting black against the dazzling light, it was a weird and wonderful scene. For about ten minutes I watched it entranced, then it slowly faded away, and the scene was changed to dense obscurity. Last night I looked out at the same hour, and saw nothing but darkness, but about midnight I was awakened by a deafening crash of thunder, followed by heavy rain. I guessed this would stir up whatever creatures caused the strange light. Perhaps they are disturbed by the rain-drops, or perhaps they receive a small electric shock which starts them all dancing. Whatever be the cause, the result proved as I expected. Ere I could reach the window, the bay was illuminated by tiny ripples of fire, which gradually increased in size and number till all was one blaze of glowing, dazzling light. This lasted for about five minutes and then died completely away.

CUMMING, *At Home in Fiji*

*

The seventh (September, 1613) in the morning much raine, with wind encreasing all day and night variable, from the East to the South, and in the night happened such a storme or Tuffon (typhoon), that I never saw the like in all my life ; neither was the like seene in this Countrey in mans memory, for it overthrew above a hundred houses in Firando, and uncovered many others ; . . . and the Sea went so high that it undermined a great Wharfe or Key at the Dutch House, and brake down the stone-wall, and carryed away their Staires, and sunke and brake them two Barkes ; as also forty or fifty other Barkes were broken and sunke in the Roade. It brake down our Kitchen wall at the English House, which was newly made, and flowed into our Oven, and brake it down and blew downe the tyles, and uncovered part both of the house and kitchen, and the house did shake like as if there had beene an Earthquake. I never passed night in all my life in such feare, for the barbarous unruly people did run up and downe the streets all night with fire-brands, that the wind carried great coales quite over the tops of houses, and some houses being carryed away, the wind whirled up the fire which was in them, and carryed it into the air in great flakes, very fearfull to behold ; so that the greatest feare I had was that all would have been consumed with fire. And verily I think it had, had it not been for the extreame raine which fell (contrary to the true nature of a Tuffon), being accompanied with lightning and thunder. Our shippe roade at anchor with five Cables, and as many Anchors, whereof one old Cable burst, but God be thanked no other hurt was done.

SARIS

*

January 1826.

While we were off Clermont Tonnere we had a narrow escape from a water-spout of more than ordinary size. It approached us amid heavy rain, thunder and lightning, and was not seen until it was very near to the ship. As soon as we were within its influence a gust of wind obliged us to take in every sail, and the topsails, which could not be furled in time, were in danger of splitting. The wind blew with great violence, momentarily changing its direction, as if it were sweeping round in short spirals; the rain, which fell in torrents, was also precipitated in curves with short intervals of cessation. Amidst this thick shower the water-spout was discovered, extending in a tapering form from a dense stratum of cloud to within thirty feet of the water, where it was hid by the foam of the sea being whirled upwards with a tremendous giration. . . . It changed its direction after it was first seen, and threatened to pass over the ship; but being diverted from its course by a heavy gust of wind, it gradually receded. On the dispersion of this magnificent phenomenon we observed the column to diminish gradually, and at length to retire to the cloud from whence it had descended, in an undulating form.

Various causes have been assigned for these formations, which appear to be intimately connected with electricity. On the present occasion a ball of fire was observed to be precipitated into the sea, and one of the boats, which was away from the ship, was so surrounded by lightning that it was thought advisable to get rid of the anchor by hanging it some fathoms under water.

BEECHEY

We had a very pleasant day; my trusty valet plied the paddle and swept us gently along the margin of the water, beneath the shades of the overhanging thickets. Fayaway and I reclined in the stern of the canoe, on the very best terms possible with one another;

the gentle nymph occasionally placing her pipe to her lip, and exhaling the mild fumes of the tobacco, to which her rosy breath added a fresh perfume. . . .

This lovely piece of water was the coolest spot in all the valley, and I now made it a place of continual resort during the hottest period of the day. One side of it lay near the termination of a long, gradually expanding gorge, which mounted to the heights that environed the vale. The strong trade wind, met in its course by these elevations, circled and eddied about their summits, and was sometimes driven down the steep ravine and swept across the valley, ruffling in its passage the otherwise tranquil surface of the lake.

One day, after we had been paddling about for some time, I disembarked Kory-Kory, and paddled the canoe to the windward side of the lake. As I turned the canoe, Fayaway, who was with me, seemed all at once to be struck with some happy idea. With a wild exclamation of delight, she disengaged from her person the ample robe of tappa which was knotted over her shoulder, and spreading it out like a sail, stood erect with upraised arms in the head of the canoe. We American sailors pride ourselves upon our straight clean spars, but a prettier little mast than Fayaway made was never shipped aboard of any craft.

MELVILLE, *Typee*

★

It was a cloudy, sultry afternoon ; the seamen were lazily lounging about the decks, or vacantly gazing over into the lead-coloured waters. Queequeg and I were mildly employed weaving what is called a sword-mat, for an additional lashing to our boat. So still and subdued, and yet somehow preluding, was all the scene, and such an incantation of revelry lurked in the air, that each silent sailor seemed resolved into his own invisible self.

I was the attendant, or page, of Queequeg, while busy at the mat. As I kept passing and repassing the filling or woof of marline between the long lines of the warp, using my own hand for the shuttle, and as Queequeg, standing sideways, ever and anon slid his heavy oaken sword between the threads, and idly looking off upon the water, carelessly and unthinkingly drove home every yarn ; I say so strange a dreaminess did there then reign all over the ship and all over the sea, only broken by the intermitting dull sound of the sword, that it seemed as if this were the Loom of Time, and I myself were a shuttle mechanically weaving and weaving away at the Fates . . . and here, thought I, with my own hand I ply my own shuttle and weave my own destiny into these unalterable threads. Meanwhile, Queequeg's impulsive, indifferent sword, sometimes hitting the woof slantingly, or crookedly, or strongly, or weakly, as the case might be ; and, by this difference in the concluding blow, producing a corresponding contrast in the final aspect of the completed fabric ; this savage's sword, thought I, which thus finally shapes and fashions both warp and woof, this easy, indifferent sword must be chance—aye, chance, free-will and necessity—no wise incompatible—all interweavingly working together. The straight warp of necessity, not to be swerved from its ultimate course—its every alternating vibration, indeed, only tending to that ; free-will still free to ply her shuttle between given threads ; and chance, though restrained in its play within the right lines of necessity, and sideways in its motions directed by free-will, though thus prescribed to by both, chance by turns rules either and has the last featuring blow at events.

. . . Thus we were weaving and weaving away when I started at a sound so strange, long drawn, and musically wild and unearthly, that the ball of free-will dropped from my hand, and I stood gazing up at the clouds, whence that voice dropped like a wing. High aloft in the cross-trees was that mad Tashtego. His body was reaching eagerly forward, his hand stretched out like a wand, and at brief sudden intervals he continued his cries. To be sure, the same sound was at that very moment, perhaps, being heard all over the seas, from hundreds of whalemen's look-outs perched as high in the air ; but from few of those lungs could that accustomed old cry have derived such a marvellous cadence as from Tashtego the Indian's.

As he stood hovering over you half suspended in air, so wildly and eagerly peering towards the horizon, you would have thought him some prophet or seer beholding the shadows of Fate, and by those wild cries announcing their coming.

' There she blows ! There ! There ! There ! She blows ! She blows ! '

MELVILLE, Moby Dick

★

Dec. 14, 1844.—. . . I now hoped to have some leisure to make inquiries on many points concerning which I felt an interest, when unfortunately I was attacked with fever. It appeared, however, of trifling character ; it went off in four or five days, and in ten I was able to walk about, apparently as well as ever. But I no longer felt the same person ; languor and lassitude took possession of both mind and body, and I seemed to pass at once into the state of those who have been long resident in hot countries, and to have acquired all their listlessness and indifference, want of energy and want of curiosity. Neither was this state of mind transient ; I could not overcome it for two or three months after we left Java, and now, for the first time, I knew how to account for and excuse what at first seemed to me the blameable inertness, indolence and indifference to anything beyond the comfort of the passing hour, the want of energy and action so almost universally characteristic of the resident in hot countries. The European, at his first arrival, brings with him the feelings and powers belonging to a temperate zone, which are acted upon by the powerful excitement of new and delightful scenes, and he wonders at and contemns the apathy of the native or the resident European. Either by the sudden attack of sickness or the gradual action of the climate, however, his own energy is undermined and he eventually falls into the same listlessness and love of repose.

Another apparent consequence of the fever was an attack of ' prickly heat,' as it is called. When slight it is of no consequence, but when it acquires the virulence with which it attacked me it becomes a real affliction. My body seemed to be surrounded by an invisible padding of the finest possible needle-points, and every motion, whether of a limb or of the muscles of the hand or face, seemed to cause them to be pressed into the skin. Drinking a glass of water, or doing anything which caused a flow of perspiration to the skin, produced this exquisitely painful sensation over the whole of it, from the crown of the head to the sole of the foot, and every motion or pressure for some minutes after sent fresh gleams of tingling flashing along it. . . . It bears the exact relation to a mortal fever that a cloud of mosquitoes does to a tiger.

JUKES

THE LANDS

BURMESE PROVERBS

If you want to travel fast keep to the old roads.

*

Any bird is handsome compared with the vulture.

*

A mountain is climbed by degrees ; property acquired by degrees ; wisdom learned by degrees.

*

The more you know the better your luck.

*

A short boat is hard to steer ; a dwarf is quick in the temper.

*

If a cock ruffles up his feathers he is easy to pluck ; if a man loses his temper he will get the worst of the argument.

THE ISLAND OF ANDAMAN

(Fourteenth Century)

Andaman is a very large island. The people are without a king
and are idolators, and no better than wild beasts. And I assure you
all the men of this island of Andaman have heads like dogs, and
teeth and eyes likewise ; in fact, in the face they are all just like big
mastiff dogs ! They have a quantity of spices ; but they are a most
cruel generation, and eat everybody that they can catch, if not of
their own race. They live on flesh and rice and milk, and have
fruits different from any of ours.

M. Polo

★

1863

Near the centre of the track of one of the greatest highways of
commerce, traversed by ships of the most civilized and enlightened
nations of modern times, lie a small group of islands, the name and
position of which may be found in the map, although our knowledge
of them is in general very limited. Forming an almost invisible
dot on the map of the world, the civilization of both the East and
the West has passed them by without in any way affecting the
condition of their inhabitants.

The Andaman Archipelago, the group of islands to which we
allude, is situated in the Bay of Bengal. All of them are clothed
with the richest tropical vegetation which, from the level of the
lowest swamp to the summit of the highest hill, grows in that

unrestrained profusion in which Nature indulges in such climates. The entire group is surrounded in every direction by a natural fortress of coral reefs which, extending for many miles, guards the approach to the islands, and in stormy weather, or in dark nights, renders it a matter of no little difficulty, and attended with considerable danger, to attempt to land upon them.

MOUAT

(1883)

The natural beauty of the scenery of the Andamans never fails to awaken the admiration of every visitor. ' Of all the places I have seen in Europe,' writes one, ' Killarney alone can convey an idea of these scenes. The blue waters, the luxuriant emerald green vegetation down the margin of the coast, and the passing showers which brighten all the aspects of nature, have their counterpart here.'

In the records of certain Arabian travellers of the ninth century we appear to find the first mention of these islands being inhabited by negritos, and Marco Polo, some four hundred years later, bears out their statement.

The modern history of the Andamans may be said to date from 1857, when the scheme of founding a penal settlement and harbour of refuge in these islands, which had been under consideration for a few years, was precipitated by the events connected with the Sepoy mutiny.

MAN

The Lands

ANGKOR

(1864)

In the province still bearing the name of Angkor are ruins of such grandeur, remains of structures which must have been raised at such an immense cost of labour that, at the first view, one is filled with profound admiration, and cannot but ask what has become of this powerful race, so civilized, so enlightened, the authors of these gigantic works ?

One of these temples—a rival to that of Solomon, and erected by some ancient Michael Angelo—might take an honourable place beside our most beautiful buildings. It is grander than anything left us by Greece or Rome, and presents a sad contrast to the state in which the nation is now plunged, and if you interrogate the Cambodians as to the founders of Angkor Wat you invariably receive one of the following replies : 'It is the work of Pra-Eun, the king of the angels,' 'It is the work of the giants,' 'It was built by the leprous king,' or else, 'It made itself.'

MOUHOT

BATAVIA

(1762)

The ground for about ten or twelve miles round Batavia is pretty well cultivated. The gentlemen have their country houses, gardens, and ponds, after the Dutch mode ; and must always keep a numerous retinue of servants well armed. The Dutch grandees have their pleasure houses and gardens on small islands in the bay, where they pass to and from one another in boats built for the purpose. These islands, being shaded with groves, are very cool and pleasant.

East Indies

(1800)

If a stranger should happen to make his first entrance into the city of Batavia about the middle of the day, he would be apt to conclude it deserted by the inhabitants. At this time the doors and windows are all shut, and not a creature, except perhaps a few slaves, is stirring in the streets. But if he should enter the city in the morning or the evening, his eye will not be less attracted by the vast crowds of people moving about in the streets than by the very great variety of dress and complexion which these crowds exhibit.

That class of men which bears a complete sway over the island is by much the least numerous ; it is rare to see a ' right honourable high-born Dutchman ' condescending to walk the streets. ' Nothing from Europe,' he observes, ' but Englishmen and dogs walk in Batavia.' Whenever he has occasion to take this kind of exercise, he puts on his full-dress suit of velvet, and is attended by a suitable retinue of slaves. But the Armenians, the Persians and the Arabs, always grave and intent on business ; the half-caste merchants from Hindostan ; and above all, the Chinese, some in long satin gowns reaching to their heels and others in large umbrella hats, short jackets and wide, long trowsers ; the Javanese loitering carelessly along, as if indifferent to everything around them ; the free Malays looking with suspicion on all who come across them ; and slaves from every nation and country of the East, condemned to trudge in the same path with the carriages—all these, in the earlier and latter parts of the day, may be seen bustling in crowds in the streets of Batavia.

BARROW, *Voyage to Cochin China*

★

If you use the pole going downstream even the crocodiles will laugh.

Malayan Proverb

(1811)

The road of Batavia is justly esteemed one of the best in the world, as well with regard to the anchoring-ground, which consists of soft clay, as to the safety it affords the ships which anchor in it, and to the number which it can contain.

The Dutch seem to have pitched upon Batavia for the convenience of water-carriage ; and in that respect it is, indeed, a second Holland, and superior to every other place in the world. There are very few streets in the city without a canal of considerable breadth running through, or rather stagnating in, them, and continuing for several miles beyond the town, intersecting, together with five or six rivers, in almost every direction, the dead flat in which it is situated ; nor is this the worst, for the fence of every field and garden is a ditch ; and interspersed among the cultivated ground are many filthy fens, bogs and morasses, as well fresh as salt ; nay, such is the influence of habit, both upon the taste and understanding, that the Governor-General, whose country house was situated upon the only rising ground near Batavia, contrived, at some trouble and expense, to enclose his own garden with a ditch. . . .

The English, who circumnavigated the globe, 1768–1770, and had experienced almost every vicissitude of climate, declared that Batavia was not only the most unhealthy place they had seen, but that this circumstance was a sufficient defence or preservative against any hostile attempts, as the troops of no nation would be able to withstand, nor would any people in their senses, without absolute necessity, venture to encounter, this pestilential atmosphere.

STOCKDALE

*

A son who knows more than his father is a light to his family.
Javanese Proverb

The Lands

(1832)

The sea near Batavia is covered with innumerable little islets, all of which are clothed with luxuriant vegetation. Native prahus, with their yellow mat sails, are occasionally seen to shoot from behind one of them, to be shielded from view immediately afterwards by the green foliage of another ; and over the tops of the trees may often be descried the white sails of some stately ship, threading the mazes of this little archipelago. As we rounded Ontang Japa point on the 2nd of September a large number of fishing-boats were coming in from sea, and standing with us into the roads ; and although we were running at the rate of seven knots an hour, they passed us with great rapidity. They had a most graceful appearance : many of them were fourteen or fifteen tons burthen, and each boat carried one immense sail. As the breeze was strong, a thick plank was thrust out to windward for an outrigger, on which several of the numerous crew sat, or stood, to prevent the press of sail they were carrying from capsizing the boat. They were occasionally hidden from our view by their passing behind some of the small islets ; but in a few seconds they would appear on the other side, having shot past so rapidly that we could scarcely fancy that we had lost sight of them at all.

EARL

★

A CHINESE VIEW

Batavia is a fertile country on the sea-shore, an extensive region in the extreme south-west. Setting sail from Amoy . . . it is calculated that the voyage is about 280 ship's watches.

The city faces the north, and is bounded on the south by a range of volcanoes, as a sort of screen, beyond which is the southern ocean. To the left lies Bantam, and to the right Cheribon, while before it are spread out the fortified islands. The gates of the city are strong, and the walls are high; the territory is extensive, and the streets are wide, merchandise is abundant, and all the tribes of foreigners assemble there; truly it is a great emporium. But the situation is low and the climate sultry, all the four seasons being as warm as our summer. The river water is, however, cool and pleasant, and bathing in it keeps off disease. . . . Articles of commerce generally come from the neighbouring states, being conveyed to Batavia for the purpose of traffic, and are not the production of the place itself.

The virtuous influence of our (Chinese) government extending far, all the foreigners have submitted, and thus mercantile intercourse is not prohibited.

The territory of Batavia originally belonged to the Javanese, but the Dutch, having by strategem got possession of the revenues, proceeded to give orders and enact laws. The Hollanders have long noses and red hair; they are deep-scheming and thoughtful, and hence they acquire such an influence over the natives. They are very much like the man who stopped his ears while stealing a bell. . . . They scarcely possess one of the five cardinal virtues. . . . Of the single quality of sincerity, however, they possess a little.

I should say that these lands of the western ocean have something agreeable in them, and something to be lamented. The climate is not cold; all the flowers are in bloom during the four seasons; in the time of our winter the nights are rainy and the days fine—truly an enchanting state of things and very agreeable. The soil is rich and fertile, and necessaries are cheap and easily procured. A peck of rice can be bought for a few cash, fowls and ducks are cheaper even than vegetables, and for a mere trifle you can obtain an attendant. This is a cheap state of things and very agreeable. But there are no writings of philosophers and poets wherewith to beguile the time; nor any friends of like mind to soothe one's feelings;

no deep caverns or lofty towers to which one could resort for an excursion ; all which is very much to be lamented.

WANG TA-HAI (abridged)

BORNEO

(1843)

THE Island of Borneo, throughout the whole of the N.E. coast, is, with few exceptions, a low land, covered with jungle ; but so beautifully verdant does it appear when viewed from some distance that you would be led to suppose that it is widely cultivated. The idea is, however, soon dispelled on a near approach, when you discover the rich groups of acacias, palms, pandani, and numerous trees as yet unknown, so luxuriant in themselves, but forming one entangled mass, alike impenetrable to European or native. What, in the distant view, we fancied a meadow, where we might relax from our long confinement, and amuse ourselves with recreation, now proved to be ranges of long damp grass interspersed with swamps and infested with venomous snakes. In short, I never yet was on a coast which, on arriving on it, promised so much, and, on landing, caused such a series of disappointments as the coast of Borneo.

MARRYAT

★

Bruni is called the Venice of the East ; and the name is so far correct that it is built in the same peculiar way, and is a most extraordinary town. It is built almost entirely on the water, where the river forms a wide and shallow estuary, and with but little regard to regularity. There are, however, two large main streets, intersecting each other in the form of an irregular cross. These divide the town into four parts, one of which is partly built upon terra firma, while the other three portions are composed of wooden houses built upon piles, and just sufficiently separated here and there to admit of the passage of a canoe. It was in the main street, and as near as possible in the centre of the town, that our steamer was anchored.

Ibid.

*

We disembarked at a Chinese village twenty-five miles from Kuchin. We remained there for the night, and the next morning proceeded further up the river and landed at another village, where we breakfasted. Our path lay through dense forests of gigantic trees, whose branches met and interlaced overhead, shading us from the burning rays of the sun. At times we would emerge from the wood, and find ourselves passing through cultivated patches of ravines, enclosed on all sides by lofty mountains, covered with foliage. In these spots we found a few natives with their families, who seemed to be contented with their perfect isolation ; for in these secluded spots generations may pass away and know no world beyond their own confines of forest jungle. At times our route was over mountains, whose appearance was so formidable that our hearts almost failed us at the prospect of having to scale them ; but we succeeded beyond our expectations, and at length arrived at the village not a little pleased at our labours being ended.

A short distance inland is a mountain called Sarambo, which seen from the village wore the appearance of a large sugar-loaf, and its sides appeared inaccessible. After a hurried breakfast we set off next morning for the foot of the mountain, our party amounting to about eighty people. The guides led the way, followed by the Europeans ; and the Dyaks with the luggage brought up the rear. In this order we commenced the ascent. Each person was provided with a bamboo, which was found indispensable ; and thus, like a party of pilgrims, we proceeded on our way ; and before we had gone very far we discovered that we were subjected to very severe penance. The mountain was nearly perpendicular. In some places we had to ascend by a single piece of wood, with rough notches for the feet, resting against a rock twenty or thirty feet above our heads ; and on either side was a precipice, so that a false step must have been certain death. In other places a single piece of bamboo was thrown over a frightful chasm, by way of bridge. This, with a slight bamboo rail for the hand, was all that we had to trust to. The careful manner in which we passed these dangers was a source of great laughter and amusement to the Dyaks who followed us. Accustomed from infancy to tread these dangerous paths, although heavily laden, they scorned to support themselves. Some of our party were nearly exhausted and a long way in the rear before we came to the village. We had to wait for them coming up, and threw ourselves under the shade of some huge trees that we might contemplate the bird's eye view beneath. It was a sight which must be seen to be appreciated. Almost as far as the eye could reach was one immense wooded plain, bounded by lofty mountains in the far distance, whose top pierced the clouds. We ourselves were far above the clouds, which would break, and open, and pass and repass over each other until, like the dissolving views, all was clear again, although the landscape was not changed.

Ibid.

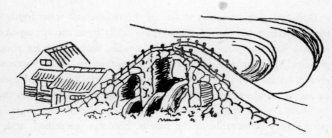

(1840)

As the sun went down the scene was beautiful, animated by the variety and picturesque appearance of the native prahus, and the praying of the Musulman, with his face in the direction of the prophet's tomb, bowing his head to the deck of his boat and absorbed in devotions, from which nothing could withdraw his attention. For a time, it being that of preparing the evening meal, no noise was made ; it was a perfect calm, and the rich foliage was reflected in the water as in a mirror ; while a small cloud of smoke ascended from each boat, to say nothing of that from my cigar, which added much to the charm I then experienced.

MUNDY

★

(1880)

A lover of nature who sees a tropical country for the first time cannot help but enjoy the bright light and heat, and the glories of flowers, fruit and leaf called forth by the rain and sunshine—of a clime where winter is unknown. And yet, with all the sunshine and showers, the tropical blossoms are in a way aristocratic and exclusive, and never mingle socially in bosky masses as do our own wildlings.

During a year's rambles in one of the richest and most fertile of tropical islands (Borneo) I saw nothing really fresh and spring-like ; nothing like the green and gold of daffodils, and the tender young grass of April, or the royal glory of a summer iris, or an autumnal crocus on its mossy bed. This much is ever lacking in the forest primeval ; and even in gardens—Eastern gardens—beautiful as they undoubtedly are in many ways, the sameness, the cloying degree of permanency observable in the forests, becomes intensified, and so still more unsatisfying. The plants seem always to present the same aspect ; and although most of them are at their best when revived by the rains, just after the dry season, yet the charm of freshness is destroyed by the number of evergreens everywhere and the driblets of bloom kept up by them nearly all the year round.

Still the beauty of tropical gardens is lovely of its kind. You have, or may have, all the tropical treasures of Kew—palms, ferns and orchids—around you in the open air ; but all this is as the beauty of a lovely woman jaded by over-enjoyment, the whirl of a whole season's gaieties. There is elegance of form, and charm of colour, all the refinement of cultured beauty. Victoria water-lilies, and dainty nymphæas in open-air pools, the fresh-tinted blooms of the sacred lotus also ; the noble amherstia, with its pendants of crimson and gold ; groves of feathery palms—all this and more is common ; but it is astonishing how soon one tires of this plethora of floral charms, and how eager becomes the longing to sniff the homely fragrance of pinks and wallflowers ; to stoop for a violet from a mossy hedge-bank, or a snowdrop from a cottage garden. Indeed, there is no denying the fact that the most lovely and satisfying, the most sociable of all flowers, are those of temperate climates.

BURBIDGE

(1881)

As our fires, though tended by three watchmen, got low from time to time, the air became illumined with the intermittent light of numerous fireflies, whose tiny torches seemed to be answered again by the less intense, but more steady, spark emitted by glow-worms, which swarmed on the damp ground.

The long night-watches are kept by these fairy-like insects dancing to the strange midnight music of the forest. Over and above the monotonous hum caused by myriads of insect wings beating the still air, resound the hoarse croaking of frogs and the livelier staccato notes of crickets. Now and again a falling nut or branch startles the birds, and a hurried flapping of wings seems to silence all minor sounds. As the darkness—which seems all the more intense on account of the brilliancy of the stars peeping through the curtain of foliage overhead, and the dazzling movements of the fireflies close around one—rapidly gives way to the light of day, the lamps of the firefly are extinguished, the crickets and frogs are hushed, the birds break out into joyous song, or loud shrieks and child-like screams, and the intermittent bark of the *kijang* (antelope) with the occasional howling and chattering of monkeys as they chase each other along the boughs overhead, renders sleep impossible.

The solitude of a night in a forest is a myth conjured from the brain of poets. Not a moment passes but some sound—strange in itself or seeming strange, even if familiar, because heard amid unaccustomed surroundings—falls on the ear. The rustling of the leaves during the silence of the night causes a soft whisper, which appears distinct from the same sound heard in similar surroundings by daylight. The pitter-patter of the rain, bringing down number-less leaves during a sudden shower, produces an entirely novel impression on the ear ; and a tropical thunderstorm at night in a forest, when the rain falls as if it would sweep every tree bare of its foliage ; when each flash of lightning seems to single out a forest giant on which to expend its force, and to set the whole forest ablaze ; when the deafening reverberations of the thunder-clap roll through and through the great aisles of the forest—such a scene is beyond the power of pen to describe or pencil to picture.

BOCK, *Headhunters* . . .

The Lands

(1886)

It is a mistake to suppose that all tropical rivers are alike, and as I floated gently up stream on a rising tide I could not help feeling how much more to my taste were others I had seen in other parts of the world, in spite of the undoubted beauty of the jungle and the enormous height of the trees. The stream, forty or fifty feet in width, looked a mere runlet beneath the huge forest giants rising so abruptly from its banks. Towering up as clean, straight, branchless trunks, often for a hundred and fifty feet or more, their tops were merged in those of others by the dense masses of creeper which had sprung from branch to branch and overwhelmed them. High up in the forks of the branches, dozens of yards above our heads, are thick, dark masses which the glasses reveal as clumps of Birds'-nest Fern, or the still more curious Elk's-horn, whose upper fronds, deeply dentate, cling to the tree with their base, from which the long, seaweed-like fronds hang pendulous. Orchids, too, are there, could we only see them, but their flowers are too small, or too dull in colour for us to distinguish them.

Not a breath of air stirs leaf or water, and the oily pea-soup-coloured river with its oozy banks looks untempting enough beneath a sun whose heat seems to penetrate to one's very marrow. Few visible signs of life appear to break the monotony of the scene, save when a party of monkeys swings chattering from bough to bough. But if there is rest for the eye, there is none for the ear. The forest is alive with sound, from the dull, hoarse cry of the hornbill and the slow *swish*, *swish* of its powerful wings, to the loud booming note of the fruit-eating pigeons and the ceaseless and ear-piercing whir-r-r-r of thousands of cicadas. It is tropical nature indeed, but in its least pleasing aspect.

GUILLEMARD

Bamboo, Lotus and Palm

The explorer who penetrates the true primeval forest in a country such as Borneo finds himself at the bottom of a subarboreal world with whose surface all communication is absolutely cut off. . . . Beneath, the forest seems gloomy, dank and devoid of life. Everything is fighting for the sun and air in which alone most flowers will come to perfection, and could we only transform ourselves into monkeys, and swing from branch to branch a couple of hundred feet from the ground, we should doubtless get a much more favourable idea of the richness of the flora of the tropics than we obtain at the foot of the trees.

Ibid.

★

. . . It was a treat to see the sea again and watch the changing panorama on shore—a relief from the everlasting forest of the interior to be able to gaze into the depths of the ocean and peer speculatingly at the hidden things of beauty that lay beneath its surface. Some of these would reveal themselves as the darkness came on. Then could be seen myriads of medusæ, discharging flashes of light like meteors in the ocean ; or a train of dim white phosphorescence—a luminous glow—gliding in serpentine movements along the surface of the dark water, indicating the presence of incalculable hosts of infusoria, too minute for human eye to detect. The gorgeous effects of sunrise and sunset, when ocean and sky were painted in manifold delicate tints ; the paler and calmer glory of the moon, casting her silvery light over the dancing waters ; followed by the hosts of stars, shining like little suns in another ocean of blue, and illumining with their brilliant rays the dark waves beneath—these afforded such scenes as, once viewed amid the surroundings of a tropical panorama of sea and land, could never be forgotten.

BOCK, *Headhunters* . . .

The Lands

BURMA

(1876)

THE traveller who has left behind him the sad-coloured and surf-bound coast of Coromandel, with its monotonous rows of palms, or the equally uninteresting sunderbunds of the Ganges, with their low-lying slimy banks, covered with dank and miasma-breeding jungle—fit abode for the alligator and the tiger, but deadly to human life—cannot fail to be struck with the rich, varied, and glorious scenery of the Golden Chersonese.

Whether his approach be through the tawny-coloured waves which mark where a great river, thickly charged with alluvial deposit, mingles with the ocean, or whether it be through the clear blue sea that washes its rock-bound coast, he is sure to be charmed.

Here a cluster of islets, covered to the water's edge with dense foliage of varied hue, with beautiful headlands and tiny inlets, the representatives in miniature of the bold bluffs and deeply indented bays of the mainland, claim his attention.

Ranges of lofty mountains, which claim relationship with the Great Himalaya, at times looming in the distance, and anon throwing out feelers into the sea, form a background of surpassing grandeur; while the nearer inspection which a sail up its rivers affords, reveals new beauties—approaching the sublime—when contrasted with what he last saw, and worthy of comparison with the most favoured places in the world.

Hills with rounded or rugged contour, whose summits, as well as every other vantage ground, are crowned with pyramidal pagodas, and quaint flagstaffs whose silvery bells tinkle in every breeze, diversified by sequestered but picturesque little nooks, planted with jack, mango, tamarind and other fruit trees, from which the triple-roofed monasteries of Buddhist monks peep forth, are conspicuous objects in the foreground.

Plains with vivid green, yellow or sombre patches, shining brilliantly in the sun's rays, or temporarily obscured by passing clouds, with curious masses of limestone scattered over them in the wildest disorder, form pleasing objects in the mid-distance. Horizons, now bounded by groups of hills that leap up behind each other till lost in the misty distance ; . . . deep rugged ravines and stupendous cliffs, often shooting up sheer two thousand feet ; streams that course down the mountain-side, forming brawling cascades ; great rivers on which the ships of all nations securely float ; combining, one and all, many of the softer beauties of wood and water with all the stern sublimity of mountain scenery, give to the landscape a character inconceivably fascinating, and taking the beholders for the nonce far away from the tropics, realize for a moment the scenes of more temperate climes, justly famed for their exquisite beauty.

McMahon

★

Rangoon was amazingly and even fascinatingly attractive. The markets were kaleidoscopic in ever-changing tint. There is no caste prejudice or purdah system among the Burmese, and the stalls and little shops were managed by the women. . . .

Everybody in Burma lives on the first storey. There is too much wet about for anyone to live on a level with the ground, and as Burma is the land of forests, of course every house is of wood, and is perched on the top of wooden arches. There is a charming variety of design. The Burman is nothing if not a woodcarver, and some of the residences I saw were, outwardly, fairy-land palaces of artistic delight.

It seemed to me that Rangoon consisted chiefly of pawnshops and pagodas. In the Chinese quarter the town bristled with pawnshops. But while the pawnshops were mean and sordid, the pagodas were glowing towers of golden magnificence. The greatest is the Shui Dagon, which, higher than St. Paul's, and resting on the summit of a hill, is a mass of dazzling splendour, guarding the land from ghouls and jinns and other fearsome monsters.

We went to see it. . . . Without warning we found ourselves on the terrace. Right in front rose the golden shaft. Around the base clustered dozens of shrines, grotesquely shaped, with pillars flower-festooned, and dark recesses where glimmering, faint ruby lights were burning and the solemn, sedate Buddha sat with unmoved countenance. An atmosphere of the marvellous hung over it, accentuated now and then by the heavy toll of great bells. One bell, the largest in the world apart from that at Moscow, was struck with a wooden mallet by every passer, so that the deep solemn peal hardly ever ceases. Huge carvings of exquisite and dainty chiselling graced every door-way. Over the lichen-covered walls one saw the swirling, muddy Irrawaddy running away into misty distance, but close at hand were curved pretty lakes. . . . It was a lovely spot, and to all Buddhists most sacred.

FOSTER-FRASER

*

(1892)

A few minutes' walk brought us to the jungle, which we at once entered, on the *qui vive* for whatever small game might turn up, the idea of encountering anything larger having, strange to say, never occurred to any of us. We were soon threading our way through an exceedingly pretty part of the jungle, amid gigantic trees with gnarled trunks, festooned with creepers, and inlaid with delicately tinted and waxy-looking orchids that peeped out everywhere from a profusion of spotless green leaves. These beautiful flowers, which always appear to me to be gifted with more expression than perhaps any other, seemed to warn us of dangers lurking within that tangled mass of vegetation, the haunts of the cruel python and other formidable creatures. There is much to be said in favour of the orchid, in spite of its lowly position in the vegetable world as a parasite. It is, in point of fact, a veritable robber, though not to the extent generally supposed ; for, though it derives its sustenance from the tree on which it grows, yet this is extracted from the effete bark, and not from the juices. In this respect, therefore, orchids are more sinned against than sinning ; sinners or no sinners, they are worthy of adoration, whether abroad in their sylvan haunts or as exotics at home.

PASKE

*

For hours (our guide) led us through the jungle. It was all a jungle should be. The grass was ten and twelve feet high, with blades the thickness of swords. Enormous trees, slim and feathery-headed, rustled aloft, and through the branches and in the leaves was the eternal swish of the rains. Gnarled trunks, blasted by lightning, blocked the narrow path, and over these and round we had to drag our mud-clogged bicycles, frequently ourselves sinking above the shoes in the black, squashy mire.

Standing in the matted thicket, I was impressed by the awful silence of the jungle. There was no rustle of beast among the grass, no scurrying squirrel, not a bird to be seen or a twitter to be heard. . . . It was always the same rank, tropical vegetation, but never a breaking twig to disturb the terrible hush.

FOSTER-FRASER

CANTON

(1762)

THE streets of Canton are so crowded that it is difficult to walk in them ; yet you will seldom see a woman of any fashion, unless by chance when coming out of their chairs. And, were it not that curiosity in the Chinese ladies makes them sometimes peep at us, we should never get a glance at one of them.

Though there are no magnificent houses in Canton, most of them being built only one, and none of them more than two, storey, yet they take up a large extent of ground, many of them having square courts within their walls.

They have all such a regard to privacy, that no windows are made towards the streets but in shops and places of public business. None of their windows look towards those of their neighbours. Within the gate to each house a skreen is placed, to prevent strangers from looking in upon the opening of the gate ; and you enter the house either on the right or left-side of this middle skreen, where there are little alleys to the right and left, from whence you pass into the several courts, which are walled on all sides.

Their entertainments are held in a sort of hall at the entrance of their houses, which have no other ornament besides a single order of painted columns which support the building. The rooms are open to the tyles, without any ceiling. In these they use no looking-glasses, hangings or fine chairs ; and their beds, which are the principal ornaments of their house, are seldom seen by strangers, who are not permitted to go farther than the first great hall.

East Indies

*

(1825)

The factories extend a considerable distance along the banks of the river, fronting the city. They consist of large and handsome houses, each having a flag-staff before it, on which is hoisted the flag of the nation to which it belongs. The English factory far surpasses the others both in elegance and extent, and commands an extensive view both up and down the river.

The streets in the suburbs are in general very narrow and confined. The principal one is denominated China-street ; it contains nothing but shops, in which are to be met with the productions of every part of the globe, and the merchants are in general extremely civil and attentive. . . . At night they all retire inside the city.

The river is somewhat broader than the Thames at London Bridge ; and for the space of four or five miles opposite Canton, is an extensive wooden town of boats stowed so close together that there is scarcely room for a large boat to pass. In these vast numbers of families reside. In the middle of the river the Chinese junks which trade to the Eastern Islands, Batavia, &c., lie moored head and stern.

Milburn

*

(1839)

The scenery in the country around Canton is rich and diversified, but does not present anything bold or grand. On the north and north-east of the city the country is hilly and mountainous. In every other direction a wide prospect opens before you. The rivers and channels, which are very numerous, abound with fish, and are covered with a variety of boats, which are continually passing to and from the neighbouring towns and villages. Southward from the city, as far as the eye can see, the waters cover a considerable portion, perhaps one-eighth, of the whole surface. Rice-fields and gardens occupy the low lands, with only here and there a few little hills and small groves of trees rising up to diversify the otherwise unbroken surface.

The city of Canton is one of the oldest in this part of the empire, and the historians of Canton are able to trace the origin of their city to the time of one of the last emperors of the Chou dynasty, who reigned two thousands years ago. . . .

Fernao Peres de Andrade seems to have been the pioneer in European commerce to China by the Cape of Good Hope. He reached Canton in 1517—during the peaceful and most prosperous times of the Ming dynasty. Spanish, Dutch, and English adventurers soon followed the Portuguese. And the ports of Canton and Macao in this province ; those of Ningpo and Chusan in Chekiang ; and that of Amoy in Fukien, became large marts for European commerce.

Description of Canton

Bamboo, Lotus and Palm

(1858-9)

The banks of the Pearl River are planted at regular intervals with
the dark-leaved *li-chi* and peach-trees now covered with blossom,
agreeably relieved with chili bushes and clumps of the pale green,
broad-leaved plantain ; while the level padi-fields, half under
water, are yellow with heavy-eared rice. The broad river flows
calmly by. Here and there, stretched out athwart the stream, are
countless fishing-stakes, extending in regular, long rows, with
black fishing-nets drying in the sun, and arranged in festoons on the
ropes which stretch from pole to pole. Little sampans are floating
like so many waterfowl on the water, drifting with the current,
and paying out their fishing-lines furnished with a hundred baited
hooks ; poor villagers, dusky, half-clothed figures, are patiently
seeking for cat-fish, or groping for mussels on the river-banks
which the tide leaves bare ; up the little narrow creeks cluster
hundreds of brown dome-roofed fishing craft, while conspicuous
over the low land are the tanned square sails of the trading junks
sailing along the distant reaches of the winding river.

ADAMS

*

(1886)

What chiefly strikes one in arriving in Canton is not so much the
temples (though of these there are, I believe, about eight hundred,
dedicated to gods and goddesses innumerable, and all more or less
richly adorned with shrines, images, fine temple-bronzes, and
elaborate wood-carving). What really fascinates the eye and
bewilders the mind is simply the common street life, which, from
morning till night, as you move through the streets, presents a
succession of pictures, each of intense interest and novelty. In all
this there is life—the real life of a great busy people, and one feels
that it is really an effort to turn aside from these to see any recognized

' sight.' In the temples there is stagnation. Their gilding and beautiful carving are defaced and incrusted with dirt ; but the interest of the streets cannot be surpassed, though most of them are dirty and all are narrow, some being only six feet wide ! Even this is further reduced by the singular but very effective manner of hanging out sign-boards at right angles to the shops, some suspended like the signs of old English inns, and some set upright in carved and gilded stands at the corners of the shop.

The streets are paved with long narrow stone slabs, but with no causeway for foot passengers, for riders are few and far between ; and as to (carrying-)chairs, they block up the street, so that the patient crowd must step close to the shops to let them pass. With the exception of a few wealthy tradesmen . . . all the crowd are dressed in blue. All are intent on their own business, and hurry to and fro, yet never seem to jostle or even touch one another.

To my uneducated eye, all these men and all these women are extraordinarily alike. The same features, the same yellow skin, the same black hair and dark eyes, and, at first sight, even the same expression. Talk of being ' as like as two peas ' ; I think we might say as like as two Chinese.

CUMMING, *Wanderings* . . .

CAPRICORN ISLANDS

(1843)

ON January 7, 1843, I landed for the first time in my life on a coral island. This was a little islet called First Bunker's Island, in the northern part of the Capricorn Group, which is an assemblage of islets and reefs on the north-east coast of Australia, the tropic of Capricorn passing through them.

The beach was composed of coarse fragments of worn corals and shells, bleached by the weather. At the back of it a ridge of the same materials, four or five feet high, and as many yards across, completely encircled the island, which was not a quarter of a mile in diameter. . . . The ridge was occupied by a belt of small trees, while on the plain grew only short scrubby vegetation, a foot or two in height. On the south-east, or weather side, of the island, was a coral reef about two miles in diameter, having the form of a circle of breakers enclosing a shallow lagoon. . . .

January 11.—Landed on ' One Tree Island,' which exhibited the same general features as First Bunker's Island, with some modifications. The external ridge of loose coral fragments was loftier and steeper, owing I believe to this island being more on the weather side of the reef. Inside, the island sloped down every way towards the centre, forming a shallow basin, in the middle of which was a small hole of salt water at or near the level of the sea. The inside slope was covered with low succulent plants (*mesembryanthemum* ?) and trailing bushes. On this green carpet were multitudes of young terns that fluttered before us like flocks of ducklings, with the old birds darting and screaming over our heads. To the northward and eastward of the island stretched the shoal lagoon, its bottom of clean white sand and patches of dead and living coral, bounded by the usual rim of snow-white breakers. Altogether I confess I was much disappointed with the first view of a coral reef, both as to its beauty and to its richness in animal life.

January 13–18.—Although there is not much variety, there is considerable beauty in a small coral reef when viewed from a ship's mast-head at a short distance in clear weather. A small island, with a white sand beach and a tuft of trees, is surrounded by a symmetrically oval space of shallow water of a bright grass-green colour, enclosed by a ring of glittering surf, as white as snow, immediately outside of which is the rich dark blue of deep water. All the sea is perfectly clear from any mixture of sand or mud ; even where it breaks on a sand beach, it retains its perfect purity, as the large grains of coral are heavy and do not break into mud, so that if a bucket full of coral sand be thrown into the sea, it may be seen gradually sinking like a white cloud without producing any discolouration in the surrounding water. It is this perfect clearness of the water which renders navigation among coral reefs at all practicable, as a shoal with even five fathoms of water on it can be discerned at a mile distance from a ship's mast-head, in consequence of its greenish hue contrasting with the blue of deep water.

JUKES

CATHAY

(1499)

CATHAY is a great country and a fair, noble and rich, and full of merchants. Thither go merchants all years for to seek spices and all manners of merchandises. And ye shall understand that merchants that come from Genoa or from Venice or from Romania or other parts of Lombardy, they go by sea and by land eleven months or twelve, or more sometime, ere they may come to the isle of Cathay that is the principal region of all parts beyond : and it is of the great Chan.

From Cathay go men toward the east by many journeys. And then men find . . . another old city toward the east. And it is in the province of Cathay. And beside that city the men of Tartary have let make another city that is clept Caydon. And it hath twelve gates, and between the two gates there is always a great mile ; so that the two cities, that is to say, the old and the new, have in circuit more than twenty mile.

In this city is the siege of the great Chan in a full great palace and the most passing fair in all the world, of which the walls be in circuit more than two mile. . . .

And within the palace, in the hall, there be twenty-four pillars of fine gold. And all the walls be covered within of red skins of beasts that men clepe panthers, that be fair beasts and well smelling : so that for the sweet odour of those skins no evil air may enter into the palace. . . . And many folk worship those beasts when they meet them first at morning, for their great virtue and for the good smell that they have. And those skins they prize more than though they were plate of fine gold.

And in the midst of this palace is the mountour for the great Chan, that is all wrought of gold and of precious stones and of great pearls. . . . And under the mountour be conduits of beverage, and beside the conduits be many vessels of gold, by which they that be of household drink at the conduit.

And the hall of the palace is full nobly arrayed, and full marvellously attired on all parts in all things that men apparel with any hall. . . . And first, is the emperor's throne, full high, where he sitteth at the meat. . . . And the emperor hath his table alone by himself, that is of gold, and of precious stones, or of crystal bordered with gold, or of lignum aloes that cometh out of paradise. And under the emperor's table sit four clerks that write all that the emperor saith, be it good, be it evil ; for all that he saith must be holden, for he may not change his word, ne revoke it.

MANDEVILLE

*

The highways throughout all this kingdome, are the best and gallantest paved that ever hath beene discovered ; they are verie plaine, yea, unto the mountaines, and they are cut by force of labour and pickaxes, and maintained with brick and stone, the which by the report of them which hath seen it, is one of the worthiest things that is in all the realme.

MENDOZA

CHUNGKING TO CHÊNGTU

(1877)

I PASSED under the western gate of Chungking on the morning of July 8th, 1877, full of the pleasurable anticipation which precedes a plunge into the unknown. The road from Chungking to the provincial capital (Chêngtu) had, it is true, been already trodden by more than one European ; but beyond that point the whole of the western border, with slight exception, was untraversed. My project was, after reaching Chêngtu, to make an excursion to the sacred mountain of Omi, and thence to descend into Yünnan by way of Chien-ch'ang—a route of which no account exists except the short notes left us by Marco Polo. . . .

Crossing the grave-covered hills outside the city, we soon reached the fortified post of Fu-t'ou-kuan, about four miles distant, a remarkably picturesque knoll protecting the isthmus of the peninsula of rock on which Chungking is built. So long as the encircling rivers are commanded and this outpost is held, Chungking is secure from attack. Here the road divides, the one which we were to follow being the great highway through Western Szechuen, and probably the finest road in China. . . .

Three days journey of 17 or 18 miles each carried us to Yung-ch'uan, the first city on the high road to the capital, through a very broken country. . . . As seen from the road, the land is rather sparsely wooded with bamboo, cypress, oak, and the wide-branching banyan, the only use of which seems to be to afford its invaluable shade to wayfarers.

Native ignorance of anything extra-Chinese in this area can only be illustrated. I once stopped to inquire, in Chinese, of course, of two men who were hoeing a field, what was the purpose of a nearby mound. After listening with evident interest to my question, one of them remarked to the other, ' How much the language of these foreigners resembles ours.'

Szechuen manners are easy and simple, and when no convenient roadside hostel was near and the breakfast hour approached, we used to enter the most commodious cottage, and spread our frugal meal there as a matter of course. We were generally received with a frank welcome, but the fear of officialdom is so strong that the arrival of my sedan chair was apt to cause uneasiness, from the suspicion that I was a military commander with a tendency to make requisitions. In such circumstances, I would open conversation by inquiring how far it was to the nearest inn, and would find an opportunity of explaining indirectly that I needed nothing but fire and water. By some such diplomacy we always gained free approach and fair accommodation.

Chêngtu, which we reached on the 20th, is one of the largest of Chinese cities, having a circuit of about 12 miles.

On the 26th July we took ship outside the East Gate on a rapid, narrow stream, apparently the city moat, which soon joins the main river a little below an antiquated wooden bridge some 90 yards long, which is in all probability that mentioned by Marco Polo.

The plain begins to break up a few miles below Mei-chou. Some hours before reaching that point my attention had been attracted to a dim but sharp-pointed object rising high above the south-western horizon, which I took to be a cloud ; but at last, noticing that its profile did not change, I pointed it out to a boatman, who replied with a certain contempt, ' Don't you know Mount Omi when you see it ? ' From the point where I first caught sight of it, the distance was more than 50 miles. How it looks from a nearer point of view I cannot affirm, for I have ascended it, travelled all round it, and three times passed close under it, without ever seeing it again, as it was always clothed in mist.

BABER

CHUSAN

(1853)

CHUSAN is a large and beautiful island, twenty miles in length and ten or twelve in breadth at the broadest part. In approaching it the view of the numerous other islands which stud the sea in all directions is striking and picturesque ; noble mountains towering above the other land, and fertile valleys sloping gradually to the ocean. The island itself is a succession of hills, valleys and glens, presenting an appearance not unlike the scenery in the Highlands of Scotland. At the head of every valley there are mountain passes, over which the inhabitants cross when they wish to visit the interior of the island. The valleys are rich and beautiful, surrounded by mountains which in many parts are covered with trees, and in others under cultivation : these, in their turn, open and expose other valleys no less fertile, rich in vegetation and watered by the clear streams from the mountains. Thus the traveller can visit the whole of the island, his way winding through valleys and over

mountain passes, until his prospect is at last arrested by the sea, of which he has had frequent glimpses during the journey. Did our island of Hong Kong possess the natural advantages and beauties of Chusan, what a splendid place it might have been made by our enterprising English merchants in a very few years !

The flora of Chusan, and all over the mainland of this part of the province of Chekiang, is very different from that of the south. Almost all the species of a tropical character have entirely disappeared, and in their places we find others related to those found in temperate climates in other parts of the world. Most people have seen and admired the beautiful azaleas which are brought to the Chiswick fêtes, but few can form any idea of the gorgeous and striking beauty of these azalea-clad mountains, where on every side, as far as our vision extends, the eye rests on masses of flowers of dazzling brightness and surpassing beauty. . . .

The green-tea shrub (*Thea viridis*) is cultivated everywhere. Every small farmer and cottager has a few plants on his premises, which he rears with considerable care, but seems to have no wish to enter

on its cultivation on a larger scale. The forests of different varieties of bamboo are very striking, and give a kind of tropical character to the Chusan scenery. I do not know anything more beautiful than the yellow bamboo, with its clean, straight stem and its graceful top and branches waving in the breeze.

The natives of Chusan are a quiet and inoffensive race, and were always civil and obliging to me.

FORTUNE, *Two Visits . . .*

*

Gods and fairies sometimes err.

Chinese Proverb

D'ENTRECASTEAUX ISLANDS

(1876)

BEFORE turning my back on Eastern New Guinea I resolved on visiting its unknown northern shores in my boat. Taking the galley, we rounded East Cape, and found ourselves floating on a deep, tranquil sea, ruffled but gently by the monsoon.

Full of pleasant excitement, we lay on our oars to take in the exquisite scene. To the eastward rose the lofty wooded D'Entre-casteaux Islands; within a hundred yards of us a large village lay peacefully among its palms and fruit trees; on and on the eye travelled to the westward, from the nearby thickly populated shores to the blue shadowy outlines of the massive New Guinea Mountains, seventy or eighty miles distant.

We turned our faces to the ship with many regrets at being forced to leave this unexplored coast, and returned, landing at some of the villages on the way, where we found the people as gentle and friendly as possible. At times I found myself drawing a contrast between the squalid poverty too often seen in England and the plenty and cleanliness that met us here at every step, where the small cane houses lay in valleys rich as the garden of Eden, and no man had to go more than a stone's throw from his own door to find all the necessities of his simple life.

They possess coco-nuts, the bread-fruit, citron, oranges and sago by the bounty of nature, and they cultivate yams, taro, bananas and other roots. They are great fishers and traders, passing from island to island in large canoes forty or fifty feet long, made of a hollowed tree, which they handle so skilfully that when we met them at sea and we were going five knots, they easily sailed round us, and, luffing under our lee, were with difficulty prevented from boarding us whilst under weigh.

What have these people to gain from civilization ? Pondering on the fate of other aboriginal races when brought into contact with the white, I was ready to wish that they had never been seen by us. But considerations of this kind cannot be entertained by those who see a simple duty before them and have means to execute it. We were not responsible for the issues, and Providence may surely be trusted to work out its own ends.

MORESBY

ELLICE ISLANDS

IT was nine in the evening before we reached the village. Once inside the enclosing reef, we saw the full size of the lagoon it shelters —a lake some eighteen miles long by nine wide. Bright white moonlight steeped the shore, making visible every leaf and frond of the trees and undergrowth that fringed it. The pure white coral surface shone like silver in the open, flecked with soft shadows from the trees, and across it a warm yellow glow came from the coco-nut oil burning in the pretty little oval huts.

I paused for a moment to look at the mingling of the two lights. It gave the sort of radiance that Corregio has in his ' Notte,' where the cold clear light of morning comes stealing through the doorway from the eastern hills, and flows over the yellow lambent flame thrown upward from the body of the infant Christ to the faces of his adorers. . . . It was like a scene in a dream—the sheet of moonlight, the graceful trees, the perfect stillness, the roar of the surf—like a silence, it was so measured—all seemed unreal, and ready to dissolve.

Ibid.

THE FLORIDAS

THE chart will show that the Floridas are a group of small islands lying out midway between Malanta and Guadalcana, which are situated on either side of the Indispensable Straits. There are three large inhabited islands in the group . . . and some fifty uninhabited islands of varying sizes, from the large island of Buona Vista, so named by the Spaniards, to tiny islets not an acre in extent.

The scenery here is very lovely. I wish I could give some idea in language of the queer-shaped hills with their fantastic peaks, their slopes covered with long yellow-green grass, and crowned with cocoa-palms or nut-trees ; the long streaks of sandy beach, dazzlingly white, meeting the pale blue water, of the tint of an Italian sky ; and, looking landward from the sea, valleys and mountains, where greens and purples blend in softening distance.

PENNY

*

The rich want most.

Chinese Proverb

FORMOSA

(1727)

FORMOSA is a noble Island, and produces many valuable Commodities, as well for the Sustenance of Mankind as for Pleasure and Luxury. It affords Plenty of Gold, raw Silk, fine white Sugar, Sugar-candy and Copper finer than in China, but coarser than in Japan. Before the Tartars subdued it, it had Kings of its own, but tributary to China. The Natives differ much from the neighbouring People of China and Luconia, both in Phisiognomy and Make. They are of a low Stature, with a large Head and Fore-head, hollow-eyed, and the Cheek-bone very high, a large Mouth, and a short flat Chin, with little or no Beard on it, long-jaw'd, and with a small long Neck, their Body short and square, their Arms and Legs long, small and ill-shaped, their Feet long, and broad at the Toes, and generally they are baker-kneed. The English and Dutch had their Factories there, but about the Year 1678, when all Fokien had submitted to the Tartars, they were ordered to withdraw their Factories from Teywon, a small Island close to the great one, on which their Factories stood. The English obeyed and removed over to Amoy, but the Dutch received supplies from Batavia, and endured a long Siege, but were at last forced to submit, tho' they sold their Factory, and many of their Men's Lives pretty dear, for the Tartars lost above 5000 Men in reducing it. It is now wholly under the Tartars.

When it was tributary to China, about the Year 1650 there was a strange Distemper raged on the Island for three Years together, for most of the Virgins between twelve and eighteen Years of Age, had a Trick of hanging themselves, in so much that very few Maidens were left on the Island, nor could any Remedy be found to prevent it, before an old China Man found one out, and address himself to the King, desiring him to make a Trial of hanging (all those that hanged themselves privately) up by one Leg on the Sides of Highways, for Passengers to gaze on. The King took his Counsel, and hanged up some so, and in one Month's Time the Maidens refrained from hanging, and have continued good Girls ever since.

HAMILTON

FUJI-YAMA

IF asked to name the most conspicuous of those physical phenomena which have exercised so great an influence on our mind, no Japanese will hesitate to mention our most beloved Fuji-yama. This is the highest and the most beautiful of all the great mountains in the main group of the Japanese islands. Gracefully conical in shape, lifting its snow-clad head against a serene background 12,365 feet above the sea, it has from the earliest time been the object of unceasing admiration for the surrounding thirteen provinces, and where it stands out of the reach of the naked eye, winged words from the poet's lyre, and flying leaves from the artist's brush have carried its praise to all the nooks and corners of the Land of the Gods.

There is many another towering mountain in Japan, but none can vie with Fuji for majestic grace. More beautiful than sublime, more serene than imposing, it has been from time immemorial a silent influence on the Japanese character.

There on the border, where the land of Kahi
Doth touch the frontier of Suruga's land,
A beauteous province stretched on either hand,
See Fuji-yama rear his head on high !

The Lands

The clouds of Heav'n in rev'rent wonder pause,
Nor may the birds those giddy heights essay,
Where melt thy snows amid thy fires away,
Or thy fierce fires lie quenched beneath thy snows.

What name might fitly tell, what accents sing,
Thy awful, godlike grandeur ? 'Tis thy breast
That holdeth Narasaha's flood at rest,
Thy side whence Fujikaha's waters spring.

Great Fuji-yama, tow'ring to the sky !
A treasure art thou giv'n to mortal man.
A god-protector watching o'er Japan :
On thee for ever let me feast mine eye !

OKAKURA, *Japanese Spirit*

*

The great beauty of Fuji consists in its rising singly out of a low
country with a beautifully curved sweep to a conical apex ; and the
atmospheric effects changing from hour to hour, as it is seen from
thirteen provinces, give such a variety to this single object that it is
rightly called by a name to express the feeling that there are not
two such in the world. The variations of atmospheric density make
it look at one time much higher than at another. It may be seen
with its head clear in the blue sky rising out of a thick base of clouds
—or the clouds rise and roll in masses about the middle, leaving the
gentle curve to be filled up by the mind's eye from the base to the
apex. Again, the whole contour, in a sort of proud, queenly sweep,
stands out against a cloudless ether, or with a little vapour drifting
to leeward of the summit giving the appearance of a crater—or,
after a cool night in September, the eye is arrested by the appearance
of the bursting downward of a flattened shell, the pure white snow
filling the valleys from the top, the haze of the morning half

49

concealing the hill beneath. Every hour brings a change upon a landscape which consists of a single object which the lover of nature can never weary of admiring, in a climate where seventy miles of atmosphere does not obscure the larger features on the face of the mountain even to the naked eye.

DICKSON

*

Turning our backs on Fujiyama, we enter a large, wide valley. The mountains are all green ; single rows of trees mark their outlines. In Japanese scenery the same elements are repeated *ad infinitum*. All these heights end in sharp sides, as steep as the blade of a knife. Between the two slopes there is only room for a single row of trees. We pass by a number of little villages, all clean, tidy and evidently prosperous. Everywhere there is the richest and most careful cultivation. In the narrow plains, which here and there wind between the mountains, are patches of rice, and quantities of mulberry trees. The road is but a path, well-kept and full of people. At every turn we meet fresh pilgrims. They walk in great and small bands, all dressed in the same white dresses and all ringing a bell. When rain threatens they put on their straw cloaks. Some are followed by their servants. Female pilgrims are rare, but are not altogether wanting. All along the road charming details abound. At the second *ri*, near a little tea-house, a stone staircase leads to some beautiful tombs shaded by a fine group of cryptomerias. Further on we stop to see a foaming cascade.

At half-past five we arrive at Yamura, a little town situated in the centre of one of the great silk districts. There are mulberry trees everywhere. The river rushes violently across the flowery meadows and flows swiftly along the edge of the rocks, covered with moss, grass, and trees. Behind us, between the green peaks, the crater of Fujiyama is still visible.

HÜBNER

THE GOLDEN CHERSONESE

THE Irrawaddy is navigable by ordinary river steamers for at least one thousand miles from the sea. The Burmese, much to their honour, were the first to prove this by the actual experiment of running a good-sized steamer as far as the point where the old caravan route from Yunnan struck the Irrawaddy—a route which, it is hoped, will ere long be revived, to result in such a measure of wealth and prosperity to the region it will affect as to enable it to claim, with some show of truth, its ancient name of the Golden Chersonese.

. . . Josephus tells us that about the time the Queen of Sheba visited Solomon ' there were brought to the King from the Aurea Chersonensus, a country so called, precious stones and pine trees, and these trees he made use of for supporting the temple and the palace, as also for the materials of musical instruments, the harps and the psalteries, that the Levites might make use of them in their hymns to God. The wood that was brought to him at the time was larger and finer than any that had been brought before ; but let no one imagine that these pine trees were like those which are now so named, and which take their denomination from the merchants who so call them, that they may procure them to be admired by those that purchase them ; for those we speak of were to the sight like the wood of the fig tree, but were whiter and more shining. Now we have said this much that no one may be ignorant of the difference between these sorts of wood, nor unacquainted with the nature of the genuine pine tree ; and we thought it both a reasonable and a humane thing when we mentioned it, to explain the difference so far as we have done.'

McMAHON

AT HAKATA

TRAVELLING by ricksha one can only see and dream. The jolting makes reading too painful ; the rattle of the wheels and the rush of the wind render conversation impossible, even when the road allows of a fellow-traveller's vehicle running beside your own. After having become familiar with the characteristics of Japanese scenery, you are not apt to notice, except at long intervals, anything novel enough to make a strong impression. Most often the way winds through a perpetual sameness of rice-fields, vegetable farms, tiny thatched hamlets—and between interminable ranges of green or blue hills. Sometimes, indeed, there are startling spreads of colour, as when you traverse a plain all burning yellow with the blossoming of the natané, or a valley all lilac with the flowering of the gengebana ; but these are the passing splendours of very short seasons. As a rule the vast green monotony appeals to no faculty ; you sink into a reverie or nod perhaps, with the wind in your face, to be wakened only by some jolt of extra violence.

Even so, on my autumn way to Hakata, I gaze and dream and nod by turns. I watch the flashing of the dragon-flies, the infinite network of rice-field paths, the slowly shifting lines of familiar peaks in the horizon glow, and the changing shapes of white which float in the vivid blue above all—asking myself how many times again must I view the same landscape, and deploring the absence of the wonderful.

Suddenly and very softly, the thought steals into my mind that the most wonderful of possible visions is really all about me in the mere common green of the world—in the ceaseless manifestations of Life.

Ever and everywhere, from beginnings invisible, green things are growing. . . . Names we have given them, and classification. The reason of the forms of their leaves, the qualities of their fruits, the colours of their flowers, we also know ; for we have learned not a little about the course of the eternal laws that give shape to all terrestrial things. But why they are—that we do not know. What is the ghostliness that seeks expression in this universal green —the mystery of that which multiplies forever issuing out of that which multiplies not ? Or is the seeming lifeless itself life—only a life more silent still, more hidden ?

But a stranger and quicker life moves upon the face of the world, peoples wind and flood. This has the ghostlier power of separating itself from earth, yet is always at last recalled thereto, and condemned to feed that which it once fed upon. . . . The green, slower life seeks being only ; but this forever struggles against non-being. We know the mechanism of its motion, the laws of its growth ; the innermost mazes of its structure have been explored. . . . But the meaning of it, who will tell us ? Out of what ultimate came it ? What is it ? Why should it know pain ? Why is it evolved by pain ?

And this life of pain is our own. Relatively, it sees, it knows. Absolutely, it is blind, and gropes, like the slow, cold, green life which supports it. But does it also support a higher existence— nourish some invisible life infinitely more active and more complex ? Is there ghostliness orbed in ghostliness—life within life without end ? Are there universes impenetrating universes ?

HEARN, *Out of the East*

HONG KONG

(1848)

THERE never was, perhaps, so rapid a rise in any settlement made by the English as that of Hong Kong, considering the very short time it has been in our possession. Where, two years back, there existed but a few huts, you now behold a well-built and improving town, with churches, hotels, stores, wharves and godowns. The capacious harbour which, but a short time ago, was only visited by some Chinese junks or English clippers, is now swarming with men-of-war and merchant ships. The town extends along the base of the mountains. Every day some improvement takes place in this fast-growing colony, but, from the scarcity of building ground, house rent is very dear, and everything has risen in proportion. The town which, from the irregularity of the ground, has but one street of importance, lies under the highest part of a rock, which is called Possession Peak.

The harbour is completely land-locked, and has two entrances. One side of it is formed by Hong Kong, the other by Kow-loon, which is part of the mainland.

But all this has its reverse. The unhealthiness of the climate is very great, and this is impressed on the stranger while at anchor in the roads ; for the first object that meets the eye is the Minden Hospital ship, with her flag continually half mast high, announcing that another poor sailor has gone to his long home. . . .

The great error of the last war was our selection of such an unhealthy and barren island as Hong Kong as our *pied-à-terre* in China. Even now it is not too late. The Chinese dislike our propinquity to their coast at Hong Kong, and the last expedition will have the effect of increasing this dislike. I think, with very little difficulty, the Chinese government would now exchange Chusan for Hong

Kong, if it were only to keep such unpleasant barbarians as the English have proved to be at a more respectable distance.

MARRYAT

(1853)

Hong Kong Bay is one of the finest which I have ever seen; it is eight or ten miles in length, and irregular in breadth; in some places two, in others, six miles wide, having excellent anchorage all over it, and perfectly free from hidden dangers. It is completely sheltered by the mountains of Hong Kong on the south, and by those of the mainland of China on the opposite shore; land-locked in fact on all sides; so that shipping can ride out the heaviest gales with perfect safety.

Hong Kong is one of the largest islands near the mouth of the Canton river. It is about eight miles from east to west, and the widest part of it is not more than six miles; but it is very irregular, some parts being only three miles in breadth, and the land jutting out here and there, forming a succession of headlands and bays. Imagine, then, an island considerably longer than it is broad, perfectly mountainous and sloping in a rugged manner to the water's edge, having here and there deep ravines, almost at equal distances along the coast, which extend from the tops of the mountains down to the sea, deepening and widening in their course. There are immense blocks of granite in these ravines, which have either been bared by the rapid currents of water in its descent during rains, or which have tumbled into them from the sides of the mountains at some former period of time.

There is very little flat ground on the island capable of being brought under cultivation ; indeed the only tract of any extent is the Happy Valley, as the English call it, and even that is not more than twenty or thirty acres in extent. . . .

From the tops of the mountains the view is grand and imposing in the extreme ; mountain is seen rising above mountain, rugged, barren and wild—the elevation of the highest being nearly two thousand feet ; the sea as far as the eye can reach is studded with islands of the same character as Hong Kong ; on one side our beautiful bay lies beneath us, crowded with shipping and boats and, on the other the far extending waters of the China Sea.

The climate of Hong Kong is far from being agreeable, and has proved very unhealthy, to both Europeans and Chinese. During the months of July and August—the hottest in the year—the maximum heat shown by my thermometer was 94° Fahr, and the minimum in the same time was 80°. In winter the thermometer sometimes sinks as low as the freezing-point, but this is a rare occurrence. Even in the midst of winter, when the sun shines it is scarcely possible to walk out without the shelter of an umbrella, and if anyone has the hardihood to attempt it he invariably suffers for his folly. The air is so dry that one can scarcely breathe, and there is no shade to break the almost vertical rays of the sun. At other times in winter fires are necessary, and at all seasons the climate is liable to sudden changes of temperature.

FORTUNE, *Two Visits* . . .

JAPAN

(1586)

'In the year of Christ 1586 Japan was shook by such dreadful earthquakes, that the like was never known before. At Nagasama, a small Town of about a thousand houses in the Kingdom Oomi, the Earth gap'd and swallowed up one half of that place, and the other half was destroyed by a fire. Another place, likewise called Nagasama by the Natives, after it had been violently shook for some days, was at last swallowed up by the Sea, the waters rising so high that they overflowed the Coasts, washed away the houses, drowned the Inhabitants, and left no foot step of that once rich and populous Town, but the place on which the Castle stood, and that even under water.'

Quoted by Kaempfer from a letter dated at Simonoseki October 15th, 1586, by
F. LEWIS DE FROES

(1728)

THE borders of this Empire (Japan) are its rocky, mountainous Coasts, and a tempestuous Sea, which by reason of its shallowness admits none but small vessels, and even those not without eminent danger, the depth of most of its Gulfs and Harbours being not yet known, and others, which the pilots of the Country are better acquainted withal, unfit for harbouring of Ships of any considerable bulk. Indeed it seems Nature purposely design'd these Islands to be a sort of little world, separate and independent of the rest, by making them of so difficult an access, and by endowing them plentifully, with whatever is requisite to make the lives of their Inhabitants both delightful and pleasant, and to enable them to subsist without a commerce with foreign Nations.

KAEMPFER

✳

(1775)

On anchoring at the entrance of the harbour, all the prayer-books and Bibles belonging to the sailors were collected and put into a chest, which was nailed down. This chest was afterwards left under the care of the Japanese till the time of our departure, when everyone received his book again. This was done to prevent the introduction of Christian or Roman Catholic books into the country.

THUNBERG

✳

The only people allowed to trade at Japan are the Chinese and the Dutch.

The Chinese have almost from time immemorial traded to Japan and are the only people in Asia who have engaged in the trade or are allowed to visit the empire. Formerly they proceeded to Osacca (Osaka) harbour, but later the Portuguese shewed them the way to Nangasacki (Nagasaki). At first the number of their vessels amounted to upwards of one hundred. The liberty which they then enjoyed is at present greatly contracted since they have been suspected by the Japanese of favouring Catholic missionaries and have made attempts to introduce into Japan Catholic books printed in China. They are therefore as much suspected and as hardly used as the Dutch.

The island of Dezima is let to the Dutch Company, and is considered merely as a street belonging to the town of Nagasaki. The island is joined to the town and main-land, and at low water is separated from it only by a ditch; at high water it becomes an island, which has communication with the town by means of a bridge. The island is only about 600 feet in length and 120 in breadth. It is planked in on all sides, and has two gates, one towards the town near the bridge and the other towards the water-side. The latter is opened only on such days as the Dutch ships are discharging or taking in their cargoes; the other is always guarded in the daytime by the Japanese and locked at night. Near it is a gate-house, where those that go in and out of the town are searched. . . . Excepting the Dutch large and fire-proof store-houses, the houses are all built of wood and clay, covered with tiles, and having paper windows and floor-mats of straw. By the sea-gate is kept in readiness every kind of apparatus for the prevention of fire, and at the other end are a pleasure and kitchen garden and a large summer-house. For the purpose of keeping a vigilant eye over the Dutch several Japanese officers, interpreters and guards are kept on the island. . . . Within this small compass the Dutch are compelled to pass their time during their stay in Japan.

MILBURN

(1854)

At the hour of the monkey (3.30 p.m.) a great shock came from the north-west, with a noise like that of a typhoon. The ground heaved like waves of water for a long time. Afterwards enormous waves rushed up the rivers, and the city of Kochi caught fire. Seventy different shocks occurred in the night. . . . By the first great convulsion the earth opened, land-slips took place from the mountains, rivers were flooded, and all dwelling-houses and fireproof storehouses were either thrown down or severely wrenched. . . . At about eight o'clock a great noise was heard, and on enquiring its cause I was told that great sea-waves were rushing in upon the land. The confusion of the moment was indescribable, the people all rushed towards the high land.

REED

These are things
An earthquake brings :
At nine of the bell they sickness foretell ;
At five and seven betoken rain ;
At four the sky is cleared thereby ;
At six and eight comes wind again.

Ibid.

✻

The Lands

(1863)

At daylight on the 12th of October, 1860, the swift little bark
'Marmora,' in which I was a passenger from China, was rapidly
approaching the coast of Japan—a country at the ends of the earth,
and well named by its inhabitants 'the Kingdom of the Origin of
the Sun.' When I came on deck in the morning the far-famed
shores of *Zipangu* lay spread before my wondering eyes for the
first time. Having heard and read so many stories of this strange
land—of its stormy coasts ; of its fearful earthquakes ; of its
luxuriant vegetation, full of strange and beautiful forms ; of its
curious inhabitants ; and last, but not least, of its salamanders !—
I had long looked upon Japan much in the same light as the
Romans regarded our own isles in the days of the ancient
Britons.

My first view of these shores, however, did a good deal towards
dispelling this delusion. It was a lovely morning. The sun rose
from behind the eastern mountains without a cloud to obscure his
rays. With a fair wind and a smooth sea we were rapidly approaching the large island of Kiusiu, on which the town of Nagasaki is
situated. The land is hilly and mountainous, and in many instances
it rises perpendicularly from the sea. These perpendicular, rocky
cliffs have a very curious appearance as one sails along. There are
also a number of queer-looking, detached little islands dotted about
which seem to have no connection with any other land near them.
Some are crowned with a scraggy pine-tree or two, and look
exactly like those bits of rock-work which are constantly met with
in the gardens of China and Japan. Others look in the distance
like ships under full sail, and in one instance I observed a pair of
them exactly like fishing-junks. Nearer the shore the islands are
richly clothed with trees and brushwood. The highest hills on this
part of the mainland are about 1500 feet above sea level, but hills of
every height, from 300 to 1500 feet, and of all forms, were exposed

to our view as we approached the entrance to the harbour of Nagasaki. Many were terraced nearly to their summits, and at this season these terraces were green with the young crops of wheat and barley.

The pretty little island of Papenberg stands as if it were a sentinel guarding the harbour of Nagasaki. Pretty it certainly is, and yet it is associated with scenes of persecution, cruelty and bloodshed of the most horrible description. . . . During the persecutions of the Christians in the seventeenth century it was the Golgotha of many martyrs to the Roman Catholic faith. . . .

As soon as our ship rounded Papenberg the harbour and town of Nagasaki came full into view—one of the most beautiful in the world. It is about a mile in width and three or four in length. When you are inside it appears to be completely land-locked, and has all the appearance of an inland lake. The hills around it are divided and broken up by long ridges and deep glens or valleys which extend far up towards the summits. These ridges and glens are for the most part richly wooded, while all the more fertile spots are terraced and under cultivation.

Nagasaki is about a mile in length, and three-quarters of a mile in width. It fills up the space between the shores of the bay and the hills which surround it. The streets are wide and clean, compared with those in Chinese towns. Although the houses of the common people have a poor and mean appearance, there are some of considerable pretensions. . . . Almost every house which has any pretensions to respectability has a flower-garden in the rear, oftentimes indeed small, but neatly arranged. As the lower parts of the Japanese houses and shops are open both before and behind, I had peeps of these pretty little gardens as I passed along the streets. Many of them are exceedingly small, some not much larger than a good-sized dining-room; but the surface is rendered varied and pleasing by means of little mounds of turf, on which are planted dwarf trees kept clipped into fancy forms, and by miniature lakes, in which gold and silver fish and tortoises disport themselves.

FORTUNE, *Yedo* . . .

*

(1886)

Perhaps one of the greatest charms Japan has for Europeans, at any rate on first acquaintance, is its unreality. As far as it affects the natural features of the country, I confess that I think the attraction fades with wonderful rapidity. I do not mean that there is no scenery of real beauty in Japan, for everyone who has seen Nikko under the reddening maples, or explored the splendid gorges of the Tenrui-gawa, must allow that their beauty is hardly likely to be surpassed in any country. But the ordinary views of village life, which are to the new-comer so attractive from their very novelty, eventually become rather more than wearisome.

GUILLEMARD

*

KYOTO,
April 16th, 1896.

The wooden shutters before my little room are pushed away ; and the morning sun immediately paints upon my *shoji*, across squares of gold light, the perfect sharp shadow of a little peach-tree. No mortal artist—not even a Japanese—could surpass that silhouette ! Limned in dark blue against the yellow glow, the marvellous image even shows stronger or fainter tones according to the varying distance of the unseen branches outside. It sets me thinking about the possible influence on Japanese art of the use of paper for house-lighting purposes.

By night a Japanese house with its *shoji* closed looks like a great paper-sided lantern—a magic-lantern making moving shadows within, instead of without itself. By day the shadows on the *shoji* are from outside only ; but they may be very wonderful at the first rising of the sun, if his beams are levelled, as in this instance, across a space of quaint garden.

There is certainly nothing absurd in that old Greek story which finds the origin of art in the first untaught attempt to trace upon some wall the outline of a lover's shadow. Very possibly all sense of art, as well as all sense of the supernatural, had its simple beginnings in the study of shadows. But shadows on *shoji* are so remarkable as to suggest an explanation of certain Japanese faculties of drawing by no means primitive, but developed beyond all parallel, and otherwise difficult to account for. Of course, the quality of Japanese paper, which takes shadows better than any frosted glass, must be considered, and also the character of the shadows themselves. Western vegetation, for example, could scarcely furnish silhouettes so gracious as those of Japanese garden trees, all trained by centuries of caressing care to look as lovely as Nature allows.

I wish the paper of my *shoji* could have been, like a photographic plate, sensitive to that first delicious impression cast by a level sun. I am already regretting distortions ; the beautiful silhouette has begun to lengthen.

HEARN, *Kokoro* . . .

★

Why should the trees be so lovely in Japan ? With us, a plum or a cherry tree in flower is not an astonishing sight ; but here it is a miracle of beauty so bewildering that, however much you may have previously read about it, the real spectacle strikes you dumb. You see no leaves,—only one filmy mist of petals. Is it that the trees have been so long domesticated and caressed by man in this land of the gods, that they have acquired souls, and strive to show their gratitude, like women loved, by making themselves more beautiful for man's sake? Assuredly they have mastered men's hearts by their loveliness, like beautiful slaves.

HEARN, *Glimpses*

From all over the city there rises into the night a sound like the bubbling and booming of great frogs in a marsh,—the echoing of the tiny drum of the dancing-girls, of the charming geisha. Like the rolling of a waterfall continually reverberates the multitudinous pattering of *geta* (clogs) upon the bridge. A new light rises in the east; the moon is wheeling up from behind the peaks, very large and weird and wan through the white vapours. Again I hear the sound of the clapping of many hands. For the wayfarers are paying obeisance to O-Tsuki-San; from the long bridge they are saluting the coming of the White Moon-Lady.

Ibid.

*

Sept. 14, 1874.—It rains in torrents. They are the first autumn rains—the disagreeable season for the inhabitants of Japanese houses. The damp pervades them all. The paper partitions come unpasted: there is no longer any protection from the wind; and although it is mild out of doors, inside one shivers. In summer one suffers terribly from the heat; in winter there is no way of guarding oneself from the cold. It is only during the short spring and towards the end of autumn that one finds oneself really comfortable.

HÜBNER

I see, rising out of darkness, a lotus in a vase. Most of the vase is invisible ; but I know that it is of bronze, and that its glimpsing handles are bodies of dragons. Only the lotus is fully illuminated : three pure white flowers, and five great leaves of gold and green,— gold above, green on the up-curling under-surface—an artificial lotus. It is bathed by a slanting stream of sunshine ; the darkness beneath and beyond is the dusk of a temple-chamber. I do not see the opening through which the radiance pours ; but I am aware that it is a small window shaped in the outline-form of a temple-bell.

The reason that I see the lotus—one memory of my first visit to a Buddhist sanctuary—is that there has come to me an odour of incense. Often when I smell incense this vision defines ; and usually thereafter other sensations of my first day in Japan revive in swift succession with almost painful acuteness.

HEARN, *In Ghostly Japan*

*

'How precious seems the firefly
Now that the lantern has gone out ! '

There are many places in Japan which are famous for fireflies,— places which people visit in summer merely to enjoy the sight of the fireflies. At present the most famous is in the neighbourhood of Uji, a pretty little town in the centre of the celebrated tea-district, and scarcely less famed for its fireflies than for its teas. Every summer brings thousands of visitors to see the fireflies. But it is on the river, several miles from the town, that the Battle of the Fireflies is to be seen.

The stream there winds between hills covered with vegetation, and myriads of fireflies dart from either bank to meet and cling above the water. At moments they so swarm together as to form a luminous cloud or a great ball of sparks. The cloud soon scatters, or the ball drops and breaks upon the surface of the current, and the fallen fireflies drift glittering away. After the 'Battle' the river, covered with the still sparkling bodies of the drifting insects, appears like the Milky Way, or as the Japanese more poetically call it, the River of Heaven.

> Is it the river only ?—Or is the darkness itself drifting ?
> Oh, the fireflies !

HEARN, Kottō

Of all peculiarly beautiful things in Japan the most beautiful are the approaches to high places of worship or of rest—the Ways that go to Nowhere and the Steps that lead to Nothing.

Perhaps the ascent begins with a sloping paved avenue, half a mile long, lined with giant trees. Stone monsters guard the way at regular intervals. Then you come to some great flight of steps ascending through green gloom to a terrace umbraged by older and vaster trees ; and other steps from thence lead to other terraces, all in shadow. And you climb and climb and climb, till at last, beyond a grey torii, the goal appears : a small, void, colourless wooden shrine—a Shinto *miya*. The shock of emptiness thus received, after the sublimity of the long approach, is very ghostliness itself.

HEARN, Kokoro . . .

JAVA

(1903)

Java,
Jan. 17, 1903.

For three long weeks not a drop of rain has fallen. It is boiling hot as it has never been before, even in the driest season.

Father is in despair : the young rice in the fields is turning brown. Oh, our poor people ! So far they have had enough to eat here, and they do not know the most frightful of all calamities a land can suffer—Famine. But what has not been, may be ; and this great drought in the time of the wet season presages anything but good. What will happen if it keeps up ? For several mornings the wind has blown as it usually does first in May. Has the turning point been reached, has the dry season begun ?

It is frightful, everyone looks on helpless. It is hard to see everything that has been sown and planted turn brown and die, without being able to turn a finger to help it, and the great heat harasses the body too ; one feels dull and listless.

What do you think of such a complaint from a child of the sun ? Oh, how frightful for the people who are working out in the fields, if for us in here it is so scalding hot, and this is the wet season. Do not be chary with your cold : could you not spare a little of it ? You may take as much of our warmth as you wish.

Kartini

The Lands

KEPPEL ISLAND

(1876)

KEPPEL ISLAND is but some four miles long by two and a half broad ; but being of coral and volcanic origin combined, it has variety, and the beauties belonging to both origins : the bold volcanic heights and the coraline bright beach and verdant flat. On strictly coral islets you see no trees but coco-nut, bread-fruit and small palms ; but here they were mixed with forest trees, and the light greens thus broken up with deeper tints.

Visitors have spoken in such enchanting terms of these coral and volcanic isles that we were prepared to be disappointed. I can only say that some of these emerald gems, shrined in by the summer sea, with sparkling beach, leafy shades, and a wealth—a waste— of fruit and flower, seemed to me like scenes in a dream of peace and beauty.

MORESBY

KIUSIU (JAPAN)

SOON I reached the head of the valley. I observed the barley was nearly all cut, and that the crops of sweet potatoes and cotton looked very promising. Half a dozen green pheasants were pecking away at the potatoes. A pair of beautiful light-green pigeons passed in front of me, their bright yellow necks shining like gold in the sun. The rough path now entered the fir-wood, which ran down on each side of the valley I had come up. Just before the trees closed over the path, I looked over the high bank of the reservoir, which is invariably found at the head of all cultivated valleys, and observed a small flock of mandarin ducks swimming about by the edge of the alder shrubs which hung over the water from the wood side.

As I passed through the wood, numbers of little yellow butterflies flitted to and fro, constantly lighting on the damp spots of ground and sucking the moisture up greedily. The wood was quite narrow at this spot, and as I emerged from it on the hillside, a beautiful copper pheasant cock rose at my feet and went off like a rocket for the cover. The path skirted round the hill, leaving the wood to the right and the grassy hill-side on the left. Sweet-scented yellow lilies were everywhere scattered about, and pretty bluebell-shaped flowers, besides the scented jessamine and azaleas in profusion, carpeted the ground.

I soon came to a clear stream running down the hill-side, in the deepest pools of which trout five or six inches long were plainly seen against the dark rocky bottom. As I stood watching them, a little green kingfisher dashed suddenly into the water ten yards up the stream, and immediately appeared with a trout about two inches in length. Numbers of painted-lady butterflies flitted about the banks of the stream, attracted, I suppose, by the warm surface of the great rocks.

The path in a short time again entered the wood, which was more open underneath, and the lovely ferns which grew in profusion were more easily seen. Here I came upon a gigantic camphor-tree, the stem of which I found to be fifty-three feet in circumference at four feet from the ground.

Passing over a sharp rise, I found myself in a large valley which ran up amongst the hills at right angles to the general direction I had been coming. A broader path led up the left side of this big valley. Great fir-trees here and there towered high over everything. A few white storks were feeding in the rice-fields, and grand birds they looked.

I trudged on to the village near the top of the valley, meaning to have a dip in the sulphur spring which I knew existed there. But

I found the bath, which was only about four feet square, already occupied by an elderly gentleman and lady, a young damsel and a youth. Not wishing to interfere with this happy though peculiar quartet, I gave up the idea of a bath and went on.

The path now led directly into an extensive range of hills covered with wood. Numerous species of fir, oak of small size, alder, Spanish chestnut and birch were the principal trees. As I passed a badger came shuffling along, and got quite near before he observed me. When he did, he appeared very little astonished, only altering his course slightly as he went by.

Myrtles and azaleas grew on all the more open places, the latter being in full bloom and forming a rich and colourful carpet. About a quarter of a mile further on another beautiful kingfisher started from a branch, and as I watched it a stag trotted from a clump of bushes and made off up the hill.

Evening was approaching, and I had still some miles to go, so getting again into the path I made the best of my way back.

ANON

KOREA

(1888)

THE country . . . grew still wilder, and the villages more sparse. Another slow ascent, following the bed of a stream, brought us to the top of another ridge, beautifully wooded and rich in ferns. The maples were exquisite, and among them were well-grown oaks, hazels, and a bush like the hazel, which has a flower said to be white with large purple stamens. The road ran for a mile or so along the crest of the hills, commanding a wide view towards Chang-söng. The drivers, like myself, felt the effect of the scenery, and dawdled on the road, with the result that we were again benighted. But being benighted is rather an advantage than otherwise when bodies of men are ready with huge hurdles of flaming reeds to show the road. The monotony of the day is then destroyed, and the beauties of daylight only give way to the weird effect of torchlight among the hills.

CARLES

*

(1885)

The houses are devoid of windows, except of the most rudimentary description. In the side streets the effect is forbidding in the extreme. On either hand are long lines of wall, protected in front by little gutter-moats and capped with a roofing of tiles. Though they scarcely look it, they are the sides of houses. Except for a few loopholes close under the eaves, they are indistinguishable from walls proper ; for all walls in Korea are as thoroughly roofed as the houses themselves. These loopholes are small square apertures, fitted with small sliding screens of paper. On the outside are not infrequently iron gratings. Only at intervals in the long line of

stone some gateway breaks the pitiless exclusion, and then but to
yield at best a melancholy glimpse into an empty courtyard.

LOWELL, *Chosön*

KUCHIN

(1848)

THE town of Kuchin is built on the left hand side of the river Sarawak
going up, and, from the windings of the river, you have to pull
twenty-five miles up the river to arrive at it, whereas it is only five
miles from the coast as the crow flies. It consists of about 800
houses, built on piles driven into the ground, the sides and roof
being enclosed with dried palm leaves.

The residence of Mr. Brooke is on the side of the river opposite
the town, as for the most part are all the houses of the Europeans.
In structure it somewhat resembles a Swiss cottage, and is erected
upon a green mound, which slopes down to the river's bank, where
there is a landing-place for boats. At the back of the house is a
garden containing almost every tree peculiar to the climate ; and
it was a novelty to us to see collected together the cotton-tree,
the areca, sago, palm, etc., with every variety of the Camellia
japonica in a state of luxurious wildness.

MARRYAT

LIUCHIU ISLANDS

THE Liquejo Islands, as they are set down in our Maps, or the Islands
of Riuku, as they are call'd by the Inhabitants . . . lie to the
Southwest of the Province Satzuma. . . . If we believe the
Japanese, they are so fruitful, as to yield the Rice harvest twice a
year. The Inhabitants, which are for the most part either husband-
men or fishermen, are a good natured merry sort of people, leading

an agreeable contented life, diverting themselves, after their work is done, with a glass of rice beer, and playing upon their musical Instruments, which they for this purpose carry out with them into the fields. They appear by their language to be of Chinese extraction. In the late great revolution in China, when the Tartars invaded and possess'd themselves of that mighty Empire, the Natives retired in great numbers, and were dispers'd all over the East Indies. Not a few fled to these islands, where they applied themselves chiefly to trade, being well skill'd in navigation, and well acquainted with those Seas.

KAEMPFER

*

(1817)

The island of Lewchew itself is situated in the happiest climate of the globe. . . . Refreshed by the sea breezes, which, from its geographical position, blow over it at every period of the year, it is free from the extremes of heat and cold which oppress many other countries ; whilst from the general configuration of the land, being more adapted to the production of rivers and streams than of bogs and marshes, one great source of disease in the warmer latitudes has no existence : and the people seemed to enjoy robust health. . . .

The verdant lawns and romantic scenery of Tinian and Juan Fernando, so well described in Anson's Voyage, are here displayed in higher perfection, and on a much more magnificent scale ; for cultivation is added to the most enchanting beauties of nature. From a commanding height above the ships, the view is in all directions picturesque and delightful. . . . On one hand are seen the distant islands, rising from a wide expanse of ocean, whilst the clearness of the water enables the eye to trace all the coral reefs which protect the anchorage immediately below. . . . Turning to the east the houses of the capital, Kintching, built in their peculiar style, are observed here and there, opening from among the lofty trees which surround and shade them, rising one above another in gentle ascent to the summit of a hill which is crowned by the king's palace. . . . To the north, as far as the eye can reach, the higher land is covered with extensive forests.

M'Leod

The island of Lewchew is about sixty miles long and twenty broad. . . . It is the principal island of a group of thirty-six, subject to the same monarch, and the seat of the government. The natives trace their history back to a period long anterior to the Christian era ; but their first communication with the rest of the world, when their accounts became fully corroborated and undisputed, was about the year 605, when they were invaded by China, who found them at that time—a time when England and the greater part of Europe were immersed in barbarism—the same kind of people they are at the present day, with the exception of a few Chinese innovations ; or, at least, they appear to have altered but in a very slight degree. Indeed, it is very obvious that a revolution in manners, and alteration of habits, are by no means so likely to occur with a people thus living in an obscure and secluded state, as among those who have a wider intercourse with other nations. The only connexion which the Lewchews have had with their neighbours, and that but very limited, has been with Japan and China, from neither of whom were they likely to receive any example of change.

Ibid.

(1889)

The scene had the Japanese peculiarity of quaintness and unreality
to a marked degree, but was at the same time strikingly beautiful.
The house, that lay before us, was placed at the edge of a miniature
lake, whose still, black waters were dotted with lotus plants. The
rich green leaves and delicate pink flowers were mirrored in its
surface with marvellous clearness, and on the opposite bank it was
hard to trace the limits of the water, so merged was the reflection
in the reality. Here a hill rose steeply, a mass of dense vegetation, in
which gnarled trunks, masses of creeper, and feathery fronds of the
tree-fern mingled in graceful confusion. A gap in the foliage
revealed the battlements of the citadel above, weather-worn and
grey with age, and over the grotesquely shaped stone bridge, whose
open balustrading was richly carved, a crowd of people poured
from the busy street.

GUILLEMARD

MACAO

(1727)

CANTON or Quantung (as the Chinese express it) is the next maritime Province ; and Maccaw, a City built by the Portugueze, was
the first place of Commerce. This City stands on a small Island,
and is almost surrounded by the Sea. Towards the Land it is
defended by three Castles built on the Tops of low Hills. By its
Situation and Strength by Nature and Art, it was once thought
impregnable. Indeed their beautiful Churches and other Buildings
give us a reflecting Idea of its ancient Grandeur, for in the Forepart
of the seventeenth Century, according to the Christian Aera, it was
the greatest Port for Trade in India or China.

The largest brass Cannon that ever I saw are mounted in proper

Batteries about the City. I measured one (amongst many) out of Curiosity, and found it 23 Foot from the Breech to the Muzzle Ring, nine Inches and a Quarter diameter in the Bore, and it was 12,250 *Rotullaes* or *lb* Weight of solid Metal.

The City contains five Churches, but the Jesuits is the best, and is dedicated to St. Paul. It has two Convents for married Women to retire to, when their Husbands are absent, and orphan Maidens are educated in them till they can catch an Husband. They have also a Nunnery for devout ladies, young or old, that are out of Conceit with the Troubles and Cares of the World.

HAMILTON

MACASSAR

(1911)

SAILORS and Swiss peasants do not rhapsodise on scenery ; but deep down somewhere the sailor, at any rate, has an inarticulate under-standing ; and every one on the ship, I noticed, had been glad when we got the orders for Macassar.

Looking at the panorama as it unfolded itself to me that beautiful clear morning, I think I understood why they liked it so much ; for the approach to Macassar is one of the faery visions of the world, and years after the inward eye can ruminate on it and return anew.

Imagine to port an opal sea, pellucid, mirror-like, studded with a thousand little atolls, each with its silvery beach and fringe of dark green palm trees, smiling under a sky of purest ultramarine shading gradually to a pearly-grey as it touched the horizon. Landward the silver shore ran sinuous in little sparkling bays and inlets, fringed, far as the eye could see, with feathery groves of slender coco-nuts, backed by serrated blue mountains shimmering in the hinterland.

Gradually as we approached native huts could be made out, nestling amongst the njamplong trees, each house a framework of

77

bamboo standing on props, with walls of latticed yellow rattan, and dark brown palm-thatched roofs. Dilapidated boat slips, a patchwork of blistered stakes and warped tinder-like planks, ran up to some of the stilted huts projecting into the water ; and sampans and dug-outs, some with, some without outriggers, lay bleaching on the strand, just beyond the lazy ripples.

On the intervening water other fishing praus were shooting about, with their peculiar-looking lozenge-shaped ' bugis ' sails swelling in the light morning zephyrs. A lotus-air of immemorial calm lay over everything.

Then came signs of civilisation—a long white red-tiled building close to the shore with a square green behind ; next a dazzling black-and-white lighthouse flying the Dutch tricolour ; nestling beneath it, glistening in the morning sun, lay a little white jetty for yachts ; and then came the long straight reach of over half a mile of black tarred wharf, almost devoid of shipping, with a row of yellow bamboo rattan-latticed ' go-downs ' behind, and again behind these the huddled red-tiled roofs of the city itself.

Several river gunboats lay anchored off the pier ; and from the red-roofed building we had first noticed a burst of military music floated to us on the morning air. It was a regimental band playing outside the officers' mess at breakfast.

ABRAHAM

The Lands

MALACCA

(1727)

THE Country produces nothing for a foreign Market but a little
Tin and Elephants Teeth, and several excellent Fruits and Roots
for the Use of the Inhabitants, and Strangers who call there for
Refreshments. The Malacca Pine-apple is accounted the best in
the World, for in other Parts, if they are eaten to a small Excess,
they are apt to give Surfeits, but those of Malacca never offend the
Stomach. The Mangostane is a delicious Fruit, almost in the Shape
of an Apple, the Skin is thick and red, being dried it is a good
Astringent. The Kernals (if I may so call them) are like Cloves of
Garlick, of a very agreeable Taste, but very cold. . . . The Durean
is another excellent Fruit, but offensive to some Peoples Noses,
but when once tasted the Smell vanishes. The Skin is thick and
yellow, and within is a Pulp like thick Cream in Colour and Consistence, but more delicious in Taste. The Pulp or Meat is very
hot and nourishing, and instead of surfeiting they fortifie the
Stomach, and are a great Incentive to Wantonness. They have
Cocoanuts in Plenty, and . . . some that are overflown with the
Sea in Spring-tides. Their Liquor and Kernal partake of the
Qualities of the Ground they grow in, being exceeding Salt. I
never saw any Cocoanuts grow in Salt Grounds but there in
Marishes, and some are so large that the Shell will hold more than
an English Quart Pot.

HAMILTON

★

Malacca, a Place of small Account, in a short Time became
famous all over India and Europe, lying almost in the Centre of

Trade, brought thither by Shipping from the rich Kingdoms of
Japon, China, Formosa, Luconia, Tonquin, Couchin-China,
Cambodia and Siam, besides what Johore produced, and Sumatra,
Java, Borneo, Macassar, Banda, Amboina, and Ternate Islands, that
produce many valuable Commodities.

As the Portugueze grew great and rich, they grew also insolent,
and so continued abusing and affronting their Neighbours till,
about the Year 1660, the Dutch had a War with Portugal, on
Account of some Losses the Dutch sustained in Brazil. . . .

The Dutch coming into the Streights of Malacca from Batavia,
with a strong Fleet and a Land-army on board of it, struck up an
Alliance with the King of Johore, offensive and defensive, as long
as the Sun and Moon gave Light to this World ; for I saw the
Treaty, and heard it read, with those Expressions in it : On which
the King of Johore assisted the Dutch with 20,000 Men, and laid
siege to (Malacca) by Land, while the Dutch distressed it by Sea ;
and yet for all that the Fleet and Army could do, they could not
have taken it by Force . . . so what they could not effect by Force,
they did by Fraud.

They heard that the Portugueze Governor was a sordid, avaricious
Fellow, and ill beloved by the Garison, so the Dutch, by secret
Conveyances, tampered with him by Letters, promising him
Mountains of Gold if he would contribute towards their gaining
the Fort. At length the Price was set of 8000 Pieces of Eight, to be
the Reward of his Treachery, and to be safely transported to Batavia
in their Fleet, and be made a free Denizon there. So he sent secret
Orders to the Dutch to make an Attack on the East-side of the
Fort, and he would act his Part, which was accordingly done . . .
and he delayed (to give orders) till the Dutch got into the Fort,
and drove the Guard from the East-gate, which they soon opened
to receive the rest of their Army, who, as soon as they were entred,
gave Quarters to none that were in Arms, and marching towards
the Governor's House, where he thought himself secure by the

Treaty, they forthwith dispatcht him to save the fourscore thousand Dollars.

Ibid.

*

At Malacca the Streights are not above 4 Leagues broad ; for tho' the opposite Shore on Sumatra is very low, yet it may easily be seen in a clear Day, which is the Reason that the Sea is always as smooth as a Mill-pond, except when it is ruffled with Squalls of Wind, which seldom come without Lightnings, Thunder and Rain ; and tho' they come with great Violence, yet they are soon over, not often exceeding an Hour.

Ibid.

*

(1847)

Malacca always seemed to me one of those old places that, having a kind of half-fabulous antiquity about them—a name and a glory long since faded—are peculiarly attractive to the imagination. I was delighted at the opportunity of being able to substitute a real image for the shadowy one that had glimmered in my mind ever since, as a boy, I had read of Malacca as the Queen of the East, in narratives of the older voyagers.

. . . Altogether I was far more pleased with the aspect of Malacca than that of Singapore. Singapore looks like one of our spick and span new colonial towns dropped by some accident into the tropics, where it is totally out of place. The trees have been most injudiciously cleared away leaving bare white houses and dusty roads gleaming in the sun. Malacca on the contrary, seems to be the natural growth of the country, a native town just sufficiently elevated by the mixture of European character, without losing its own. Its houses seem to have grown up under the trees that shelter them, and its narrow, shadowy alleys and green lanes form a most delightful contrast to the glaring streets of Singapore. To a stranger

81

like myself unemployed in business, the very air of indolence and contentment that Malacca wears is far preferable to the stir and bustle of its rival. This character seems fully appreciated by its inhabitants, as on my asking a native boatman one day, which he liked best, he said he had been at Singapore, but did not like it at all ; adding in his own language, ' Everybody was running here, running there, and doing something all the day long, and there was too much noise.'

JUKES

*

St. Francis Xavier reached Malacca at the end of September, 1545.

' Since I have been at Malacca,' he wrote to the Society in Portugal, ' which is a city on the sea, a famous and crowded mart for merchants, I have had no lack of holy occupations. On Sundays I preach to the people, though I admire my own sermons much less than those do who are so good as to listen to them. Every day for an hour, and sometimes more, I teach the children the usual prayers, I live in the hospital, I hear the confessions of the sick, say mass for them, and give them holy communion. I am so overwhelmed by the number of persons who come to confess, that I cannot satisfy them all by any means.'

' When I was at Malacca,' he wrote later, ' I established the custom that at the beginning of night the souls in Purgatory and the souls of the living who are in a state of worldly sin, should be recommended to the prayers of the pious in all the streets. This practice not only encouraged the good, but threw terror into the wicked. The city appointed a man for the purpose, to go round the town, with a lantern in one hand and a bell in the other, and calling out from time to time in a loud voice, " Pray for the souls of the faithful Christians who are suffering in Purgatory, and pray also for those who, lying under the burthern of mortal sin, take no pains to be delivered from it." '

COLERIDGE

The Lands

MANCHURIA

(1859)

ON the 12th of September we landed on a projecting point marked on the charts as an island, on the eastern side of the Gulf of Liao-tung. On leaving the boat we approached a rounded knoll, on the summit of which was a square watch-tower with Tartar horsemen grouped picturesquely around it. In the distance were the angular, cold, grey peaks and ridges of a barren mountain range, with here and there little rivers running down their sides, gleaming like quicksilver as the sun shone on the water-courses and little winding streams. At the base of these lifeless granite masses stretched a level

plain, green and fertile, where little straggling hamlets of low, flat-topped mud houses were snugly sheltered in long groves of trees. To this succeeded a sterile sandy belt, with a chain of fresh-water ponds, shallow and full of weeds, and with muddy open spaces between them—the natural resort of the curlew, the whimbrel, the plover and the snipe. Here also we saw the spotted crake, a sly little fellow, keeping close in the cover of the reeds and grass. The pretty but scentless Chinese pink, a little blue-flowered iris, and a yellow, red and white mixture of the blossoms of the tormentil, the heads of sanguisorba, and the loose corymbs of the flower of yarrow, completed nearly all the plants that redeemed the sandy soil from sameness and utter sterility. Nearer the sea, long salt-water lagoons and shallow swamps extended, covered in some parts with a white-flowered sea-lavender and the blue stars of *aster tripolium.* From these the great white heron slowly rose, and after a few lazy flaps with his huge curved wings, alighted again to resume his interrupted fishing. Equally familiar was his yet larger cousin in grey, the common heron, and, standing on one leg, her loose, snowy plumes waving in the breeze, the elegant white egret dreamed of frogs and fishes. Sandpipers and greenshanks ran piping and probing about the margin, and gulls and little terns screamed, quarrelled and hovered over the heads of both bipeds and birds.

ADAMS

I had pictured Manchuria as bleak and barren, but I found myself as it were in a great garden run wild. From the sandy banks of a small trout stream, where plenty of fish were rising, I was surrounded by large crimson roses, white-flowered peonies, spotted tiger-lilies, a scarlet, single-flowered lychnis, clusters of clematis with dark, hairy, bell-shaped blossoms, lilies of the valley, tall, blue-flowered Polymoniums, and the bright yellow blossoms of *Trollius asiaticus.* The rest of the vegetation was made up of oak-scrub, plume-like sedges, tall grasses, and the stems of a giant Archangelica, with here and there *Geranium pratense* and a pretty red Valerian.

Ibid.

The Lands

(1898)

A main road in Manchuria in winter is a busy scene. . . . I counted in a single day's march over eight hundred carts, all heavily laden and drawn by teams of at least two, and many of them nine animals, ponies or mules. These strings of carts rolling along on a frosty morning, with the jingling bells of the teams and the drivers shouting at their animals, were signs of animation which we had hardly expected to see after our first experience on the heavy, muddy roads in the summer.

The country we passed through was pretty even in winter, and must have been beautiful in summer. It was undulating, well covered with trees, and intersected with many little streams and rivers. At this season all was under snow, but one morning we saw one of the most perfectly lovely sights I have ever seen—a *frozen* mist. As the sun rose we found the whole air glittering with brilliant particles sparkling in the rays of the sun—and the mist had encrusted everything, all the trunks of the trees and all the delicate tracery of their outlines, with a coating like hoar frost. The earth, the trees, and everything around was glistening white, and the whole air sparkling in the sunlight. It lasted but a short while, for as the sun rose the mist melted away ; but for the time one seemed to be verily in a fairyland.

YOUNGHUSBAND

MANILLA

(1727)

LUCONIA is the largest of all the Philippine Islands, and is richest in its Productions, for it affords Corn, Fruits and Roots in great Plenty, as well as wild Game and Fowl. It produces Gold, but of a low Touch. It is not half conquered yet by the Spaniards, tho' they are possest of all the Sea-coast, as the Dutch are of Zealoan ; and the Natives lose no Opportunity of cutting off their Lords the Spaniards, when they can do it without Danger. They have fortified their Mountains and Vallies so well with thick Hedges of Bambows, that the Spaniards cannot easily molest them, tho' they have secret Ways to sally out and disturb their Enemy.

The chief City in Luconia is Manhila or Manilla, the Residence of the Spanish Viceroy, and the Port where all the Galleons that come yearly from New-spain resort to. The Harbour is spacious, commodious and safe. They admit of Trade from India and China, but not with any European Nation. The Mahometans are tolerated in their Religion, but not the Pagans, so that all Chinese that go there for Commerce, get a little Brass Image hung about their Neck, with a String of Beads in their Hands, and learning to cross themselves, cry *Jesu sancta Malia* (for they cannot pronounce *Maria*, because the Letter R is excluded the Chinese Alphabet). I say, when they have got all those fore-named Qualifications, they are good Spanish Christians.

And when they have feathered their Nest by cheating the Spaniard, and taken their Leave of Manilla or Manhila, at their passing by a Mountain dedicated to the Virgin Mary, they throw their Beads over board, and thank the Virgin for her Kindness to them.

HAMILTON

MINDANAO

(1727)

MINDANAO is both the southernmost and easternmost of all the Philippines. It has little or no Commerce with Strangers, and I never heard of any European Ship that went to it since Captain Swan called there in his Way from Panama to India, when Captain Dampier was with him, who, no Doubt, has given a good Account of it in his Travels : And I know no more of it, but that it is divided into many small Principalities, and that the Sea-Worm eats so greedily Ships Bottoms, that in three or four Months they eat quite thro', and that there is Abundance of Rice and other Provisions to be had very cheap there, and that it produces very good *Cassia-lignum*, or bastard Cinnamon. It is about 140 Leagues in Length, but of very unequal Breadth, having many large deep Bays running into it, which afford many Harbours for Shipping.

HAMILTON

*

(1911)

All the next morning we were racing along the coast of Mindanao, a mass of serrated, blue-grey mountain-peaks against a sky capped by golden cumuli, with vast forests of dark green pine running down the mountain-sides to the sea, and here and there the smoke of a great forest fire rising in the tremulous haze.

Flying catamarans manned by coppery Filipinos once or twice came close ; but we had not time to stop to buy their fish.

The temperature was 90° F. in the shade ; but all the morning the cool breeze, blowing off the shore, kept us quite comfortable. At noon, however, we had passed Mindanao and sighted Sarangani (5°19′ N., 125°19′ E.) ; we were clear away from the land ; and now the starboard side felt like an oven, and the heat-waves could almost be seen beating through the awnings as a big dragon-fly from the land spread his iridescent wings and preened himself on the rail before me.

Now and again, as I lay watching, a dolphin would raise his nose out of the water just behind a scurrying flying fish, which had taken to the air to avoid him ; whilst further out a line of splashing white-flecked spots indicated a school of bonito jumping.

ABRAHAM

MOTU MOTU

(1890)

DURING the fortnight spent at Motu Motu my two natives simply revelled in a most welcome change of diet. For not only did the sea and river yield a plentiful harvest of whiting, garfish, flounder, soles, eells, mullet, bream and schnapper, as well as rainbow-tinted tropical piscine eccentricities innumerable ; but the perfervid, seething soil brought forth luscious bananas, mealy yams, and refreshing coconuts in profusion. The very pigs grow so fat and monstrous in that land of rolling plenty that they can hardly move. The life of the Motu Motuans would be that of the true lotus-eaters ; they might even degenerate into the phlegmatic condition of their own pigs were it not for the little rift within the lute, *i.e.*, their fear of spirit or devil-worship (in other words, their inability to escape from the *shadow of themselves*), and a perennial internecine feud with the Moviavians, who live some little distance down the Williams River.

BEVAN

The Lands

NAGASAKI

(1728)

THIS Town is never without a great deal of noise. In the day time victuals, and other merchandise, are cried up and down the streets. Day labourers encourage one another to work with a certain sound. The Seamen in the harbour measure the progress of their work according to another loud tune. In the night time the watchmen and Soldiers upon duty, both in the streets and harbour, shew their vigilance, and at the same time indicate the hours of the night, by beating two strong pieces of wood one against another. The Chinese also contribute their share, chiefly in the evening, when they burn some pieces of gilt paper, and throw them into the Sea, as an offering or sacrifice, to their Idol . . . or when they carry the said Idol about its Temple, both which they do with beating of drums and cymbals. But all this is little in comparison to the clamour and bawling of the Priests and relations of dying, or dead, Persons, who, either in the house where the corpse lies, or else upon certain days sacred to the deceased's memory, sing a *Namanda* with a loud voice, and ringing of bells, for the relief of his soul.

KAEMPFER

THE ISLAND OF NICOBAR

(FOURTEENTH CENTURY)

WHEN you leave the island of Java the Less and the kingdom of Lambri, you sail north about one hundred and fifty miles and then you come to two islands, one of which is called Nicobar. In this island they have no king or chief, but live like beasts. And I tell you they all go naked, both men and women, and do not use the slightest covering of any kind. They are idolators. Their woods

89

are of all noble and valuable kinds of trees ; such as Red Sanders and indian nut and cloves and brazil and sundry other good spices.

There is nothing else worth relating ; so we will go on, and I will tell you of an island called Andaman.

Marco Polo

NINGPO

(1891)

The life of a Chinese country gentleman, or farmer, or farm-labourer, is a monotonous one for the most part, but not unbroken by strange and sudden excitement.

How fair beyond description is a morning in April or early May in the fields or on the slopes near Ningpo. The sun is up, and is fast dispersing the low white mist over the land. The sharp metallic cry of the pheasant is heard ; and looking from the boat-head, there, almost glorious in the sunshine which lights up every dew-drop on the grass around him, the great red bird is standing flapping his wings and rejoicing in the morning air. The beans are in full bloom, and as the sun warms the flowers, and the breeze wafts the odour, the air is deliciously fragrant. The wheat is tall and luxuriant, as it is only one month till harvest time. Great masses of red clover are in flower, and ready to be ploughed into the half-submerged soil which is being prepared for the rice crops. We pass brilliant emerald patches, the seed-beds for the early rice plants, which will soon be transplanted into the wider acres of the prepared ground. Narrow raised paths run round each field ; and the country is traversed by larger paths, paved with rough round pebbles or slabs of stone. . . .

The lines of the water-courses which traverse the plain are shaded with trees—willow, or Pride of India, or large camphor trees, or the tallow tree, so brilliant in autumn with scarlet leaves and snow-white berries. Fine trees also shade the water-pumps, which are now taken out of their winter shelters in temple-yard or shed, and are fixed for the summer's ceaseless toil along the canal-banks. The yellow oxen, which blind-folded turn the flat wheels of these pumps, are enjoying rest and fresh pasture now on the low hill-sides or amongst the clover and buttercups which clothe the tombs ; and as our boat nears the hills, red bunches of azaleas hang from the bank and mirror themselves in the water of the inundated rice-land below.

The hills are in their full beauty. Besides the great carpet of azaleas, wisteria crowns the rocks, and sometimes camphor trees, thirty or forty feet high, are festooned from the summit to the ground by branches of this beautiful and fragrant creeper, falling and trailing amongst the green of the young camphor leaves. Single camellias also abound, and blue borage ; and the fir-trees are in bloom ; and women and girls are busy gathering the bloom to mix in their cakes.

The blackbird and the Chinese yellow-eyebrowed thrush make the hills resound with melody ; the wood-pigeons murmur ; and the soaring cry of rooks and the croak of the raven are heard ; besides many sweet notes peculiar to these beautiful hills and plains of China.

MOULE

NORFOLK ISLAND

As a rule, I think, much-praised scenery is disappointing, at any rate at first sight. But Norfolk Island is an exception. No description that I have read of this island exaggerates its loveliness. On shore the broad sweeps of grass land, broken here and there into valleys and undulations, give it a park-like appearance, while the clusters of Norfolk Island pines, their picturesque forms sharply defined in the yellow sunlight, with depths of restful shadows, seem to be the result of artistic cultivation rather than chance disposition.

Looking seaward the scene is not less fair. Bays with white, sandy beaches and crested waves. Rocky chasms where the long swell dashes itself into foam. Rocks and islets, fantastic in form and rich in colour. While burning with brilliance, as if it had drunk in every bright glow of sunset, Philip Island stands out of the many tints of blue and opal of the surrounding sea.

. . . The station has been long abandoned, and the present inhabitants came from Pitcairn's Island. They were brought to Norfolk Island by the order of the Queen (Victoria), and endowed with houses and lands, when the convict settlement was abandoned, Pitcairn's Island having become too small for their rapidly increasing numbers.

No greater boon, one would suppose, could have been conferred upon these descendants of the mutineers of the *Bounty*, whose exemplary conduct had brought them under the Sovereign's favourable notice ; but some were dissatisfied with the change. Norfolk Island, small as it was, oppressed them with its vastness, with its roads (there was only a wheel-barrow track at Pitcairn), and especially with its stone houses, in which the echo of their voices was a novelty too startling for their nerves ; and so this minority elected to return to their old home, leaving to their more canny compatriots an appreciably increased share in the good things at Norfolk Island.

The community principle is still in practice to a considerable extent. In the early days at Pitcairn this answered well enough, and it is difficult to abolish it now, when almost everyone is more or less nearly related to everyone else, but it bars the way to improvement in the condition of the people, both morally and socially, which is greatly needed. Because the Norfolkers of to-day may be divided into two classes; those who work and those who don't. If it were not for the community principle the scripture rule would be carried out, and a man who has work to do and won't do it would have to starve. Instead of this the industrious ones keep the lazy ones.

PENNY (abridged)

PEGU

(1586)

PEGU is a citie very great, strong, and very faire, with walles of stone, and great ditches round about it. There are two townes, the old towne and the newe. In the old towne are all the merchants strangers, and very many merchants of the countrey. All the goods are sold in the olde towne which is very great, and hath many suburbs round about it, and all the houses are made of Canes which they call Bambos and bee covered with strawe. In your house you have a warehouse which they call Godon, which is made of bricke to put your goods in, for often times they take fire and burne in an houre four or five hundred houses : so that if the Godon were not you should bee in danger to have all burned, if any winde should rise, at a trice. It is a citie very great and populous, and is made square with very faire walles and a great ditch round about it full of water, with many crocodiles in it. The streets are the fairest that ever I saw, as straight as a line from one gate to the other, and so broad that ten or twelve men may ride a front thorow them. At both sides of them at every mans doore is set a palmer tree which is the nut tree, which make a very faire shew and a very commodious shadow, so that a man may walke in the shade all day.

The kings house is in the citie, and the buildings are made of wood and sumptuously gilded. Within the first gate of the kings house is a great large roome on both sides whereof are houses made for the kings elephants, which are brought up to warres and in service of the king. And among the rest he hath foure white elephants, which are very strange and rare. . . . They do very great service unto these white elephants; every one of them standeth in an house gilded with gold, and they do feed in vessels of silver and gilt.

RYLEY (abridged)

PEKING

(SIXTEENTH CENTURY)

'They that have seen little beleeve not much, whereas they that have seen much beleeve the more.'—PINTO.

THE City of Pequin, whereof I have promised to speak more amply then yet I have done, is so prodigious, and the things therein so remarkable, as I do almost repent me for undertaking to discourse of it, because to speak the truth, I know not where to begin, that I may be as good as my word ; for one must not imagine it to be, either as the City of Rome, or Constantinople, or Venice, or Paris, or London, or Sevill, or Lisbon, or that any of the cities of Europe are comparable unto it, how famous and populous soever they be : nay, I will say further, that one must not think it to be like to Grand Cairo in Egypt, Tauris in Persia, Amadaba in Cambaya, Bisnagar in Narsingua, Goura in Bengala, Ava in Chaleu, Timplan in Calaminhan, Martaban and Bagou in Pegu, Guimpel and Tinlau in Siammon, Odia in the Kingdom of Sornau, Passarvan and Dema in the Island of Jaoa, Pangor in the country of the Lequiens, Usangea in the Grand Cauchin, Lancama in Tartaria, and Meaco in Jappun, all which Cities are the Capitals of many great Kingdoms ; for I dare well affirm, that all those same are not to be compared to the least part of the wonderful City of Pequin, much less to the greatness and magnificence of that which is most excellent in it, whereby I understand her stately buildings, her inward riches, her excessive abundance of all that is necessary for the entertaining of life, also the world of people, the infinite number of Barques and Vessels that are there, the Commerce, the Courts of Justice, the Government and the State of the *Tutons* . . . and *Bracanons* who rule whole Kingdoms and very spacious Provinces, with great pentions, and are ordinarily resident in this city. . . . But setting these things aside, I say that this City is thirty leagues in circuit, not comprehending therein the buildings of the other inclosure that is without it, and is invironed with a double wall, having three hundred and three score gates, each of which is a small Fort. . . .

The principal streets of this City are all very long and broad, with fair houses of two or three stories high, and inclosed at both ends with ballisters of iron and lattin. . . . Moreover this great City (if credit may be given to that which the said book, so often before mentioned by me, records) hath an hundred and twenty canals, which are three fathom deep and twelve broad, crossing through the whole length and bredth of the City. . . . It is said that the Bridges over these hundred and twenty Canals or Aqueducts, are in number eighteen hundred, and that if one of them is fair and rich the other is yet more, as well for the fashion as for the rest of the workmanship thereof.

Now during the two months time we were at liberty in this City, we saw eleven or twelve public Fairs, where were an infinite company of people that out of boxes hanging about their necks sold all things that well neer can be named, besides the ordinary shops of rich merchants, where was to be seen a world of silk stuffs, tinsels, cloth of gold, linnen and cotton-cloth, sables, ermine, musk, aloes, fine pourcelain, gold and silver plate, pearl, seed-pearl, gold in powder, and lingots. But if I should speak in particular of all the other commodities that were to be sold there, as of iron, steel, lead, copper, tin, latin, corral, cornalin, crystal, quicksilver, vermillion, ivory, cloves, nutmegs, mace, ginger, tamarinds, cinnamon, pepper, cardamone, borax, hony, wax, sanders, sugar, conserves, acates, fruit, meal, rice, flesh, venison, fish, pulse and herbs ; there was such abundance of them as it is scarce possible to express it in words. The Chineses also assured us that this City hath an hundred and three score Butchers shambles, and in each of them an hundred stalls, full of all kinds of flesh that the earth produceth, as veal, mutton, pork, goat, the flesh of horses, buffles, rhinoceros, tygers, lions, dogs, mules, asses, otters, shamois, bodgers, and finally of all other beasts whatever. . . . There are withal many Taverns, where excellent fare is always to be had, and cellers full of gammons of bacon, dried tongues, poudered geese and other savoury viands, for to relish ones drink, all in so great abundance that it would be very superfluous to say more of it ; but what I speak is to shew how liberally God hath imparted to these miserable blinded wretches the good things which he hath created on the earth, to the end that his holy name may therefore be blessed for ever.

PINTO

★

(1862)

March 26th, 1862.—Though the sky was clouded, the forenoon, for the present season of the year, was unusually hot and sultry, the thermometer about noon having risen to 70°. Towards the afternoon a strong wind began to rise, and gradually one of the ordinary sandstorms, common in this region, was produced. A remarkable fall in the thermometer then suddenly took place, and at ten minutes to three a dark brown cloud was seen to be rapidly approaching the town, which was soon enveloped by it in comparative darkness. The wind howled, and the whole air was pregnant with a minute and searching dust which penetrated every crevice. A strong sulphurous odour was at the same time very apparent. At five minutes to three, though sitting at a table close to a window, I could not see to write, and it was with difficulty that I could even make out what the hour was, so dark had it become. In a very few minutes every portion of the building was filled with dust, from which there was no escape. The atmosphere outside was suffocating, and it was almost impossible to walk a hundred yards against the wind, which I did, being anxious to see the condition of the electrometer, which I found showed at the time negative electricity, the conducting wire emitting from its lower end a constant succession of blue sparks, which were very apparent in the darkness that prevailed ; the shocks on the knuckle also, when presented to it, were very severe. From three in the afternoon the darkness was so great as to abbreviate daylight by three and a half hours. At night the darkness was complete, not the most imperfect ray of light being visible.

March 27th.—The storm raged during the night, the wind blowing in gusts like a hurricane, and threatening to sweep the buildings down, partitions and window-frames giving way in every direction. The condition of the interior of the rooms it would be difficult to describe, from the amount of fine dust with which everything was coated, and every individual also.

Rennie

PENANG

(1821)

Penang is about sixteen miles in length from north to south, and from seven to eight in breadth. By far the greater part of the island is mountainous, rocky, sterile, and covered with a forest of tall trees. A portion of the south and of the east parts is level, and these alone constitute the cultivated and inhabited quarter of the island. The highest hills are above two thousand feet in height, and on these the thermometer is about ten degrees lower than on the plain. The harbour, which was the principal inducement to its occupation, is formed by the island, with the mainland two miles distant. The whole island, like the countries in its neighbourhood, is one mass of granite, exhibiting very little variety. The seasons are irregular : rain is frequent throughout the year ; but the regular wet season is of short continuance, beginning with September and ending with November. The coldest months are December and January ; and the hottest June and July. In rural economy the rainy season is the spring of the year ; and January, February and March constitute autumn. . . .

When the English took possession of Penang in 1786 it was wholly uncultivated, and had no other inhabitants than a few occasional Malayan fishermen. It now contains about 39,000 people, including Indian islanders, Chinese, natives of the Coromandel and Malabar coasts, natives of Bengal, Burmans and Siamese, Europeans, and their descendants, with a few Arabs, Armenians, Parsees and African negroes. The Indian islanders consist of Malays, Achinese, Battaks and Bugis, who find employment as fishermen, woodcutters, builders of native houses, and field-labourers. . . .

The history of this little establishment is very shortly told. After the war which ended in the peace of 1783, and during which we had had to struggle for naval superiority with the French, the want of a good harbour in the Bay of Bengal as a resort for our ships of war became evident, and Penang, after other abortive and injudicious attempts had been made, was at length fixed upon under the administration of Sir John Macpherson. The person who recommended it to the attention of the Government of India was a Mr. Francis Light, who had traded and resided for a number of years at Siam and Queda. . . . The settlement was formed in the year 1786, and this gentleman appointed to the charge of it, under the title of Superintendent. There is no foundation whatever for the idle story of Mr. Light's having received Penang as a dowry with a daughter of the King of Queda. It was made over to the East India Company in consideration of a yearly payment of 6000 Spanish dollars to compensate for any loss of revenue which might arise to this petty prince from its occupation. It soon rose to considerable prosperity ; and in the year 1791 we were already at war with the Prince of Queda on account of it. In the year 1800 we received an increase of territory by accession of waste and uninhabited land on the opposite shore.

CRAWFURD, *Journal . . . Siam*

*

Jan. 1st, 1822.—Visited Mount Palmer, on the south coast of Prince of Wales' Island (Penang).

4th.—We returned on board the vessel, carrying with us two boxes of nutmeg plants for the King of Siam.

5th.—Sailed out by the South passage ; for several days following we were for the most part becalmed within sight of land.

Nothing is more singular in these seas than their phosphorescent appearance by night, the ocean showing like a vast lake of liquid fire, melted sulphur, or phosphorus. In many of the bays the bodies which emit this singular light exist in such vast quantity that a boat may readily be distinguished at a distance of several miles by the brilliant light, resembling that of a torch, proceeding from the water agitated by her bow and oars. We have seen the sea rendered of a green colour and slimy appearance, by day, so that it might have been taken for the green vegetable matter common on stagnant pools. We have taken up a quantity of this green coloured water, and by keeping it till night, have ascertained that the green colour by day and the phosphorescent appearance by night were occasioned by the same substance.

FINLAYSON

PERAK

(1878)

PRIOR to 1875 the state of Perak was, to a majority of people, a *terra incognita*. They knew, of course, that the Malay peninsula was a long tongue of land stretching nearly to the equator, and that it was in close proximity to Sumatra and Java, with innumerable islands generally known as the Malay archipelago. But few people were aware that a large and rich territory, ruled over by a sultan and his petty chiefs, had been placed under the wing of the British Government, whose representatives were at the court of the ruler, to counsel and advise for the better management of the country.

Picture this tropical land. Not a sun-baked region of parched desert and insufferable drought ; but a rich, moist country, almost touching the equator but rarely suffering from excessive heat ; a land of eternal summer, where refreshing rains fall ; where the monsoons blow regularly ; where the frightful tempests of the east are unknown ; and which is, for the most part, covered with a luxuriant vegetation, the produce of a fertile soil.

This Perak—pronounced as though it were spelt Payrah—is one of the largest of the native states into which the Malay peninsula is divided, and lies upon the western coast, having there, for its ninety miles' boundary-line, the bright prau-traversed waters of the Straits of Malacca.

Perak signifies silver—a name derived probably from the vast amount of silvery looking tin which has been, and promises still to be, one of its principal productions.

The nature of the country may be seen if we take a rapid glance through it by means of its great water-ways. Sailing, steaming, or even paddling, up one of these Perak rivers, we have on either side, if the tide be down, the regular mud-banks of a tropical shore, with the dense mangrove forest standing in its labyrinth of water-washed roots, as if nature had set the example, followed by the dwellers in the land, of building a rough scaffold on which to support the tree trunks, high and dry above the flood. If, on the contrary, the tide be up, right and left the mangrove forest seems to be growing directly out of the river, the stream passing unhindered among the roots. The silence is solemn in its intensity; for, save the plashing of the water to paddle or screw, not a sound is to be heard, and the traveller seems to be penetrating into one of nature's unexplored retreats.

As the boat glides on and on, beyond the tidal influence, the mangroves give place to jungle growth, and on either side, columnar and beautiful, rise the stately growths of palm, with their wondrously straight trunks and tufted heads.

Suddenly the first trace of human habitation appears, in the shape of a Malay village—a cluster of houses of wood or bamboo in a grove of coco-nut palms and fruit-trees. The huts are raised on posts, so as to be beyond the reach of flood and noxious beast, while, secured to bamboo posts or run safely on the mud, are the boats of the villagers. These boats play a prominent part in the daily life of the Malay; for in Perak the rivers are the highways, and the roads are only a few elephant-tracks and pathways through the jungle known to the country people alone.

McNair

*

It is well to remember that to be encyclopedic in giving information is to become a bore. Speaking of Perak, it will not help the enquirer to tell him it is near Penang, because Penang is not so well known as Perak, except to a few people of sixty years and upwards. Early in the seventies Sir Arthur Birch re-discovered Penang and made it known to his friends, but his interest in the Island was fleeting, and it takes a good deal to make a lasting impression on the minds of the English people. Since that time there has been a little war in Perak, but nothing of special importance has taken place in Penang. . . . It is British not to know, and also British not to wish to know. Perhaps it is as well ; too many questions are often trying.

SWETTENHAM

PORT MORESBY

AFTER a week or two spent at Port Moresby, Ah Gim and I took a small boat and cruised some fifty miles to the eastward as far as Keranpuno, in Hood Bay, visiting numerous coast villages *en route*.

Both the spear-grass and the heat are adverse to sheep-farming along this part of the littoral of New Guinea, but behind the coast range, in the undulating forest country, dotted with stunted Australian gum and abounding in wallabies, horses do wonderfully well, and where they succeed cattle may reasonably be expected to thrive.

The river-banks are almost invariably thickly timbered with a joint Australian-Malayan flora, in which the presence of the banyan, mango, casuarinas, eucalyptus, acacias, Leichardt pine, white cedar, the feathery bamboo, also very numerous palms and cycads testify to the suitability of the soil for the growth of tropical products, including sugar-cane. . . .

This part of the country is unsurpassed for natural beauty and romantic formation ; hills, ranges, peaks and mamelon-shaped bluffs, alternating with open forests and thick, rich scrubs, sloping spurs, splendid rolling downs—covered with fine young grass in abundance—and broad well-watered valleys, clothed in perpetual glossy green. The soil is of the finest description, covered with the most luxuriant growth of kangaroo grass, often breast high. Slender spiral columns of smoke here and there betray the presence of man ; and behind this lovely scenery (at a distance of ten to twenty miles) the steep and rocky cliffs of the Astrolabe range, like frowning battlements, may be seen projecting clear-cut against the skyline ; while the sun may be counted upon to shine on some portion of this panorama during part at least of every day in the year.

BEVAN

SINGAPORE

Jan. 20th, 1822.—Arrived at the new settlement of Singapore.

The selection of this island for the purpose of a commercial settlement has been extremely happy. It is placed in the direct route from Bengal towards China and the numerous islands in the eastern part of the Archipelago. It is from its situation calculated to become the centre of the trade carried on in the China Seas, and neighbouring countries, the kingdoms of Cochin China, Siam, etc., as well as that of the Malayan Peninsula and the western parts of India. It affords a safe and convenient anchorage at all seasons of the year ; while from its insular situation, and being surrounded on every hand by innumerable islands, it is alike exempted from the destructive typhoons so common in the China Seas and the scarce less furious tempests that occur on the coasts of India. Here indeed the atmosphere throughout the year is serene and placid, to a degree unknown, perhaps, in any other part of the globe. The smooth expanse of the sea is scarcely ruffled by the wind. Storms are here felt as it were by reflection. The regular and periodical influence of the monsoons is but little, if at all, felt, the winds partaking more of the nature of what have been called sea and land breezes. Few days elapse without the occurrence of showers, which produce the most agreeable effect in reducing the temperature and cherishing vegetation.

Finlayson

(1843)

Sincapore, like all new settlements, is composed of so mixed a community that there is but little hospitality and less gaiety. Every one is waiting to ascertain what is to be his position in society, and till then is afraid of committing himself by friendly intercourse; moreover, every body is too busy making money. The consequence is that a ball is so rare that it becomes the subject of conversation for months. There are some good-looking girls at Sincapore, but prudery is the order of the day, and this is carried to such an extent from non-intercourse that at a farewell ball given to the Cambrians the women would only polka and waltz with each other.

Marryat

The Lands

(1875)

Singapore has beauties of its own such as few other lands can boast. Low hills lend variety to the landscape, and high-roads are carried in broad, even lines along the intervening plains. We may travel by these roads for miles through avenues of fruit-trees, or beneath an over-arching canopy of ever-green palms to red-tiled foreign houses on the slopes and crowns of these hills, behind hedges of wild heliotrope which form compact barriers of green leaves which blossom with gold and purple flowers.

Behind these hedges broad bananas nod their bending leaves, and fan the hot path beneath, while cooler breezes ripple among the palm-trees high above our heads.

If it be early morning there is an unspeakable charm about the spot. The air is cool, even bracing ; and beneath the shade of a group of forest trees we see the rich blossoms of orchids hanging from the boughs and breathe an atmosphere saturated with their perfume. Here and there the slender stem of the aloe, rising from an armoury of spiked leaves, lifts its cone of white bells, or the deep orange pine-apple peeps out from a belt of fleshy green foliage and breathes its ripe fragrance around. On one side a wall of dark foliage casts its shade across the house, and on the other we can see through leafy spaces the rising sun casting long shadows over hill and dale, or mark its faint pencillings of golden light on the distant palm-covered islands that are gradually emerging from the morning mists in the far-off waters of the Straits.

THOMSON, J.

(1884)

In June, 1881, I found myself once more in the East, sweltering in the moist heat of the island settlement of Singapore, and longing for the signal for the steamship *Kongsee* to start, hoping that her progress through the motionless air might in some degree compensate for the absence of the slightest breath of wind to temper the fierce rays of the equatorial sun. The shimmering sea seemed to intensify rather than alleviate, as the presence of water usually does, the oppressiveness of the atmosphere, for its glassy surface, like a polished mirror, reflected the bright light of the sun and seemed to focus his rays as in a lens.

BOCK, *Temples . . .*

SOLOMON ISLANDS

(1867)

WITH the first sight of the tropical islands, I was, I confess, disappointed; the dense masses of foliage, the dull, dark colour of the trees, did not come up to my expectations of what a tropical island would be like.

. . . The Solomon Islands are different in appearance from the Banks and the New Hebrides. There is the same predominating feature of dense, dark-green foliage, but it is varied in some islands by large open spaces covered only by grass of a colour much lighter than that of the trees ; and the size of the islands, some more than a hundred miles long, and the height of the mountain ranges, some of which rise to eight thousand feet above the sea, make so great a contrast to the smaller islands that my ideas of tropical scenery were thereby more fully realized.

PENNY

★

(1887)

Some of my pleasantest memories are associated with my journeys across these smaller islands. After forcing my way during some hours through a tangled forest, irritated by the numerous obstructions in my course and sweltering under the oppressive heat, I have suddenly emerged from the trees on the weather coast of the island, where an invigorating blast of the trade in a few moments restores the equilibrium of mind and body as one drinks in the healthful breeze. After such an experience I have found myself with my native companions standing on the brink of a bold line of coral-limestone cliff with the surf breaking below us, which even in the calmest weather sends up one continued roar, whilst away to sea-ward, across the blue expanse of water, extended the horizon, unbroken by any distant land. On the edge of the cliff the pandanus and the cycad competed with each other for possession of the seaward margin of the island. The scene was peculiarly Pacific ; and as we sat alone on the brink of the cliffs enjoying a smoke and contemplating the scene set out before us, I fancied even my natives shared with me that feeling of awe with which one views the grander of nature's forces in actual operation. . . . Equally pleasant are my recollections of numerous tramps during the fine weather along the sandy beaches on the windward coasts of coral islands. On such occasions the sea itself seemed to revel in the glory of the day. Wave after wave, white-tipped, and reflecting the brightest of the sun's rays, pursued each other merrily over the surface of its unfathomable blue. Against the edge of the reef the surf broke unceasingly, sending its whitened spray high into the air, and joining its hoarse bass with the hum of insect life from the neighbouring wood.

GUPPY

*

With the night-fall the concert of frogs, lizards and insects began. One could readily distinguish amongst the notes of the various contributors in the evening chorus the ' koo-roo ' of the lizard, and the ' appa-appa ' of the frog, sounds from which the native names of these creatures are derived. Numerous fireflies lit up the recesses of the forest, as if to disclose the hiding-places of the performers in the general discord, but to no purpose ; and soon, fatigued by our day's exertions, we fell asleep.

Ibid.

*

Bush-walking, where there is no native track, is a very tedious process, and requires the constant use of the compass. In districts of coral limestone, such traverses are equally trying to the soles of one's boots and to the measure of one's temper. After being provokingly entangled in a thicket for some minutes the persevering traveller walks briskly along through a comparatively clear space, when a creeper suddenly trips up his feet and over he goes to the ground. Picking himself up, he no sooner starts again than he finds his face in the middle of a strong web which some huge-bodied spider has been laboriously constructing. However, clearing away the web from his features, he struggles along until, coming to the fallen trunk of some giant tree, he plants his foot firmly on it, and sinks knee-deep into rotten wood. With resignation he lifts his foot out of the mess and proceeds on his way, when he feels an uncomfortable sensation inside his helmet, in which, on removing it from his head, he finds his old friend the spider, with a body as big as a filbert, quite at ease. Shaking it out in a hurry, he hastens along with his composure of mind somewhat ruffled. Going down a steep slope he clasps a stout-looking areca palm to prevent himself falling, when down comes the rotten palm, and the long-suffering traveller finds himself once more on the ground. To these inconveniences must be added the peculiarly oppressive heat of a tropical forest, and the frequent difficulty of getting water.

Ibid.

SOURABAYA

(1832)

SOURABAYA is situated on the main-land of Java, on the shores of a narrow strait, which divides it from the large island of Madura. It is the only perfectly secure harbour on the north coast of Java, and the only one also in which the shipping can be well defended by batteries on shore. . . . The town itself, which is a mile and a half from the sea, is divided by a river thirty yards wide, which is navigable by boats one hundred miles from the sea. The land in the vicinity is little above the level of the sea ; but it is not of so swampy a nature as that of the site of Batavia.

During the period of my sojourn at Sourabaya, my mornings were generally occupied in visiting the Chinese and native portions of the town, and my evenings were chiefly spent at the residence of an English merchant, whose hospitality rendered his house the rendezvous of all the conversable part of the European community. My stay at Sourabaya proved altogether more agreeable than that at Batavia, where the insalubrity of the climate kept me in constant dread of an attack of fever, and I had by this time acquired a tolerable knowledge of the Malay language, and therefore was enabled to derive much amusement from my conversations with the natives.

EARL

SULU ISLANDS

IF the reader will consult a map he will notice that the north-eastern part of Borneo presents a more or less straight coast-line, from the eastern end of which the Sulu Archipelago runs like a chain connecting it with the Philippines. . . .

. . . Beautiful as are almost all tropical islands, I do not think I have ever seen one more captivating than Cagayan Sulu—'true gem of the ocean,' as it has been called—and as the boat glided over the coral-gardens, bright with vividly coloured fish, I felt as if I could cast off European civilisation and clothes alike and cultivate my mealie-patch and grove of coconuts with the natives for the rest of my life. . . . In the little valleys, or along the seashore, the mat-shed houses, elevated on piles, are shaded in pleasant groves of banana, coconut, jack-fruit and durian trees.

GUILLEMARD

The Lands

SUMATRA

(*c.* 1300)

So you must know that when you leave the kingdom of Pasei
you come to another kingdom called Sumatra, on the same island.
And in that kingdom Messer Marco Polo was detained five months
by the weather, which would not allow of his going on. And I
tell you that here again neither the polestar nor the stars of the
Maestro were to be seen, much or little. The people here are wild
idolators ; they have a king who is great and rich ; but they also
call themselves subjects of the great Khan. When Messer Mark
was detained on this island by contrary winds he landed with about
two thousand men in his company ; they dug large ditches on the
landward side to encompass the party, resting at either end on the
sea haven, and within these ditches they made bulwarks or stockades
of timber for fear of those brutes of man eaters ; . . . and the
islanders, having confidence in the party, supplied them with
victuals and other things needful. There is abundance of fish to
be had, the best in the world. The people have no wheat, but live
on rice. Nor have they any wine except such as they derive from
a certain kind of tree.

When they want wine they cut a branch of this tree, and attach
a great pot to the stem of the tree at the place where the branch
was cut ; in a day and a night they will find the pot filled. This
wine is an excellent drink and is got both white and red. It is of
such surpassing virtue that it cures dropsy and tisick and spleen.

M. POLO

TAVIUNI

(1862)

THE island off which we were now anchored is properly called Taviuni, erroneously Vuna. It is the third island in size of the Vitian (Fijian) group, being about twenty-four miles long and nine broad, running from south-west to north-east, and being traversed by a chain of mountains about two thousand feet high, the tops of which are nearly always enveloped in clouds. Stately cocoa-nut palms gird the beach, whilst the mountain sides are covered by dense forests full of fine timber, and abounding in wild pigeons and a species of paroquet valued on account of its scarlet feathers, by the Tonguese, and still more by the Samoans, for ornamenting mats. Numerous streams and mountain-torrents, fed principally by a lake at the summit, descend in every direction and greatly add to the beauty of the scenery. The northern shores especially teem with vegetation and present a picture of extreme fertility. The trees and bushes are very thick, and everywhere overgrown by white, pink, and blue convolvulus and other creepers, often entwined in graceful festoons. Here and there the eye descries patches of cultivation, or low brushwood, overtopped by the feathery crowns of magnificent tree-ferns ; villages nestling among them. The air is laden with moisture, and there is scarcely a day without a shower of rain.

SEEMAN

TERNATE AND NEIGHBOURING ISLANDS

(c. 1578)

THE 14 of November we fell in with the Islands of Maluco, belonging to the King of Ternate . . . whereupon our Generall resolved to runne with Ternate, where the next morning early we came to anchor.

The King purposing to come to our ship, sent before four great and large canoas, in every one whereof were certaine of his greatest states that were about him, attired in white lawne of cloth of Calicut, having over their heads, from one end of the canoa to the other, a covering of thinne perfumed mats, borne up with a frame made of reedes for the same use, under which every one did sit in his order according to his dignitie, to keepe him from the heate of the Sunne, divers of whom beeing of a goode age and gravitie, did make an ancient and fatherly shew.

Soone after the King himself repaired, accompanied with six grand and ancient persons, who did their obeisance with marveilous humilitie. The King was a man of tall stature, and seemed much delighted with the sound of our musicke. To all our Generall gave presents, wherewith they were passing well contented.

The same night we received of them meale, which they call Sagu, made of the tops of certaine trees, tasting in the mouth like sowre curds, but melteth like sugar. We had of them store of rice, hennes, unperfect and liquid sugar, sugar canes and a fruite which they call Figo, with store of cloves.

This Island is the chiefest of all the islands of Maluco, and the King hereof is King of seventie islands besides.

After we had heere, by the favour of the King, received all necessary things that the place could yeeld us, our Generall, considering the great distance, and how farre he was yet off from his countrey, thought it not best to linger the time longer, but waying his anchors, set out of Ternate, and sayled to a certaine little Island to the Southwards of Celebes. This Island is thoroughly growen with wood of a large and high growth, very straighte and without boughes, save only in the head or top. Amongst these trees, night by night, through the whole land, did shew themselves an infinite swarme of fiery wormes flying in the ayre, whose body being no bigger than our common English flies, did make such a shew and light, as if every twigge or tree had bene a candle.

Here we graved our ship, and continued twenty-six days. . . . And when we had ended our business we waide and set sail to runne for the Malucos.

DRAKE

TSUSHIMA THE BEAUTIFUL

WE proceeded through groves of dark, clustering cryptomerias and tangled bushes of yellow-fruited raspberries. Our course was partly along the scooped-out, rugged banks of an old, shallow, rocky watercourse, where the trout were seen leaping after flies, and where ugly, bull-headed fish were dimly discerned deep down in clear dark pools between the rounded boulders. Sometimes we had to pick our way through patches of peas and barley, and over fields of sweet potatoes, gathering as we proceeded the sweet-scented flowers of syringa. . . . We ascended the gully, still following the course of the tumbling burn which flowed along the bottom. Above and around, clumps of light green oaks were mingled with sombre-spreading fir trees, with occasional patches of elder, and here and there with soft billowy clusters of *Cryptomeria japonica*. Impending overhead were grey slate-stone rocks peeping out from among the trees, while high aloft, conspicuous by her gorgeous head of crowded fox-glove blossoms, towered the *Paulownia Imperialis*—truly a sylvan queen.

As we emerged suddenly from our bowery chasm we encountered quite a different scene. In the bight of a sheltered bay lay the brown thatched houses of a village. The sea was clear and calm, and the sun shone bright on the wooded hills on the opposite shore. Some slender, sharp-prowed boats, propelled by bare-headed islanders clothed in blue, reminded us that we were now in Japan.

ADAMS

THE YANGTZU

'IF you really want excitement,' said our friends in Chungking, 'go down the Yangtze.'

A flimsy, leaky boat was hired. It was punt-shaped, and in the centre was a kind of box, hooded with a rush awning in which one man of modest length might lie. We had four oarsmen, a helmsman, and a smirking boy, who, we were told, could cook. . . . We shouted adieus to our friends, and when shouting was of no avail, we waved our handkerchiefs till Chungking grew hazy under its veil of reek, and our cockle-shell of a punt was swept madly down the waters of the Yangtze River.

We were travelling with the stream, racing, swirling, sweeping, as though there was a wager. We huddled in our bunk, and took things as easily as the constant prospect of being smashed against the rocks would permit. The four oarsmen stood to their work, pushing instead of pulling the oars. They were well-built, muscular, cheery men, a contrast to the pucker-faced helmsman, who stood stolidly the whole day long, reminding me of the statue of Polyphemus with his eye out. These five men worked from the break of dawn till darkness set in, and all they received from the owner of the boat in return was their rice on the way. This is the custom on the Yangtze. There are hundreds of thousands, nay, millions of boatmen, and they take the boats down to Ichang for practically nothing. There they are employed as trackers to pull the loaded junks back to Chungking, a journey occupying from three to five months, and for which they receive their rice and a sum total of from five to seven shillings. . . .

It was exciting to watch a huge, hump-backed junk towed slowly yard by yard against the battling, foaming torrent. You see two hundred men pulling at the tow-line, made of spliced bamboo. It is a tug-of-war between men and river. When the river seems like winning the men get on all-fours, straining every muscle. A man on the junk begins thumping a drum. When the boat yields and lurches ahead a roar goes up from the trackers. When the line breaks the men are shot ahead as from a bow. The junk then careers off to the nearest rock and commits suicide.

FOSTER-FRASER

YULE ISLAND

YULE ISLAND was the headquarters of D'Albertis, and it is not surprising that it attracted the attention of the Italian explorer as a suitable base for his explorations in New Guinea, for it is a lovely gem upon the water, and wears quite a fairy-like appearance. It is not very large, and yet it has beautiful green hills, with crests of trees upon their summits from which one can look abroad upon a wide, shining expanse of sea, or landwards, upon the immense delta of a river which rises in far-off ranges of mountains whose secrets have not yet been disclosed to white men, but whence have come strange stories sufficient to create an intense longing to know more of this interesting land. Or one may stroll through green glades, wander among palms, revel in the shade and the delicious coolness produced by broad-leaved trees, many of them bearing fruit, and luxurious creeping plants, some with gay blossoms, and all clinging to the trees and rocks or running along the ground in rich festoons. And there are secluded bits of sandy beach where the rocks and the vegetation cluster, and form delightful nooks known only to a few natives who live in the vicinity, and to the birds.

LYNE

ZIPANGU (JAPAN)

(THIRTEENTH CENTURY)

ZIPANGU is an island in the eastern ocean. It is of considerable size ; its inhabitants have fair complexions, are well made, and are civilised in their manners. Their religion is the worship of idols. They are independent of every foreign power, and governed only by their own kings. They have gold in the greatest abundance, its sources being inexhaustible, but as the king does not allow of its being exported, few merchants visit the country, nor is it frequented by much shipping from other parts. To this circumstance we are to attribute the extraordinary richness of the sovereign's palace, according to what we are told by those who have access to the place. The entire roof is covered with a plating of gold, in the

same manner as we cover houses, or more properly churches, with lead. The ceilings of the halls are of the same precious metal; many of the apartments have small tables of pure gold considerably thick; and the windows also have golden ornaments. So vast, indeed, are the riches of the palace, that it is impossible to convey an idea of them.

In this island there are pearls also, in large quantities of a red (pink) colour, round in shape, and of great size; equal in value to, or even exceeding, that of the white pearls. It is customary with one part of the inhabitants to bury their dead, and with another part, to burn them. The former have a practice of putting one of these pearls into the mouth of the corpse.

Of so great celebrity was the wealth of this island, that a desire was excited in the breast of the Grand Khan, Kublai, now reigning, to make the conquest of it, and to annex it to his dominions. In order to effect this, he fitted out a numerous fleet, and embarked a large body of troops under two of his principal officers. . . . The expedition sailed from the ports of Zaitun (?Amoy) and Kinsai (?Hangchou, or its port, Ningpo), and crossing the intermediate sea, reached the island in safety; but in consequence of the jealousy that arose between the two commanders . . . they were unable to gain possession of any city or fortified place, with the exception of one only, which was carried by assault, the garrison having refused to surrender.

MARSDEN, *Marco Polo*

東方朔

TUNG-FANG SO

CHINESE PROVERBS

Ceremony is the smoke of friendship.

★

The pleasure of doing good is the only one that never wears out.

★

The happiest mother of daughters is she who has only sons.

★

The minds of women are quicksilver and their hearts wax.

★

The most curious of women will willingly cast down her eyes to be looked at.

★

When men foregather they listen to each other ; when women meet they look at one another.

★

The tree overthrown by the wind had more branches than roots.

★

The dog in the kennel barks at his fleas ; the dog which is hunting does not feel them.

★

The way to glory is through the palace ; to fortune through the market ; to virtue through the desert.

THE PEOPLES

SIAMESE PROVERBS

When you go to the forest don't leave your axe behind.

*

If you decide to land you may run into a tiger ; if you stay in the boat you may come upon a crocodile.

*

Noble birth shows pedigree, but manners make the man.

*

Who fears the rain who lives in the open ?

*

If a dog bite you, don't bite back.

THE AINU

Ainu men love inaction, as far as work in the gardens is concerned. But there is nothing an Ainu loves so much as hunting, except, perhaps, getting intoxicated. Thus, whilst the women are hard at work in their gardens, the men, if not fishing, or hunting, or drinking, or sleeping, or gossiping, or riding horses, may possibly be found helping their wives, either with their hands or with their advice.

It would be a calumny to assert that all the hard-working Ainu women are ugly. Some of them, especially the younger ones, are quite good-looking. Their features are a little round, perhaps, and the cheek-bones rather high ; but their complexion is of a pleasant, rosy kind. They are shy before men, and fix their eyes on the ground, and place a hand over their lips, as a sign of reverence and respect. Before women, however, they are not so shy. Their smile then is pleasing and their eyes dark and sparkling ; their voices are soft and musical, and their figures well formed. It is the tattooing of their mouths, foreheads and hands that makes the elder women so unpleasing to the eye.

BATCHELOR, *Ainu* . . .

*

Ainu women are very fond of their children. But from about a month old, they are often left quite alone in the hut, suspended from the roof in their cradle. Nevertheless, this is not from want of feeling ; to let a child lie and cry is not only thought to be good for its lungs, but is part of its education. 'Babies,' they say, 'are like talkative men and women ; they must have their say.'

The Ainu have their recognised forms of etiquette which must be observed by all. Personal behaviour is a subject in which they are always careful to instruct their youth.

When a person desires to visit a hut he may not enter without invitation. But as there are no wooden doors to knock at he makes a noise as if clearing his throat. If he belongs to the village he then enters without more ceremony; but if he is a stranger he must wait till someone comes out to take him in. Once inside, he must go through the palm-rubbing, beard-stroking and all the formalities of salutation. Men always go out of a hut sideways after making a call, but women must walk backwards, for it is impolite for a woman to turn her back upon a man.

There are many minor rules which must be observed. Never enter a hut with a head-dress on. Never rush in or out, but move steadily and softly. Never look into a hut through the window, especially the end window. Never eavesdrop. Never address a stranger before he speaks to you. These rules are binding on men, women and children alike.

Ibid.

THE BALINESE

(1837)

THE Balinese entertaining a great aversion to a maritime life, are more rarely to be met with at the European ports than the natives of the other islands to the eastward. They are fairer in complexion, stouter in frame, and more energetic in their dispositions than the Javanese, and in appearance and dress bear a great resemblance to the natives of Siam, from whom it is probable they are descended. The entire population of Bali, amounting to about one million, profess the Hindoo religion, and the burning of widows amongst them is carried to an extent unknown in India. The slaves of a great man are also consumed upon his funeral pile, and when the immense annual loss of life produced by these frightful practices is considered, it is surprising that the island possesses so large a population.

EARL

THE BURMESE

THE Burman is a firm believer in amusement, in relaxation, in holidays. He sees no good in a too strenuous and incessant application to the serious business of life. He likes to take life easily, and to see plenty of change. Even his religious duties usually blend amusement with the seeking after merit. The numerous festivals and religious observances serve for frequent holidays, and whatever he may fancy in the way of diversion. The Burman is indolent, casual, and not to be depended upon. He does not readily conform to discipline or restraint. It is difficult to get him into a routine of any kind. . . .

If the Burman has the faults of a careless happy-go-lucky race, he has the virtues also. He has been called the Irishman of the East. His manners have the ease and polish of a ' gentleman born.' He is most affable and approachable and in religion tolerant of the opinions of others. He is hospitable, and will help the destitute stranger without making too many inquiries.

If it is one of the marks of a gentleman to be able in an easy and natural manner to place himself on a level with you, the Burman has this in a high degree.

WINSTON

Marriage among the Burmese is a most peculiar institution, and the ' marriage knot ' is very easily undone. If two persons are tired of each other's society they dissolve partnership in the following simple and touching but conclusive manner : They respectively light two candles, and shutting up their hut, sit down and wait quietly till they burn out. The one whose candle burns out first gets up at once and leaves the house (and for ever), taking nothing but the clothes he or she may have on at the time. All else then becomes the property of the other party.

VINCENT

THE PEOPLE OF CELEBES

THE men and women of Celebes are not tall, nor handsome in their persons, but short and thick-set. They have a flattish face, but not thick lips. Their colour is of a yellowish copper, or reddish yellow ; their manners are not graceful ; and they are revengeful and jealous.

The men are very ingenious with edged tools. They are warriors, attend to the field, and the building of houses, canoes and proas, in which they are very expert. The women are engaged in cooking, pounding rice and corn, going to the gardens, and attending to all domestic concerns. The children are kept under no fear or order and are punished from the whim or caprice of their parents. I have seen a mother, when displeased, throw stones and billets of wood at her children.

The men are capable of carrying great burdens on their backs, enduring great fatigues, and of fasting a long time ; and will with ease travel forty or fifty miles a day. They are long-lived and live temperately. Their modes of life are simple, and their disorders are few. They do not understand much of physic. They pretend to cure a great deal by enchantment. The betel-nut is their principal medicine.

The Peoples

If any part of the body be in pain, the patient sends for the *raje*, who, on his arrival, feels the place, and taking a large quid of the betel-nut, and pronouncing some words to himself, blows it on the place affected ; which is esteemed a perfect cure. But if the complaint be a fever, they often bring in a drum, which is beaten by two men, one at each end. If that do not succeed, they sometimes beat a brass kettle, which they continue beating till the recovery or death of the patient. If the latter, the kettle and drum are immediately thrown out of the house ; the drummer and physician are turned out also.

WOODARD

The Malays have a notion that if a man can eat when he is sick he will recover ; if not, that he will die.

The men bathe twice a day in fresh-water rivers. The women bathe twice a day : once in the morning, immediately after rising. When bathing the hair is put up in a smooth manner ; they then pick a flower or sprig of some kind, which they fasten on top of the head. They also gather two little blossoms just in bloom and put them in their ears, through the holes where they wear their ear-rings.

The men are courageous, cunning and enterprising. They despise cowards. Prisoners taken in war are made slaves and sold at from twenty to thirty dollars each.

A man is allowed to marry as many wives as he can maintain. He builds a house for every woman, as two wives never live together.

Ibid.

THE CHINESE

(1589)

BOTH men and women of this countrie are of a good disposition of their bodies, well proportioned and gallant men, somewhat tall : they are all for the most part brode faced, little eyes and flat noses, and without bearde save only upon the ball of the chinne : but yet there be some that have great eyes and goodly beardes, and their faces well proportioned, yet of these sorts (in respect of the others) are verie few : and it is to bee beleeved that these kinde of people doo proceede of some strange nation, who in times past when it was lawfull to deale out of that countrie, did joyne one with another.

MENDOZA

(1745)

The Mandarins, richly habited, are carried in a Sedan, gilded and open, borne upon the Shoulders of eight or sixteen Persons, accompanied with all the Officers of their Tribunal, who surround them with Umbrellas and other Marks of their Dignity. Some walk before them two and two, bearing Chains, Fasces, and Escutcheons of varnished Wood, upon which may be read, in large Gold Characters, all the Titles of Honour annex'd to their Places of Trust, together with a brazen Bason, upon which they beat a certain Number of Strokes according to the Rank they bear in the Province. They continually speak aloud and threaten the People to make way. Other Officers follow in the same Order, and sometimes four or five Gentlemen on Horseback bring up the Rear. Some Mandarins

BASHŌ

never appear in publick without a Train of Three or Fourscore Domesticks.

THOMAS

*

(1751)

The persons of rank in this country teach their children from their earliest years the dictates of virtue and honesty, and spare no expenses towards a good education : but the common sort of people train up their children with their dogs ; for which reason neither of them can bear strangers.

OSBECK

*

(1762)

. Two qualities are absolutely necessary to a young woman : attention to the duties of her station, and a respectful fear. Learn then more particularly what those duties are. In the house be up first in the morning ; and don't retire to your repose at night till after all the rest ; be constant to such business as is proper to your sex ; to you belongs the care of the lesser domestic expenses ; watch attentively that the rice, the flour, the oil, the salt, the dishes and the other utensils be carefully locked up in the places destined to them ; that there reign an air of neatness, not only in your cloathes but also in the meats which you cause to be dressed, and that nothing be seen which may disgust the eye. Otherwise you will be ranked with the most dirty animals.

The head, the face, the hands, the feet, are the four seats of female beauty : but it is modesty that must set off these natural perfections. This virtue must have the lead in your Air, your Mein, your Looks, your words, and in the gestures. If you speak without reflection, . . . if you are continually tossing yourself about, and are full of gesticulations, you will be taken for an actress or a dancer on the stage. What will be the consequence then, if you take certain liberties, if you study to see and be seen, if you look upon men by stealth, if you are heard to hum a song, or give other like marks of a giddy, volatile spirit? What idea will then be entertained of your virtue?

Remember that in their intrinsic value, a bushel of pearls is not worth a measure of rice. The more you charge your silken head-dress with flowers and other ornaments, the more labour you will have to unsew them when they are to be made clean. To what purpose is it to embroider your cloaths with so many flowers and so many different birds? Their entire beauty ought to consist in simplicity and neatness. Ornaments add nothing to merit and virtue. A woman who hath neither address, nor understanding, were she covered with gold and silver ; had she her head loaded with pearls and bodkins of gold, is far inferior to a woman of merit, who is clad in linen-cloth, and whose head is decked with the most simple ornaments.

Miscellaneous Pieces : Chinese Rules of Conduct

*

A Chinese writer, speaking of the ignorance of Chinese females, and consequent unamiableness of wives, exhorts husbands not to desist from teaching them, for 'even monkeys may be taught to play antics ; dogs may be taught to tread a mill ; rats may be taught to run round a cylinder ; and parrots may be taught to recite verses ; since then it is manifest that even birds and beasts may be taught to understand human affairs, how much more may young wives, who, after all, are human beings.'

GUTZLAFF

*

A beautiful woman is one who has cheeks red as the almond flower, a mouth like peach-blossom, a waist slender as a willow-leaf, eyes bright as autumn ripples, and feet like the flower of the water-lily.

BRIDGEMAN

*

'If any man should make a collection of all the inventions and all the productions, that every nation which now is or ever has been upon the face of the globe, the whole would fall far short, either as to number or quality, of what is to be met with in China.' These, or something similar, are the words of the learned Isaac Vossius.

The testimony given by the celebrated authors of the *Encyclopedie des Connaissances humaines* is almost equally strong : 'The Chinese who, by common consent, are superior to all the Asiatic nations, in antiquity, in genius, in the progress of the sciences, in wisdom, in government, and in true philosophy : may moreover, in the opinion of some authors, enter the lists on all these points with the most enlightened nations of Europe.'

The late Sir William Jones, indeed, who deservedly took the lead in oriental literature, had observed, in speaking of the Chinese, that, ' By some they have been extolled as the oldest and wisest, as the most learned, and most ingenious, of nations ; whilst others have derided their pretensions to antiquity, condemned their government as abominable, and arraigned their manners as inhuman ; without allowing them an element of science, or a single art, for which they have not been indebted to some more ancient and more civilised race of men.'

BARROW, *Travels* . . .

(1851)

' I felicitate myself,' wrote a Chinese, ' that I was born in China ! It constantly occurs to me, what if I had been born beyond the sea, in some remote part of the earth, where the cold freezes, or the heat scorches : where the people are clothed with the leaves of plants, eat wood, dwell in the wilderness, lie in holes of the earth ;

are far removed from the converting maxims of the ancient kings, and are ignorant of the domestic relations : though born as one of the generation of men, I should not have been different from a beast. But how happily I have been born in China ! I have a house to live in, have drink and food, and commodious furniture. I have clothing and caps, and infinite blessings. Truly the highest felicity is mine.'

Chinese Gleaner

*

The progress and advancement of the Chinese in agriculture as an art has been greatly exaggerated by many who have adverted to this subject in their writings. . . . Some who were probably able to form a correct opinion on the subject were prevented from doing so, and were led away by the fertility of their imaginations, while on the other hand, the Roman Catholic missionaries who travelled and resided in the interior were evidently ignorant of the art itself, as well as of the progress it had made in other countries. But it must also be borne in mind that, whilst agriculture has been advancing rapidly towards perfection amongst the nations of the western world, the Chinese with this, as in most other things, have remained stationary, and hence there must be a much greater disparity between us and them now than there was when the early writers on China published their works. . . . I have no doubt that as a nation, they surpass the natives of India and other half-civilised states in this art, as they do in most other peaceful accomplishments but it is ridiculous, now, at least, to compare them for a moment with our intelligent farmers in England or Scotland. As well might we compare their coasting junks with the navy of England, or their merchants with ours, whose ships are met with on every sea, and whose commercial operations extend to every quarter of the world.

FORTUNE, *Two Visits* . . .

The Chinese have lived so much in peace that they have acquired by habit and education a more than common horror of political disorder. 'Better be a dog in peace than a man in anarchy,' is a common maxim. At the same time, that only check of Asiatic despotism—the endurance of the people—appears from their history to have exercised a salutary influence. The first emperor of the Ming family observed, 'The bowstring drawn violently will break; the people pressed hard will rebel.' Another sovereign observed to his heir, 'You see that the boat in which we sit is supported by the water, which at the same time is able, if roused, to overwhelm it: remember that the water represents the people and the emperor only the boat.'

DAVIS

(1855)

There is much talk of universal fraternity; but let those who have it in their hearts, and not merely on their lips, exert themselves in the beautiful work of the propagation of the faith.

On the day before our departure we received a great number of visitors all belonging to the highest society of the town. Whilst we had resided at the mission we had been mostly in communication with the lower classes; in the country with peasants; in the town with artisans. We were happy therefore to have this opportunity of forming an acquaintance with the higher classes of this curious nation. The well-bred Chinese are very pleasing in their manners.

Their politeness is not fatiguing and tiresome as is sometimes supposed, but has really something fascinating in it, and only falls into affectation with the pretenders to elegance, who know little of refined society. . . . There was especially a group of young men amongst our visitors who excited our admiration ; their behaviour was modest, though unconstrained, showing a mixture of timidity and confidence which suited their age perfectly. They spoke little, and only when they were first spoken to, but showed their interest in the conversation by the animation of their faces and their graceful gestures. Their fans too were managed by our guests with so much elegance and dexterity, that they were quite becoming. Of course we also had on our best manners, in order to show that French urbanity was not inferior to the ceremonious politeness of China.

Huc

*

The public promenade is a thing unknown to the Chinese, who cannot perceive either its charms or its wholesomeness. Those who have some notion of European manners think it very singular, if not utterly absurd, that we should find pleasure in walking for its own sake. When they hear that we consider it a refreshment and amusement, they regard us as very eccentric, or entirely devoid of common sense.

The Chinese of the interior, whom business takes to Canton or Macao, always go the first thing to look at the Europeans on the promenade. They squat in rows along the sides of the quays, smoking their pipes and fanning themselves, contemplating the while with a satirical and contemptuous eye the English and Americans who promenade up and down from one end to the other. Europeans who go to China are apt to consider the inhabitants of the Celestial Empire very odd and supremely ridiculous, and the provincial Chinese at Canton and Macao pay back this sentiment with interest. When they see Europeans spend hours in walking for the mere sake of the exercise, they ask if it is not more conformable to civilised ideas to sit down quietly to smoke and drink tea when you have nothing else to do, or, still better, to go to bed at once.

Ibid.

The astonishing calmness with which the Chinese see the approach of death does not fail when the last moment arrives. They expire with the most incomparable tranquillity, without any of the emotions, the agitations, the agonies that usually render the moment of death so terrific. Their life goes out gently like a lamp that has no more oil. . . . It appears to us that this peaceable death of the Chinese is to be attributed, first, to their soft and lymphatic temperament, and secondly, to their entire want of religious feeling. The apprehensions connected with a future life, and the bitterness of separation, cannot exist for those who have never loved anyone

much, and who have passed their lives without thinking of God
or their souls.

Ibid.

*

(1878)

The following particulars, gleaned from the elaborate treatises
by the professors of the art, give some idea of Chinese
physiognomy :

A round head, with hair growing well from a high forehead,
eyebrows thin, and of equal length, large and thick ears, the upper
parts of which extend above the eye-brows, a large mouth in the
male and a small one in the female, a large chin, a high and firm
nose, high cheek bones, a silky beard, a dark moustache with a
tendency to curl upwards, a large neck, a powerful voice, and eyes
long and angular, and with much expression, are regarded as most
favourable indications. Where such features are wanting various
degrees of trouble and misery are predicted. Thus, a person whose
head is not round or whose eye-brows are thick, is told that he must
remain in a subordinate position all his life. One whose forehead
is singularly low is likely to suffer punishment from the magistrate
and is invariably advised to seek the retirement of the cloister. A
man whose ears are neither large nor thick is told that he will die
at an age varying from fifty to sixty years, and that, should he
continue to live beyond that age he will die in a state of destitution.
One with a small chin will be overtaken by dire misfortunes should
he reach old age ; and a woman with a large mouth has a life of
shame predicted for her. A man with a small nose and distended
nostrils is born to beggary ; and to be without high cheek bones
is to be weak in character and to be shut out from the hope of
attaining any post of trust or honour. The wife of a thin-necked
man will die shortly after marriage ; and an effeminate voice

indicates the slave of vicious practices, who cannot attain a good old age. Eyes long and angular, with large round pupils full of expression foreshadow much good fortune; while eyes lacking these characteristics indicate a strong propensity to steal.

An examination of the hand generally follows that of the face. A thick hand with a soft red palm without wrinkles is a sign of much good fortune, and the opposite qualities bring corresponding trouble. When the fingers fit closely together it is regarded as an indication of a happy and prosperous life.

GRAY

*

No elbow bends outwards. (Every man for himself.)

Chinese Proverb

Bamboo, Lotus and Palm

(1898)

From Lien Chi Altangi, *to* Fum Hoam, first President of the Ceremonial Academy at Pekin, in China

' Our scholars of China have a most profound veneration for forms. A first-rate beauty never studied the decorums of dress with more assiduity ; they may properly enough be said to be clothed with wisdom from head to foot ; they have their philosophical whiskers, their philosophical slippers, and philosophical fans ; there is even a philosophical standard for measuring the nails ; and yet, with all this seeming wisdom they are often found to be mere empty pretenders.

' A philosophical beau is not so frequent in Europe ; yet I am told that such characters are found here. I mean such as punctually support all the decorums of learning, without being really very profound, or naturally possessed of a fine understanding ; who labour hard to obtain the titular honours attending literary merit ; who flatter others, in order to be flattered in turn ; and only study to be thought students.

' A character of this kind generally receives company in his study, in all the pensive formality of slippers, night-gown, and easy chair. The table is covered with a large book, which is always kept open, and never read ; his solitary hours being dedicated to dozing, mending pens, feeling his pulse, peeping through the microscope

and sometimes reading amusing books, which he condemns in company. His library is preserved with the most religious neatness ; and is generally a repository of scarce books, which bear an high price, because too dull or useless to become common by the ordinary methods of publication.

' Such men are generally candidates for admittance into literary clubs, academies, and institutions, where they regularly meet to give and receive a little instruction and a great deal of praise. In conversation they never betray ignorance, because they never seem to receive information. Offer a new observation, they have heard it before ; pinch them in an argument, and they reply with a sneer.

' Yet how trifling soever these little arts may appear, they answer one valuable purpose, of gaining the practisers the esteem they wish for. The bounds of a man's knowledge are easily concealed, if he has but prudence ; but all can readily see and admire a gilt library, a set of long nails, a silver standish, or a well-combed whisker, who are incapable of distinguishing a dunce.

' When Father Matthew, the first European Missioner, entered China, the court was informed that he possessed great skill in astronomy ; he was therefore sent for, and examined. The established astronomers of state undertook this task ; and made their report to the Emperor, that his skill was but very superficial, and no way comparable to their own. The Missioner, however, appealed from their judgement to experience, and challenged them to calculate an eclipse of the moon, that was to happen a few nights following. " What," said some, " shall a Barbarian, without nails, pretend to vie with men in astronomy, who have made it the study of their lives, with men who know half the knowable characters of words, who wear scientifical caps and slippers, and who have gone through every literary degree with applause ? " They accepted the challenge, confident of success. The eclipse began ; the Chinese produced a most splendid apparatus, and were fifteen minutes wrong ; the Missioner, with a single instrument, was exact to a second. This was convincing ; but the court astronomers were not to be convinced ; instead of acknowledging their error, they assured the Emperor that their calculations were certainly exact, but that the stranger without nails had actually bewitched the moon. "*Well then,*" cried the good Emperor, smiling at their ignorance, "*you shall still continue to be servants of the moon ; but I constitute this man her Controller.*"

' China is thus replete with men, whose only pretensions to knowledge arise from external circumstances ; and in Europe every country abounds with them in proportion to its ignorance. Spain and Flanders, who are behind the rest of Europe in learning, at least three centuries, have twenty literary titles and marks of distinction unknown in France or England : they have their Clarissimi and Preclarissimi, their Accuratissimi and Milutissimi ; a round cap entitles one student to argue, and a square cap permits another to teach ; while a cap with a tassel almost sanctifies the head it happens to cover. But where true knowledge is cultivated, these formalities begin to disappear ; the ermined cowl, the solemn beard, and sweeping train are laid aside ; philosophers dress, and talk, and think like other men ; and lamb-skin dressers, and cap-makers, and tail-carriers, now deplore a literary age.

' For my own part, my friend, I have seen enough of presuming ignorance, never to venerate wisdom but where it actually appears. I have received literary titles and distinctions myself ; and, by the quantity of my own wisdom, know how very little wisdom they can confer. Adieu.'

GOLDSMITH

The Chinese sailor never goes to sea without first presenting an offering to the gods, to propitiate them, in order that the voyage may be a speedy and successful one. The cabin of the junk is set in order, and the tables covered with dishes of pork, mutton, fruits and vegetables. Candles and incense are burned upon the tables for a short time, and the whole business has something solemn and imposing about it. The cook, on this occasion, conducted all the ceremonies. On other days as well as this, it was part of his duty to light the candles in the little temple where the gods were kept, as well as to burn incense and prostrate himself before them.

FORTUNE, *Two Visits . . .*

*

Good doctrines need no miracles.

Japanese Proverb

145

COCHIN-CHINESE

(1856)

THE inhabitants of the kingdom of Cochin-China consist of two nations, the Anam, or civilised people, which occupies Tonquin or Cochin-China proper, and the Kambojan, the principal inhabitants of Kamboja, with several wild races inhabiting the mountains known to the civilised inhabitants under the common name of Ke-moi. The Anam, or dominant people, may be described as men of short stature as compared with the Chinese, with well-formed limbs, features of the Chinese form, and a cheerful expression. It is probable that they are, in fact, of the same race with their neighbours the Kambojans and Siamese, although to strangers their appearance be disguised by their wearing the ancient costume of China.

In character the Cochin-Chinese are a mild and docile people. The manners of the lower classes are mild and sprightly beyond what is usual in the east, while the higher imitate the solemn and formal demeanour of the Chinese. In their habits and persons, the Cochin-Chinese are an uncleanly people : their diet is indiscriminate, for no kind of animal food comes amiss to them ; it includes flesh and eggs of the alligator, and hatched eggs are a dainty with them. Their national vanity at least equals that of the Siamese : they consider themselves the first people in the world, the Chinese being the only foreign nation that they are disposed to consider respectable. Their rude condition is implied by their treatment of women, of which a writer gives the following account : ' The rich regard them as destined to serve as the instruments of their pleasure, and the poor of their wants. For this reason, they are devoted to offices which require the greatest bodily fatigue, and are under such a submission to the lords of creation, that they cannot have a will of their own. The labours of the field are ordinarily their portion ; they guide the plough and handle the spade and mattock. From morning till evening they wade in water, transplanting rice. They carry provisions to market ; they cultivate and manufacture the cotton and silk for the use of their families ; and they often take the principal share in commercial affairs.'

Crawfurd, Journal . . . Siam

DYAK WOMEN

The Dyak women were much shorter than European women, but well made ; very interesting in their appearance, and affable and friendly in their manners. Their eyes were dark and piercing, and I may say there was something wicked in their furtive glances ; their noses were but slightly flattened ; the mouth rather large ; but when I beheld the magnificent teeth which required all its size to display, I thought this rather an advantage. The hair was superlatively beautiful, and would have been envied by many a courtly dame. It was jet black, and of the finest texture, and hung in graceful masses down the back, nearly reaching to the ground. A mountain Dyak girl, if not a beauty, has many most beautiful points ; and, at all events, is very interesting and, I may say, pretty. They have good eyes, good teeth, and good hair—more than good : I may say splendid ;—and they have good manners and know how to make use of their eyes.

MARRYAT

THE FIJIANS

(1860)

IN social diplomacy the Fijian is very cautious and clever. That he ever paid a visit merely *en passant* is hard to believe. If no request leaves his lips, he has brought the desire, and only waits for a good chance to present it now or prepare the way for its reception at some other time. His face and voice are all pleasantness, and he has the rare skill of finding out just the subject on which you most like to talk, or sees at once if you desire silence. Rarely will he fail to read your countenance ; and the case must be urgent indeed which obliges him to ask a favour when he sees a frown. The more important he feels his business the more earnestly he protests that he has none at all ; and the subject uppermost in his thoughts comes last to his lips, or is not even named ; for he will make a second or even a third visit rather than risk a failure through precipitancy. He seems to read other men by intuition, especially where selfishness or lust are prominent traits. If it serves his purpose he will study difficult and peculiar characters, reserving the results for future use : if afterwards he wishes to please them he will know how ; and if to annoy them it will be done most exactly.

WILLIAMS

*

If you have a great canoe
Great will be your labour too.

Fijian Proverb

The Peoples

THE JAPANESE

(Sixteenth Century)

The Inhabitantes shewe a notable witte, and an incredible pacience in sufferinge, labour and sorowes. They take greate and diligent care lest, either in worde or deede, they shoulde shewe either feare, or dulnesse of mynde, and lest they shoulde make any man (whosoever he be) partaker of their troubles and wantes. . . . They suffer not the least injurie to passe unrevenged. For gravitie and curtesie they gyve not place to the Spainardes. They are generally affable and full of compliments. . . . They will as soone lose a limbe as omit one ceremonie in welcoming a friend. . . . The most parte of them that dwell in cyties can write and reade. They only studie martiall feates and are delighted in armes.

RUNDALL

*

(1611)

The people of this Iland of Japon are of good nature, curteous above measure, and valiant in warre : their justice is severely executed without any partialitie upon transgressors of the law. They are governed in great civilitie. I meane, not a land in the world is better governed by civille policie. The people be very superstitious in their religion, and are of divers opinions. . . .

Thus, in breife, I am constrained to write, hoping that by one meanes or other, in processe of time, I shall heare of my wyfe and children : and so with pacience I wait the good will and pleasure of Allmighty God. . . .

Dated in Japan, the two and twentieth of October 1611.

William Adams
Ibid.

In the early intercourse which existed between the empire of Japon and the states of the west, the government of Japon is exhibited in a most favourable light. It was distinguished, at that period, by high-bred courtesy : combined with refined liberality in principle, and generous hospitality in practice. Without any reservation in regard to circumstances, rank, calling or nation, the hand of good-fellowship was, then, cordially extended to the stranger. The lowly-born William Adams . . . became the esteemed councillor of the sagacious and powerful monarch by whom the land that had afforded him shelter was ruled. Merchants, for a century, found a free and open market for their wares. Missionaries were allowed to commence a career of proselytism ; and they pursued it with zeal and success.

Unhappily, this desirable state of affairs has ceased to exist. Since the middle of the seventeenth century, *exclusiveness* is an element of the polity of the empire that has been obtruded on observation. The government of Japon is now regarded as little, if in any degree, removed from barbarism. It is viewed as mean, selfish, and arbitrary : as acting ungenerously towards the foreigner by depriving him of the just reward of commercial enterprize ; and as inflicting injustice on the native, by depriving him of commodities with which the foreigner, if he were permitted, would willingly supply him. By one section of the public in the Western hemisphere, it is thought that coercive measures may justifiably be applied against a government of the character ascribed to that of Japon. Another section, not advocating absolute hostilities, is of opinion, that ' *Justice to them* (of Japon) *and the good of mankind, may imperiously demand the interference of civilised nations* ' ; or, that the treatment experienced by strangers attempting to visit the empire, ' *may call for explanations which may end in opening a door long and obstinately closed to the Merchant and the Missionary*.' Adverting to the profession of the parties by whom these opinions are promulgated, it must be presumed they are dictated by feelings of the purest

benevolence, and with the best intentions ; but doubts may be entertained, whether the means suggested are really calculated to promote the objects in view. The right of ' *interference* ' may be denied : the character of the ' *explanations* ' demanded, may be misunderstood : feelings of exasperation may ensue on both sides ; and consequences may result as little calculated to exalt the character of Christianity, as to promote the interests of commerce.

Ibid.

*

(1728)

Many will call it malice to divide the globe of our Earth, small as it is, and they will think it a crime equal to murder, to break through the society and mutual communication which ought to be among Men. All nature pleads for Society. To declaim and reason against it is, in fact, to reflect on the Author of nature. We all behold one Sun, we all tread on the same ground, we breathe all the same air, nature hath set us no bounds, nor hath the Creator established any laws, but what tend to mutual association. Should men be born to a worse condition than storks and swallows ? Is it not enough for our Soul, that noblest part of ourselves, which partakes of the liberty of the Supreme and All-free mind, to be confined to our body ? Must the Body also be kept prisoner in one Country, and the Soul denied the liberty to make it, and herself with it, enjoy the pleasure of others ? The very Stars, dispers'd through the boundless Heaven, argue for it. Many believe, that such majestick, such noble bodies, have not been left naked and empty, but are inhabited by various kinds of living creatures, which prais'd the All-wise Creator of all things, before even the foundations of our Earth were laid. . . . Whosoever dares, from the low and vulgar notions of schoolmen, to raise his mind to nobler and higher thoughts, will not scruple, nor think it derogatory to the bounty and wisdom of the Supreme Being, to assert that these Heavenly bodies are like so many great towns, inaccessible indeed to one another, because of the vast extent of the fluid wherein they float, but for that very reason fit to be, what it is not unlikely they are, inhabited by creatures of various kinds, differing in their nature, frame, and degrees of perfection. As conformable to truth, as it is highly probable this assertion is, so reasonable will it appear on the other hand, that those creatures which the All-wise Creator hath made of the same nature and substance, and which he hath confined to any one of these globes, as within the walls of a town, should live in a friendly communication together, a communication, which it cannot but be highly criminal to break through.

How justly therefore, how deservedly accused, stand the Japanese of a signal breach of the laws of nature, of an open disregard to the Supreme Will of the All-wise Creator, of a wilful infraction of the laws of society, which it was his intention should be for ever among men ? *To shut up the Empire, as they do ; to deny all accession and commerce to foreigners ; to repel them by force, if any there be who attempt to enter ; to keep the natives, as it were, prisoners within the bounds of their own Country ; to condemn to the Cross those who leave the Country of their own choice, either out of dissatisfaction or with an intent to see other transmarine parts of the world ; to imprison those who may have the misfortune to be driven upon their coasts by storms and shipwrecks :* What is it else but breaking through the laws of nature, and the All-wise order which the Supreme Being established in the world ?

Whoever hath a mind to offer these, and perhaps many more arguments and objections of this kind, against the truth of what I propose to demonstrate in this enquiry, with regard to the advantages, that must and do accrue to the Japanese from the present condition of their Empire . . . shall not by me be denied that liberty. But in the mean time I must beg leave as freely to declare that I am, for many good and plausible reasons, inclined to believe that it is by no means inconsistent with the divine Wisdom and Providence that this globe of our Earth should be inhabited, as it is, by nations of different languages, customs and inclinations. Hath not God himself, in that dreadful confusion of tongues at Babel, where men as yet made up one society, given the strongest proofs of his will and intention, that their intimacy and mutual communication should be broke, and that thence forward different Countries should be inhabited by different nations ? Such is the perversity of human nature, that whenever we are become one body, one kingdom, one common-wealth, where one and the same language is spoken, we are naturally inclined to hate our neighbours who speak another language, and to envy their state and condition. . . . Happy would have been the condition of men, if nature had so blessed each Country with all the necessaries of life, that the inhabitants, fully satisfied with their situation, should have no reason to entertain any thoughts of invading the rights and properties of others.

Japan, by the natives called *Nipon*, which signifies the support or foundation of the Sun, is properly speaking not one, but a whole set of islands. Nature herself hath done the best part towards making this Empire invincible, by making it almost inaccessible, and by surrounding it with a dangerous and exceedingly tempestuous sea. . . .

The Japanese are not wanting something, which I don't know whether I shall call it boldness or Heroism ; I mean, such a contempt of their life, that when they have been subdued and conquered by an enemy or when they find it out of their power to revenge some scorn or injury done to them, they do not scruple, with an undaunted stoicism, to lay violent hands upon themselves. . . . It cannot be supposed that courage and resolution in war should be wanting in a nation, where love as well as hatred, esteem and contempt, are handed down to posterity, where wrongs and injuries are resented by succeeding generations, where mutual enmities do seldom cease but with the death and total destruction of one of the parties concerned. . . . In short, to do justice to the Japanese nation, it must be owned, and so I believe, it will appear in ages to come, that they are not wanting prudence, resolution, and conduct in war, nor good order in their military expeditions, nor a due and cheerful obedience to their commanding officers. . . .

The Japanese are very industrious and enured to hardships. Very

little will satisfy them. The generality live on plants and roots, tortoises, shell-fish, sea-weeds and the like. Water is their common drink. They go bare-headed and bare-legg'd. They wear no shirts. They have no soft pillows to lay their heads on. They sleep on the ground, laying their heads, instead of a pillow, on a piece of wood, or a wooden box, somewhat depress'd in the middle. They can pass whole nights without sleeping, and suffer all manner of hardships. But otherwise they are great lovers of civility and good manners, and very nice in keeping themselves, their cloaths and houses, clean and neat. . . .

Happy and flourishing as is the condition of the Japanese, they must be convinced that *their Country* was never happier than it now is, governed by an arbitrary Monarch, shut up, and kept from all Commerce and Communication with foreign nations.

KAEMPFER

*

In so low a condition is at present the credit of foreigners in Japan : The Dutch, who are suffered to trade there, have found it by long experience, and are of opinion that it is impossible for them to procure any information concerning the present condition of the Empire. . . . The difficulties, I own, are great and considerable, but not altogether insuperable. They may be overcome by proper management, even notwithstanding all the precautions the Japanese government hath taken to the contrary. The Japanese, a prudent and valiant nation, are not so easily to be bound by an oath taken to such Gods, or Spirits, as are not worship'd by many, and unknown to most. If they do comply with it, 'tis more for fear of the punishment, which would inevitably attend them, if betray'd. Besides, their pride and war-like humour being set aside, they are as civil, as polite and curious a nation as any in the world, naturally inclined to commerce and familiarity with foreigners, and desirous, to excess, to be informed of their histories, arts and sciences.

Ibid.

*

United and peaceable, the Japanese are taught to give due worship to the Gods, due obedience to the Laws, due submission to their Superiors, due love and regard to their Neighbours. They are civil, obliging, virtuous ; in art and industry excelling all other nations, possess'd of an excellent country, enrich'd by mutual trade and commerce among themselves ; courageous, abundantly supplied with all the necessaries of life ; and withal, they enjoy the fruits of peace and tranquillity.

Ibid.

*

(1775)

The Japanese are in general intelligent and provident, free and unconstrained, obedient and courteous, curious and inquisitive, industrious and ingenious, frugal and sober, cleanly, good-natured, upright and just, trusty and honest, mistrustful, superstitious, proud and haughty, unforgiving, brave and invincible.

The Japanese nations shews *Sense* and steadiness in all its undertakings, so far as the light of science, by whose brighter rays it has not yet had the good fortune to be illumined, can ever guide it.

Liberty is the soul of the Japanese, not that which degenerates into licentiousness and riotous excess, but a liberty under strict subjection of the laws.

The rights and liberties of the higher and lower class of people are equally protected by the laws ; and the uncommon severity of these laws, joined to the inevitable execution of them, serves to keep everyone within proper bounds.

. . . Frugality has its principal seat in Japan. It is a virtue as highly esteemed in the imperial palace as in the poorest cottage. It is in consequence of this that the middling class of people are contented with their little pittance ; and that accumulated stores of the rich are not dissipated in wantonness and luxury. It is in consequence of this that dearth and famine are strangers to this country.

THUNBERG

The Japanese are in the highest degree suspicious of the Europeans, and at all times very fearful of granting them anything without a precedent. Having requested leave to botanize, the Japanese journals were searched to see if any Dutchman had ever obtained such a privilege, and upon finding that a surgeon, a long time before, had had that liberty at a period when disorders prevailed and there had begun to be a scarcity of medicines, leave was granted me, without hesitation, to wander about the town of Nagasake in order to collect them. But on a closer examination, it was found that this surgeon had only been a surgeon's mate, and consequently I, as principal surgeon, could not enjoy the same privilege.

Autumn was all this time advancing with hasty strides, and I daily endeavoured to convince them that a surgeon is first a mate, and that in case of his death, the latter succeeds him in the appointment. This had so great an effect that I again obtained permission ; but so very late that I could not make any use of it before the beginning of February.

Ibid.

*

(1819)

The Japanese are deficient in only one quality, which we reckon among the virtues, namely, bravery or courage. If the Japanese are timid, this is merely in consequence of the peaceful character of their government, of the long repose which the nation has enjoyed, or rather of their being unaccustomed to shed blood ; but that the whole people are by nature timid is what I can by no means allow, whether I may be right or wrong. Are there not nations, now sunk in the profoundest torpor, whose ancestors were the terror of the world a few centuries back ? In my own country (Russia) a whole village often flies into the woods from a single robber and his brace of pistols, and the same peasants afterwards mount batteries, and storm fortresses which were considered as impregnable. Does the uniform alone make the hero ? Is it not rather the innate spirit of bravery ? The Japanese, therefore, cannot be said to be naturally cowards.

GOLOVNIN

(1850)

To sum up the character of the Japonese. They carry notions of honour to the verge of fanaticism ; they are haughty, vindictive, and licentious. On the other hand, brawlers, braggarts, and back-biters are held in the most supreme contempt. The slightest infraction of truth is punished with severity ; they are open-hearted, hospitable, and as friends, faithful to death. It is represented, there is no peril a Japonese will not encounter to serve a friend : that no torture will compel him to betray a trust ; that even the stranger who seeks aid will be protected to the last drop of blood. The nation, with all their faults and vices, had qualities that won the hearts, and commanded the esteem of the missionary-fathers. Saint François Xavier concludes one of his letters by saying, ' I am loth to finish when I discourse of Japons, who verily are the delight of my heart.'

RUNDALL

(1863)

Nothing is so difficult as to get any kind of information, political, statistical or scientific, in Japan ; partly, I believe, in consequence of the dense ignorance of everyone on any subject not immediately concerning his own life and business ; partly also due to our imperfect knowledge of the language, but chiefly to their inveterate propensity to deceive and mislead the foreigner. It is enough that he should desire information on any subject, no matter how trivial or apparently unimportant, to make it their business or their pleasure, either to deny all knowledge, or tell him a falsehood, no matter how palpable.

ALCOCK, *Capital of the Tycoon* . . .

*

(1876)

No ladies [*sic*] excel the Japanese in that innate love of beauty, order, neatness, household adornment and management, and the amenities of dress and etiquette as prescribed by their own standard. In maternal affection, tenderness, anxiety, patience, and long-suffering, the Japanese mothers need fear no comparison with those in other climes. As educators of their children, the Japanese women are peers to the mothers of any civilisation in the care and minuteness of their training of, and affectionate tenderness and self-sacrificing devotion to, offspring, within the limits of their light and knowledge . . . . and if unvarying obedience, acquiescence, submission, the utter absorption of her personality into that of her husband, constitute the ideal of the perfect woman, then the Japanese married women approach so near that ideal as to be practically perfect, and in this respect are, as foreign women will cheerfully grant to them, unquestionably superior.

HÜBNER

The Japanese dislike formal lines corresponding to each other, either numerically or by measurement ; and this feeling underlies all their artistic work. Their ideas of symmetry are something quite different from those that prevail among Western nations, but it does not follow that they have a less perfect conception of symmetrical order and harmony. They have derived their fundamental ideas of symmetry from a close study of Nature, and her processes in providing for variety. It is mainly to these two sources, their love of Nature and their love of variety, that Japanese art owes

much of its special charm as well as its originality. They have gone to the ornamental part of Nature's works—to the combination of forms and colours observable in plants, flowers, and leaves, in the painting of butterflies' wings, the skins of animals, the plumage of birds, the markings of shells—for their models. It was natural that, in profound sympathy with Nature and admiration of all her works, in which beauty and variety are the leading and characteristic features, they should contract a corresponding aversion to sameness, and to any appearance of regularity or uniformity, which was nowhere to be found in Nature.

ALCOCK, *Art . . . in Japan*

(1891)

Special in their love and use of wood, the Japanese are also as peculiar and as much apart from the West in their regard for, and their dealings with, flowers. But by ' flowers ' they mean less and more than we. They include all handsome and ornamental leaves, branches, and even stumps and roots. The blossom is for them, though they love colour, rather a detail than the central point ; and a great spray of pine, of cedar, or of maple, ranks above most mere blooms. There is an aristocracy of flowers with them, very severely defined. The seven princely or primary flowers are the chrysanthemum, the narcissus, the maple, the cherry, the peony, the wistaria, and the evergreen rhodea. The iris is also of princely dignity but must not be employed at weddings because of its purple colour.

What the Japanese love and strive for in arranging flowers is that which they most value in all their arts, namely balance and beauty of line. The charm of their dancing springs from the same ' language of line,' and he who does not know and feel the subtle secrets of this will vainly seek to derive from Japanese art of any kind the exquisite pleasure it can impart to the eye and mind.

ARNOLD, Japonica

★

(1894)

Here are Hokusai's own figures walking about in straw rain-coats, immense mushroom-shaped hats of straw, and straw sandals—bare-limbed peasants, deeply tanned by wind and sun ; patient-faced mothers with smiling bald babies on their backs, toddling by upon their *geta* or high, noisy, wooden clogs ; and robed merchants squatting and smoking their little brass pipes among the countless riddles of their shops.

HEARN, *Glimpses . . .*

*

The Japanese go upon pilgrimages because they thoroughly enjoy themselves in the process, the piety incidental to the act simply relieving them from compunction at having so good a time. Sociability is the keynote of the affair from start to finish. To pool one's pleasure is always to increase it, and for a Japanese to pool his purse is a matter of as much account. For a Japanese is not only poor but impecunious. His personal property of impersonality is only matched by the impersonality of his personal property. For what a Japanese appears to possess is, ten to one, borrowed of a friend, and what he really owns, pledged to a neighbour. He is, in short, but a transition stage in one long shift of loan. We talk of our far-reaching system of mercantile credits. It is financial self-sufficiency beside the every-day state of far-eastern affairs. Everybody there lives as a matter of course upon somebody else. To these states of mind and money are due the founding of the pilgrim clubs.

LOWELL, *Occult Japan*

The standard of beauty naturally fluctuates a little according to locality. But, as a whole, there is only one ideal throughout the Empire. So let me enumerate the qualities considered necessary to make a beautiful woman : She is to possess a body not much exceeding five feet in height, with comparatively fair skin and proportionally well-developed limbs ; a head covered with long, thick, and jet-black hair ; an oval face with a long straight nose, high and narrow ; rather large eyes, with large, deep-brown pupils and thick eye-lashes ; a small mouth, hiding behind its red, but not thin lips, even rows of small white teeth ; ears not altogether small ; and long, thick eye-brows forming two horizontal but slightly curved lines, with a space left between them and the eyes. Of the four ways in which hair can grow round the upper edge of the forehead, viz. horned, square, round and Fuji-shaped, one of the last two is preferred, a high as well as a very low forehead being considered not attractive. Eyes and eyebrows with the outer ends turning considerably upwards, with which your artists depict us, are due to those Japanese colour prints which strongly accentuate our dislike of the reverse, for straight eyes and eyebrows suggest weakness, lasciviousness and so on.

OKAKURA, *Japanese Spirit*

Not even Mount Fuji looks beautiful to one who is cold and hungry.

Japanese Proverb

The Peoples

THE JAVANESE

(1830)

AN uninstructed people are often credulous, and the Javanese are remarkable for their unsuspecting and almost infantine credulity. Susceptible of every impression that artifice may attempt to make upon them, and liable to every delusion propagated by the prejudiced or the designing, they not inaptly compare themselves to a piece of pure white cloth, on which any dye or shade of colour may be laid. They lend an easy credence to omens, to prognostics, to prophets, and to quacks. They easily become the dupes of any religious fanatic, and credit, without scruple or examination, his claim to supernatural powers.

They are great observers of lucky or unlucky days, or natural phenomena, and undertake no journey or enterprize without attending to them. It is unlucky to go anywhere on the day you hear of the death of a friend ; the sight of two crows fighting is unlucky ; two small birds, fighting near a house, foretell the arrival of a friend from a distance.

• RAFFLES

*

Hospitality is universal among the Javanese. It is enjoined by their most ancient institutions, and practised with readiness and zeal. The Javanese are exceedingly sensible to praise or shame and ambitious of power and distinction, but they are more remarkable for passive fortitude than active courage, and endure privations with patience rather than make exertions with spirit and enterprize. . . . Of their nationality it may be observed, that ever since the first arrival of Europeans, they have neglected no opportunity of attempting to regain their independence. In the great cause of national independence all would unite. Quiet and peaceable as they now are,

were they once aroused to insurrection their blood would rapidly
boil, and they would no doubt be guilty of many excesses.

Ibid.

★

(1837)

When by themselves the seamen generally row to a chorus which
exercises a very animating influence over them ; but if there should
be an European officer in the boat, a dead silence is maintained, a
noise of any kind being considered disrespectful. Some of their
songs are very melodious, and the sound produces a pleasing effect
when heard at a distance.

EARL

(1856)

The village community constitutes the most important part of
Javanese institutions. The Javanese village, like the Hindu, is an
incorporation, in which the powers of self-government are to a
large extent inherent. In the structure of Javanese society there is
no other distinction of classes than that of nobles and commonalty,
or, as the Javanese express it, the head and the foot, or sometimes

' the whole ' and ' the broken ' grains of rice. There are several words for a slave, but they are obsolete, unless to express a servant or retainer, or as a pronoun of the first person in the polite or ceremonial dialect.

CRAWFURD, *Descriptive Dictionary*

★

We saw here in the evening a marriage procession of the poorer classes. . . . Two men came first beating a kind of drum, then came several men carrying a frame-work that was covered with garlands of flowers, and lighted up with tapers. Next to these came the bride and bridegroom ; he was in his gayest clothes, his face, neck and hands smeared with yellow paste. The bride was ornamented with chaplets of flowers, and on each side were several bridesmaids similarly ornamented. Behind these walked a troop of girls each carrying a small lighted taper and screaming at the top of her voice, and then came a crowd of boys and young men all singing.

JUKES

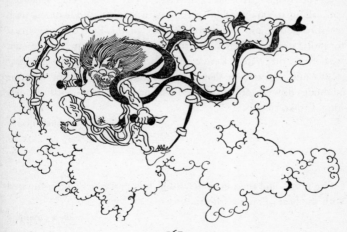

The road to Soerabaya is an open book, with living illustrations of the life and habits of the people ; for the Malay has solved the problem of existence by living practically out of doors. There is no need of thick walls, and a complicated system of heating to keep out the cold in a country where the temperature practically never falls below 85 F., and consequently the home of the Malay is not a fortress against the elements, but a cool retreat where, sheltered from the sun, in his hours of ease he may chew the betel of happiness in somnolent content ; for, like his brethren in the lower planes of evolutionary life, the fowls of the air and the beasts of the field, sun, wind, and rain are but adjuncts to his physical needs, not enemies of his body. He is the primitive man, Antæus-like, deriving his strength from the touch of the warm, brown, kindly earth, his mother.

It was a little after sunrise when I started from the landing stage ; and the activities of the day were just commencing. The men had already had their morning swim in the canal ; and the sun was now brightening to a livelier green the tamarinds on the further bank. Little boys and girls, like glistening bronze fauns, were splashing and calling to one another in the warm water ; and women with the slim bodies and wonderful carriage of the East, wearing great turquoise earrings, their softly rounded shoulders bared to the sun, fresh from the water, were coiling their glistening coal-black hair in pyramids above their shapely heads, putting in jessamine, rose, or tandjong flowers on either side behind their ears with slender, long, brown fingers.

ABRAHAM

*

Fire is hot, and the sun hotter still ; but neither is to be compared with the heat of a man's heart.

Javanese saying

THE KOREANS

(1885)

WHEN we consider that the climate, as regards heat and cold, is very much like our own, with rather more accentuation, we perceive a part of the reason why the dress must be peculiarly warm at one season and peculiarly airy at another. The other half of the same need of warmth lies in the genius of the people. Hurry finds no place in Eastern thought. The only thing worthy devotion is study; and that requires contemplation, not bustle. A dignified demeanour is their ideal of action. Exercise—the passionate pursuit of a section of the Western world and the *bête noire* of a necessity to another portion—is utterly unknown to them. Walking or riding is only undertaken because for some immediate object it becomes necessary. In olden times it was made use of in war; but nowadays even this has died out. Their object, therefore, in apparel, apart from display, is to be comfortable in repose; and this, after personal experience of the comparative comfort possible under their system and our own, I can affirm to be realized.

LOWELL, *Chosön*

*

Time is purely a Western necessity. The very impersonality and consequent individuality of the far-Oriental renders him superior to it. He has no engagements to meet, and therefore he needs no punctuality to meet them. Perhaps no better comment upon the far-Eastern want of this last virtue need be made than to mention that the Japanese invariably appear at any entertainment an hour and a half before the time for which they are invited. Such mature unpunctuality used at first to cause me, as unprepared host, no slight embarrassment. In Korea these surprise parties fortunately do not happen, but simply because all day is given up to the feast, and there is no such thing as being too early.

Ibid.

*

To suppose, however, either from the temperament or the dress, that the Koreans are not a people who travel, would be a mistake. Although far-Orientals are slow in their actions, as compared even with the European middle classes, not to speak of energetic and nervous Americans, they are, in no sense, people that stay at home. Travel in China, Korea, or Japan surpasses that in olden times in Europe ; and even in these days of travelling facilities, rapid transit, and studied accommodation, the practice is probably quite as much in vogue in the far-East, if we reckon it—as of course we should, where it is the spirit of travelling we are considering—from the time spent, and not the distance traversed.

To what causes this ant-like activity is due it is not easy to determine, especially in Korea. In Japan the pilgrims furnish the largest contingent to the travelling class ; but the pilgrimage itself is more of an excuse than an end. The journey is quite as much a pleasurable excursion as a religious devotion. The latter gives, as it were, a sanction to what would otherwise be looked upon, however enjoyable it might be, as an unpardonable waste of time ; for it is principally the working middle classes who undertake it. In fact, most of the pilgrims belong to so poor a class that they could not afford to travel were the journey at their own expense. They enroll themselves as members of associations to which they annually contribute their mites. and these enable a certain number to make the pilgrimage every year. A different set are sent out the next ummer ; and so the list is gone through, until eventually each member has had his journey.

But in Korea the travelling public is differently constituted. You annot take it for granted that those you meet are the picturesque ransmutation of the force of faith into the energy of action. On he contrary, you see here the result of purely secular causes, and ot a reflection, however dimmed, of deeds which shall profit in *æcula sæculorum*. Nor are the white-robed wanderers principally edlars, though such exist. In addition to itinerant hucksters that hrive by perambulating, the world over, there is a large class in Korea who journey either for pleasure or for some other reason

han trade upon the road. If we define a traveller par excellence s a man who is singular enough to journey for his good and not is goods, a large proportion of those we meet would still have a ight to the name. In the first place, the Koreans are passionately ond of scenery. The possessions of each province in this respect re not only thoroughly known, but they are systematically classified nd catalogued. A grove of trees is celebrated here, the precipices of mountain there, the moonlight falling on a pool of water in a iird spot, and so on. Such places people come from long distances o see. Then, again, every year it is fitting to visit the tombs of ne's ancestors ; and all who can afford to make the journey do so. nnually, also, the literary examination is held at the capital, and udents gather from all parts of the country to attend it. Several undreds in this way journey as many tens of hundreds of miles,

and then return again, the greater part unsuccessful in the contes
to their homes, to try their luck once more another year.   Lastl
among the official class there is a good deal of promiscuous travellir
hither and thither, either to get a place, or to keep one's place, «
to wring money out of some one else who holds a place l
threatening to defame and oust him unless he pays.

Ibid.

THE MALAYS

(1839)

THE courteous demeanour of the Malay is entirely divested of t
fulsome adulation that characterises the supple native of Ind
After the performance of the introductory forms, they are remar
ably independent in bearing and conversation.   They appear gra
and apathetic, because it is not considered etiquette to expr
surprise or curiosity at anything, however new or strange.   Th
reflect before speaking, and deliver themselves slowly, but witho
appearing in the slightest degree at a loss for ideas, or words whe
with to clothe them.   They have much family pride, and b
bodily pain with great firmness.   Death, when believed to
inevitable, is met with stoical indifference.

NEWBOLD

The Peoples

(1893)

' He was the mildest manner'd man
That ever scuttled ship or cut a throat.'
BYRON, *Don Juan*

To begin to understand the Malay you must live in his country, speak his language, respect his faith, be interested in his interests, humour his prejudices, sympathise with and help him in trouble, and share his pleasures and possibly his risks.

The real Malay is a short, thick-set, well-built man with straight black hair, a dark brown complexion, thick nose and lips, and bright intelligent eyes. His disposition is generally kindly, his manners are polite and easy. Never cringing, he is reserved with strangers and suspicious, though he does not show it. He is courageous and trustworthy in the discharge of an undertaking ; but he is extravagant, fond of borrowing money, and very slow in repaying it. He is a good talker, speaks in parables, quotes proverbs and wise saws, and is very fond of a good joke. He takes an interest in the affairs of his neighbours and is consequently a gossip. He is a Muhammadan and a fatalist, but he is also very superstitious. He never drinks intoxicants, he is rarely an opium smoker. But he is fond of gambling, cock-fighting and kindred sports. He is by nature a sportsman, catches and tames elephants, is a skilful fisherman, and thoroughly at home in a boat. Above all things, he is conservative to a degree, is proud and fond of his country and his people, venerates his ancient customs and traditions, fears his Rajas and has a proper respect for constituted authority—while he looks askance on all innovations and will resist their sudden introduction. But if he has time to examine them carefully and they are not thrust upon him he is willing to be convinced of their advantage. At the same time he is a good imitative learner, and when he has energy and ambition enough, makes a good mechanic. He is, however, lazy to a degree, is without method or order of any kind, knows no regularity even in the hour of his meals, and considers time of no importance.

The Malay has often been called treacherous. I question whether he deserves the reproach. He is courteous and expects courtesy in return, and he understands only one method of wiping out insults.

SWETTENHAM

THE SIAMESE

(1898)

ONE could not but be struck by the patient resignation and cheerful indifference generally displayed in the face of all misfortunes by the ordinary country people. Like true fatalists, they were convinced there was no help for it ; and so it was best taken unconcernedly and good-humouredly.

Among Western nations oppression and injustice may awaken great qualities and may form noble characters, but among Easterns an imperturbable indifference is the result. The peacefully minded bow down without a struggle, the harder hearts are driven to join the dacoit gangs, The 'blessedness of sorrow' is not for the Buddhist of Siam ; he takes it differently ; he laments his want of 'merit' from the last sphere of existence, and, as mental anguish or triumph are beyond his ken, his sufferings, like his ambitions and enjoyments, are purely physical, and with any digression are soon forgotten.

SMYTH

*

At the time Jesus Christ lived, and still later in Mahomet's time, there was no law of monogamy. Mahomet limited the number of wives to four, and after a time Europeans instituted monogamy by law, not from religious motives, but from conviction of its expediency, considering that plurality of wives was unfair to women, and gave rise to jealousy and murder, and constant trouble.

The religion of Buddha highly commends a life of chastity. Buddha also censured polygamy, as involving ignorance and lust, but he did not absolutely forbid it, because he could not say there

was any actual wrong in a man having a number of wives properly acquired.

Polygamy is extensively practised in Siam, the kings setting an example. The late king's life affords an instance of both celibacy and polygamy. At the age of twenty, his Majesty, who had been already married for some years, entered the priesthood and remained a monk for twenty-seven years ; he then came to the throne, and accepting the custom of polygamy as suitable for his new position, he was, within the next sixteen years, blessed with a family of seventy-nine children. The number of his wives we could not ascertain. So far as our own observation goes, this polygamy, accompanied by a facility for divorcement, is not attended by very evil results. There is a great deal of domestic happiness in Siam, and suicides and husband and wife murders are rare there. Nevertheless, many of the best men we have known there were theoretical admirers of monogamy, and one practised it.

ALABASTER

THE SUMATRANS

(1794)

THE Malay and native Sumatran differ more in the features of their mind than in those of their person. Although we know not that this island ever made a distinguished figure in the history of the world (for the Achenese, though powerful in the sixteenth century, were low in point of civilisation), yet the Malay inhabitants have an appearance of degeneracy, and this renders their character totally different from that which we conceive of a savage, however justly their ferocious spirit of plunder on the eastern coast may have drawn upon them that name. They seem rather to be sinking into obscurity, though with opportunities of improvement, than emerging from thence, to a state of civil or political importance. They retain a strong share of pride, but not of that laudable kind which restrains men from the commission of mean and fraudulent actions.

The original Sumatran, though he partakes in some degree of the the Malay vices, and partly from the contagion of example, possesses many exclusive virtues ; but they are more properly of the negative than the positive kind. He is mild, peaceable and forbearing, unless his anger is roused by violent provocation, when he is implacable in his resentments. He is temperate and sober, being equally abstemious in meat and drink. The diet of the natives is mostly vegetable ; water is their only beverage ; and though they will kill a fowl or a goat for a stranger, whom perhaps they never saw before nor ever expect to see again, they are rarely guilty of that extravagance for themselves ; nor even at their festivals, where there is plenty of meat, do they eat much of anything but rice. Their hospitality is extreme, and bounded by their ability alone. Their manners are simple ; they are generally, except among the chiefs, devoid of cunning and chicane ; yet endued with a quickness of apprehension, and on many occasions discovering a considerable degree of penetration and sagacity. In respect to women, they are remarkably continent, without any share of insensibility. They are modest ; particularly guarded in their expressions ; courteous in their behaviour ; grave in their deportment, being seldom or never excited to laughter ; and patient to a great degree. On the other hand, they are litigious ; indolent ; addicted to gaming ; dishonest in their dealings with strangers, which they esteem no moral defect ; suspicious ; regardless of truth ; mean in their transactions ; servile ; and though cleanly in their persons dirty in their apparel, which they never wash. They are careless and improvident of the future, because their wants are few, for though poor, they are not necessitous, nature supplying with extraordinary facility, whatever she has made requisite for their existence. Science and the arts have not, by extending their views, contributed to enlarge the circle of their desires ; and the various refinements of luxury, which in polished societies become necessaries of life, are totally unknown to them.

MARSDEN, *History of Sumatra*

JAPANESE PROVERBS

Convince thyself that imperfection and inconvenience are the lot of mortals and thou shalt have no room in thy heart for discontent or despair.

*

The voice speaks, the echo answers.

*

You can't fasten the door tightly enough to shut out trouble.

*

When the reeds begin to die and the wild geese fly south, put on an extra garment.

*

To a blind man all colours are alike.

*

You can't dispel a fog by waving a fan.

THEIR THOUGHTS AND WAYS

CHINESE PROVERBS

Talk is emptiness ; a stroke of the brush makes certain.

*

The best memory is not as good as the most awkward pen.

*

If turnips are selling briskly there is no need to wash off the mud.

*

When a dumb man eats gentian he tastes bitterness inside.

*

It is better to move the lips than to move the legs. (To ask questions saves running about.)

*

Even a tiger may nod.

'ANIMAL, VEGETABLE OR MINERAL'

THERE are some things which possess form but are devoid of sound, as for instance jade and stones ; others have sound but are without form, such as wind and thunder ; others again have both form and sound, such as men and animals ; and lastly, there is a class devoid of both, namely devils and spirits.

HAN YÜ

China

AVARICE

AVARICE is the enemy of prosperity and may even lead to death. A certain hunter was in the habit of shooting elephants to feed his wife and family. One day he discharged his bow at an elephant, which, struck by his arrow and maddened by the pain of the wound, pursued him in order to kill him. To escape the onslaught the hunter climbed on to a white-ant hill, on which lay a snake that bit him. Enraged, he slew the snake. The elephant still came on, but the arrow by which he had been struck being poisoned, he fell dead beside the ant-hill and the hunter himself died of the bite of the snake, leaving his bow still strung. Meanwhile a wolf in search of prey came to the spot and rejoiced exceedingly at what he saw before him. ' Behold me rich,' said he, ' for good fortune has befallen me. The elephant will last me three months—the man seven days,—and I will make two meals of the snake. But,' he added, ' why should the bow-string go to waste ? Better to eat it first of all and appease my hunger.' Thus meditating, he bit the string ; but the bow, rebounding, broke his skull, and he perished on the spot.

CRAWFURD, *Descriptive Dictionary*

Siam

THE BAMBOO

THE Bamboo, the Coconut-palm and the Sugar-cane were born of the same father, and all were equally dry, straight and without sap. Then one day the whole family set off on a long journey. When they had walked some distance they came to a pool, and their father told them to drink because the next stage of their road was both long and hot. The Coconut and the Sugar-cane did as they were bid, but the Bamboo, always a little arrogant and obstinate, refused, saying, ' I will drink when I am thirsty, but not now.'

When they reached their destination, no water was to be had, so that as they walked homeward the Bamboo looked forward more and more eagerly to reaching the little pool where he had refused to drink on the outward journey. ' This time,' he thought, ' I will drink my fill.'

But, alas, when they reached the pool it had completely dried up ; so while the Coconut produces delicious refreshing milk, and the Sugar-cane is filled with sweet and succulent juice, the Bamboo remains to this day a dry and sapless cane.

HADFIELD (*adapted*)

Melanesia

'THE BAMBOO OF THE WIND'

ON our right, there was a succession of neat cottages amongst cocoa-nut trees, forming the village of Kandang. On nearing one of these, our ears were saluted by the most melodious sounds, some soft and liquid, like the notes of a flute, and others full like the tones of an organ. These sounds were sometimes interrupted or even single, but presently they would swell into a grand burst of mingled melody. I can hardly express the feelings of astonishment with which I paused to listen to and look for the source of music so wild and ravishing in such a spot. It seemed to proceed from a grove of

trees at a little distance, but I could see neither musician nor instrument, and the sounds varied so much in their strength, and their origin seemed now at one place, and now at another, as if they sometimes came from the mid-air, and sometimes swelled from amidst the dark foliage, or hovered faint and fitful around it. On drawing nearer to the grove of trees, my companions (Malays) pointed out a slender bamboo which rose above the branches of the trees, and from which they said the music proceeded, and when the notes had died away in the distance, our ears were suddenly penetrated by a crash of grand and thrilling tones which seemed to grow out of the air that surrounded us, instead of pursuing us. A brisk breeze which soon followed, agitating the dark and heavy leaves of the fronds of the gomuti palms, explained this mystery, while it prolonged the powerful swell. As we went on our way, the sounds decreased in strength, and gradually became faint, but it was not until we left ' the bamboo of the wind ' far behind us, and long hidden by intervening trees and cottages, that we ceased to hear it. The instrument which produced these fine effects was a bamboo cane, rough from the jungle, thirty or forty feet long, perforated with holes and stuck in the ground. This is certainly a very simple contrivance, but one which would not have occurred to any people who had not a natural taste for music.

DENNYS, *Descriptive Dictionary*

Malaya

BETROTHAL LETTER

(*Old Style*)

' WINTER sets in, and the wild geese now fly about in large flocks. The Feng-t'ai begins to bud, and ere long its branches will be thickly covered with flowers. This day the second quarter of winter begins, and your presents on the occasion were accepted with warm thanks. I beg most respectfully to congratulate you, venerable sir, whose honourable family formerly resided in Fukien, but is now settled in the provincial capital of Kuangtung. Your illustrious name is famous and your many virtues are highly commended by the learned. I have therefore at all times regarded your incomparable good conduct as ranging high above that of your fellow-men as high as the crane flies above the earth. Your manners too are without parallel, being as gentle as the vapour compared with the stormy winds. I am so poor as to be unable to maintain myself, neither can I find means to escape from the many troubles by which I am beset. The disposition of your son is benevolent. His mind, which is highly cultivated, is as lofty as the heaven is high above the earth. My daughter, who was born in a poor cottage and is without education, rejoiced much on hearing the words of the match-maker to the effect that you were anxious that I should agree to give her in marriage to your son. Thus your son and my daughter are bound by this marriage contract. The presents which you sent me are rare and precious, and I am sorry that I cannot in return present you with a similar compliment. These ceremonies are the signs of increasing generations. When your son and my daughter are united in marriage there will be unbounded affection between them.'

GRAY

China

BUDDHIST PARADISE

THE bodies of the saints reproduced from the lotus are pure and fragrant, their countenances fair and well-formed, their hearts full of wisdom and without vexation. They dress not, and yet are not cold ; they dress, and yet are not made hot. They eat not, and yet are not hungry ; they eat and yet are not satiated. They are without pain, irritation, and sickness, and they become not old. . . . They behold the lotus flowers and trees of gems delightfully waving, like the motion of a vast sheet of embroidered silk. Looking up, they see the firmament full of the To-lo flowers, falling in beautiful confusion like rain. The felicity of that kingdom may justly be called superlative, and the age of its inhabitants is without measure. This is the place called the paradise of the west.

DAVIS

China

BORO-BOEDOR

I WAS exceedingly anxious to get ashore at Samarang, not so much on account of the place as because there are some famous Buddhist pyramids near. The centre of Java is studded with these wonderful temples, relics of a bygone civilization. At Boro-Boedor there is one covering as large an area as the great pyramid of Gizeh ; but, unlike the Egyptian pyramids, these are studded with hundreds of the most elaborately carved statues and miles on miles of bas-reliefs. This great temple was discovered buried in jungle vegetation, forgotten even by the natives, by Sir Stamford Raffles during the English occupation. The Dutch had held the country for two hundred years, and did not know of its existence. It has over five hundred carved Buddhas arranged around its walls, and is probably the most wonderful work of its kind in the world.

Legend, as is natural, has been busy with the site ; and the tale told is something as follows. At the time when William the Norman was parcelling out England amongst his robber barons there dwelt a Prince in Boro-Boedor who was great and wise, very learned, and a profound philosopher. And, as is often the way with wise men, he loved the frivolous, gay, and witty daughter of a neighbouring Prince, the Lord of Mendoet, courting her with grave and stately words and most respectful manner. And she, after the manner of women, cared not for any of these stately ways, but wanted to be wooed with hot words of passion, with verses pulsing from the heart, with impetuous advances hard to be repelled—for the maiden was young and very beautiful, and a thing to set men's hearts afire. And so his courtship found her cold and unaffected. But nevertheless she could not ignore him, for his principality marched with that of her father, she was the heiress, and her father favoured an alliance that would preserve the succession safely after his death. And so he pressed his daughter to pledge her troth to the Prince of Boro-Boedor in order that he might go down to the grave in peace. At the last, then, because of the importunity of her father, and because no other man had touched her heart, she consented, stipulating, however, that he should build a temple in the honour of Gautama and Loro-Jongran greater than any in Java, and in a certain definite space of time which she made as short as was possible next to impossibility. And the Prince of Boro-Boedor, because of his great love for her, consented, and, stimulated by his love, hurried on the workmen so that he had it completed within the allotted time, putting all the sweetness of his affection, the lofty thoughts, the noble impulses he could not give expression to in words, into the perfect details of the great temple. And when it was all finished he sent to let the maiden know. But in the interval the Prince, her father, had died; and she was now the Princess of Mendoet, and had repented of her promise.

Nevertheless she came and gazed on its wonderful loveliness, saw its vast perfection, and knew it had all been done for love of her.

Yet was her heart not touched. She turned to the Prince, waiting with tense desire for her answer, and said :

'Truly, O Prince, these images are beautiful ; but they are dead. I cannot love you any more than I can them.'

And the Prince bowed his head and said never a word, for he loved her greatly, and knew by this that she was unworthy.

ABRAHAM

Java

BURMESE MAGIC

MAGIC is practised in order to confuse the five senses, as well as to confer invulnerability. Certain potent specifics are used in the practice of magic, and the following is said to be an effective prescription :

Take equal quantities of the livers of a man, a monkey, a black dog, a goat, a cobra, an owl, and pound together with a whole lizard from midnight till dawn. The mixture should be kept in a gold or silver box and used as required :

To make witches and ghosts visible rub a little on the left eye.

To turn night into day, rub on the right eye.

To make human beings look like monkeys, rub on the chin.

To become invisible, rub a little on the forehead and sit down.

To become fleet of foot, rub it on your legs.

To annihilate an enemy, rub the forefinger in it and point it at him.

To open a steel safe without the key, rub a little on the hand and strike the safe.

Rub it on a tamarind, and it will become a beetle.

Rub it on any inanimate object and it will come to life and follow you.

Mix it with the blood of the person you love and he (or she) will love you.

Gold rubbed with it will be turned into lead.

Rub a bamboo with it and bury it on the road, and all who pass over it will find themselves without their clothes.

A dead cock rubbed with it will revive and crow.

If you cut yourself with a sword which has been annointed with it, you will not be wounded.

A leaf blown by the wind can, if rubbed with it, be turned at will into a tiger or an elephant.

Rub it on a lotus flower and it will become a woman, or on a lotus bud and it will be turned into a man.

TAW SEIN KO (adapted)

BUSHIDO

BU-SHI-DO, the spirit of chivalry, literally means 'Military-Knight-Ways,' and was the *noblesse oblige* of the *samurai* or warrior class of feudal days, 'when knighthood was in flower.' It was the ethical system of the *bushi* or *samurai*, an unwritten and unuttered code, the growth of centuries of military rule. It developed a sense of fair play in dealing with an enemy, and a consideration for the feelings of others, its essence being justice, courage, loyalty, honour, veracity, fortitude, benevolence, and self-control.

DE GARIS (adapted)

Japan

BUTTERFLIES

' When I saw the fallen flower return to the branch—
' Lo ! it was only a butterfly.'

It is possible that some weird Japanese beliefs about butterflies are of Chinese derivation. The most interesting one, I think, is that the soul of a *living* person may wander about in the form of a butterfly. . . . If a butterfly enters your guest-room and perches behind the bamboo screen, the person whom you most love is coming to see you.

However, in Japanese belief, a butterfly may be the soul of a dead person as well as of a living person. Indeed, it is a custom of souls to take butterfly-shape in order to announce their final departure from the body ; and for this reason any butterfly that enters the house should be kindly treated.

On the pink flower a white butterfly . . .
Whose spirit is it, I wonder ?

HEARN, *Kwaidan* (*adapted*)

Japan

CANOEING

In smooth weather canoe-sailing is pleasant enough ; but in a sea and heavy wind the deck inclines at a most uncomfortable angle to the water. When running with the small end foremost a beautiful jet of water, ever changing its form, is thrown up in front to the height of a yard ; or, sometimes, the body of the canoe is driven along beneath the surface, and only seen occasionally—a dark outline in a bed of foam. When this is the case a landsman is safest sitting still, but the native sailors move about with surprising security.

Canoe-sailing is not silent work. The sail is hoisted and the canoe put about with merry shouts ; a brisk interchange of jest and raillery is kept up while poling over shoal reefs, and the heavier task of sculling is lightened by mutual encouragement to exertion, and loud thanks to the scullers as each set is relieved at intervals of five or ten minutes. A dead calm is enlivened by playful invitations addressed to the wind most wanted, the slightest breath being greeted with cries of ' Welcome ! Welcome on board ! '

If there should be drums on board their clatter is added to the general noise. The announcement to the helmsman of each approaching wave, with the order to ' keep her away,' and the accompanying ' one, two, and another to come,' by which the measured advance of the waves is counted, with passing comments on their good or ill demeanour, keep all alive and in good humour. If the canoe is sound nothing but bad weather can spoil the enjoyment of such voyaging.

Generally my crews were careful to avoid the dangers of the deep : but sailors are allowed occasional freaks, and mine had theirs. On more trips than one they broke off their course and, forgetful of the primary object of the voyage, engaged in an absorbing chase after a shark, or sting-ray, or turtle, apparently willing to wreck the canoe rather than lose the fish.

The sailors are very superstitious. Certain parts of the ocean, through fear of the spirits of the deep, they pass over in silence with uncovered heads, and careful that no fragment of food or part of their dress shall fall into the water. The common tropic-bird is the shrine of one of their gods, and the shark of another ; and should the one fly over their heads, or the other swim past, those who wore turbans would doff them, and all utter the word of respect. A shark lying athwart their course is an omen which fills them with fear. A basket of bitter oranges in a canoe is believed to diminish its speed. On one of their canoes it is *tabu* to eat food in the hold ; on another, in the house-on-deck ; on another on the platform over the house. Canoes have been lost because the crew, instead of exerting themselves in a storm, have quitted their posts to pray to their gods and throw whales' teeth at the waves to propitiate them.

WILLIAMS

Fiji

A CHINESE FEAST

THE main feature of a Chinese feast seems to lie in the preponderance of gelatinous food, *e.g.* sharks' fins, *bêche-de-mer*, sea-weed, isinglass in the form of birds'-nest soup ; fat pork and fat duck are also favourite food.

On the present occasion everything was exquisitely refined, and of such unquestionable cleanliness, that the curiosity of tasting new dishes might be indulged without alloy. My host desired that as each dish was brought in, an attendant should provide me with a neat little red ticket whereon was inscribed its name both in English and Chinese, so I was able duly and intelligently to study the respective merits of birds'-nest soup with doves' eggs, sharks'-fin soup, mushroom, turtle, and duck soups, in which last floated delicate small pieces of bamboo, somewhat resembling asparagus, Then came soup of *bêche-de-mer*, *alias* sea-slugs, . . . soup of lotus seeds, and of ducks' tongues, after which followed ragouts of every conceivable meat except beef, which is too valuable to the farmer to be consigned to the butcher, But what with roofs of the mouths of pigs, dragon's beard, vegetables, long-life fairy rice, Chinese macaroni, smoked duck and cucumber, salted shrimps, shrimps with leeks and sweet pickle, a very oily stew of sharks' fins, whales' sinews, pigeons' eggs, fish-brains, crabs, roast ducks and mushrooms, stewed crab, fish with pickled fir-tree cones, pickled chicken with bamboo-sprouts, ham stewed in honey, soles of pigeons' feet, ' bellies of fat fish,' sucking pig served whole, fried egg-plant, sliced lily-bulbs, etc., we found an ample succession of gastronomic interests.

CUMMING, *Wanderings* . . .

THE CROW

WHEN God created the world the Evil One did all he could to frustrate His designs, especially as they concerned human beings. Now, when all was made that was made, the Evil One perceived that men could not possibly live without the light and warmth of the sun. He therefore made up his mind to destroy God's most majestic creation, and got up one morning with the intention of swallowing it. But God knew of his design and made a crow to circumvent it. As the sun rose the Evil One opened his mouth to swallow it; but the crow, who was lying in wait, flew down his throat and so saved the sun. Hence the crows, remembering the benefit once conferred upon the race of men by their ancestor, have an idea that they can do just what they like with them, and live upon the food men provide for themselves and their families. But since they have good cause for being so bold and saucy, it is not for men to say that crows are useless creatures.

BATCHELOR, *Ainu* . . . (*adapted*)

Japan

CHINESE SUPERSTITION

THE Chinese in Java consult their idol when they set about any important undertaking. This divination is done by means of two small longitudinal pieces of wood, flat on one side and round on the other. They hold these with the flat sides towards each other, and then letting them fall on the ground, augur of the effect of their prayers, and the good or bad result of their proposed enterprise by the manner in which they lie, with the round or flat sides upwards. If the presage be favourable, they offer a wax candle to their god, which the priest, or bonze, who attends at the temple, immediately turns into ready money.

In the temple I saw a Chinese who let the little sticks fall above twenty times before they promised him success ; he seemed to be but very little pleased with these repeated evil prognostications, and shaking his head every time with a most discontented look, he threw himself upon the ground and bumped his head against it till at last the omen proved agreeable to his wishes ; and then he joyfully lighted a thick wax candle and placed it on the altar.

STOCKDALE

Java

CURIOSITY

WHEN the world was newly made all was unsettled and dangerous, for the crust of the earth was still thin. It was burning underneath, so that people could not even venture to leave their huts in search of food, as their feet could not bear the great heat.

The plight of the newly-made people on the earth would have been sad indeed, had not their necessities been relieved by the God Oki-kurumi, who fished for them daily and sent his lovely wife to deliver the catch through the window, on condition that none should dare to look upon her face or to ask any question.

All went well until one day a certain Ainu, more curious than the rest, must needs disobey the God's command. Determined to see the lovely goddess, he waited for the moment when she laid the fish upon the window-ledge, then seized her hand and dragged her in, disregarding her screams. No sooner was she inside the hut than she turned into a wriggling sea-monster. The sky darkened, thunder crashed, the monster vanished, and hut and man were consumed by lightning.

Ever since that day the Ainu have been a poor and miserable people.

After CHAMBERLAIN

Japan

THE CHINESE DRAGON

THE dragon, says a Chinese writer, has the head of a camel, the horns of a deer, the eyes of a hare, the ears of a bull, the neck of a snake, the belly of an iguanodon, the scales of a carp, the claws of an eagle, and the paws of a tiger. Its scales number eighty-one, being nine by nine, the extreme lucky number. Its voice resembles the beating of a gong. On each side of its mouth are whiskers, under its chin is a bright pearl, and under its throat the scales are reversed. On top of its head is the *po-shan*, sometimes called the wooden foot-rule, without which it cannot ascend into the skies. When its breath escapes it forms clouds, which sometimes change into rain and sometimes into fire.

The dragon can, at will, become the size of a silkworm, or swell till it fills the space of Heaven and Earth. It desires to mount—it rises till it affronts the clouds ; to sink—it descends till it is hidden below the fountains of the deep.

BALL

THE DRAGON OF RED RIVER

AT the bottom of the Red River lies an enormous shining dragon whose maw gapes always unsatisfied, and the throne of Annam is reserved for the man who is able to carry there the bones of his dead father and lay them between the dragon's jaws. But this is not an easy achievement, since whosoever sets eyes upon the dragon is immediately struck blind.

A wise man who desired to become ruler one day said to himself, ' If I cover one eye and risk the loss of the other I should be able to achieve my purpose.' So he covered one side of his face with his hand, dived into the water, and laid the bones of his father in the dragon's jaws. Thus, though blinded in one eye, he was able to become the founder of a dynasty.

Some time later a Chinese general who possessed magical powers wished to make a passage for his troops across the Red River, which was very dangerous to junks because of the many rocks hidden beneath the water. He succeeded by means of a thunderbolt in opening a passage, but his violent action opened the veins of the dragon, and since that time the waters of the river have flowed red with its blood.

DUMOUTIER, *adapted and trans. by E.D.E.*

Indo-China

THE DURIAN

(1869)

THE Durian grows on a large and lofty forest tree, somewhat resembling an elm in its general character, but with a more smooth and scaly bark. The fruit is round or slightly oval, about the size of a large cocoanut, of a green colour, and covered all over with short stout spines, the bases of which touch each other and are consequently somewhat hexagonal, while the points are very strong and sharp. It is so completely armed that if the stalk is broken off it is a difficult matter to lift one from the ground. The outer rind is so thick and tough that from whatever height it may fall it is never broken. From the base to the apex five very faint lines may be traced, over which the spines arch a little ; these are the sutures of the carpels, and show where the fruit may be divided with a heavy knife and a strong hand. The five cells are satiny white within, and are each filled with an oval mass of cream-coloured pulp, imbedded in which are two or three seeds about the size of chestnuts. This pulp is the edible part, and its consistence and flavour are indescribable. A rich butter-like custard highly flavoured with almonds gives the best general idea of it, but intermingled with it come wafts of flavour that call to mind cream cheese, onion-sauce, brown sherry and other incongruities. Then there is a rich glutinous smoothness in the pulp which nothing else possesses, but which adds to its delicacy. It is neither acid, nor sweet nor juicy, yet one feels the want of none of these qualities, for it is perfect as it is. It produces no nausea or other bad effects, and the more you eat of it the less you feel inclined to stop. In fact to eat Durians is a new sensation, worth a voyage to the East to experience.

WALLACE

Malaya

★

(1878)

A high official, on his way from England to China, was sumptu-ously entertained by the then resident councillor at Penang, who was a great admirer of the durian and had one of the very best his garden could produce placed upon the table. On his lordship being asked his opinion of it, he replied sharply to his host : ' It may have been very good last season, Mr L., but if you will excuse me, I would rather not venture on it now.'

McNAIR

Malaya

(1880)

. . . The durian is a natural *macédoine* of fruits—one of Dame Nature's ' made dishes '—and if it be possible for you to imagine the flavour of a combination of cornflour and rotten cheese, nectarines, crushed filberts, a dash of pineapple, a spoonful of old dry sherry, thick cream, apricot-pulp, and a *soupçon* of garlic, all reduced to the consistency of a rich custard, you have a glimmering idea of the durian.

BURBIDGE

Borneo

DWARFING TREES

THE art of dwarfing trees, as commonly practised both in China and Japan is in reality very simple and easily understood. It is based upon one of the commonest principles of vegetable physiology. Anything which has a tendency to retard or check the flow of the sap in trees also prevents, to a certain extent, the formation of wood and leaves. This may be done by grafting, by confining the roots in a small space, by witholding water, by bending the branches, and in a hundred other ways, which proceed upon the same principle. This principle is perfectly understood by the Japanese, and they take advantage of it to make Nature subservient to this particular whim of theirs. They are said to select the smallest seeds from the smallest plants, which I do not think at all unlikely. I have frequently seen Chinese gardeners selecting suckers for this purpose from the plants of their gardens. Stunted varieties were generally chosen, particularly if they had the side branches opposite or regular, for a one-sided dwarf tree is of no value. The main stem was then twisted in a zigzag form, which process checked the flow of the sap, and at the same time encouraged the production of side branches at those parts of the stem where they were most desired. The pots in which they were planted were narrow and shallow, so that they held but a small quantity of soil compared with the wants of the

plants, and no more water was given than was actually necessary to keep them alive. When new branches were in the act of formation they were tied down and twisted in various ways ; and the points of the leaders and strong-growing ones were generally nipped out to discourage the production of young shoots possessing any degree of vigour. Nature generally struggles against this treatment for a while, until her powers seem to be in a great measure exhausted, when she quietly yields to the power of Art. The artist, however, must be ever on the watch ; for should the roots of his plants get through the pots into the ground, or happen to receive a liberal supply of moisture, or should the young shoots be allowed to grow in their natural position for a time, the vigour of the plant will be restored and the fairest specimens of Oriental dwarfing be destroyed. It is a curious fact that when plants, from any cause, become stunted or unhealthy, they almost invariably produce flower and fruit, and thus endeavour to propagate and perpetuate their kind. This principle is of great value in dwarfing trees. Flowering trees— peaches and plums for example—produce their blossoms most profusely under the treatment I have described, and as they expend their energies in this way, they have little inclination to make vigorous growth.

FORTUNE, *Yedo . . .*

Japan

FAIRIES

THE Fijian peoples with invisible beings every remarkable spot, the lonely dell, the gloomy cave, the desolate rock and the deep forest. Many of these, he believes, are on the alert to do him harm ; therefore, in passing their territory he throws down a few green leaves to propitiate the demon of the place.

Among the principal objects of Fijian superstition are demons, ghosts, witches, wizards, fairies, evil-eyes, and priests, all of whom he believes to possess supernatural power. A very old Fijian used to talk to me of ' those little gods ' with a faith as strong as that of a Highlander in his fairies. And these ' little gods ' are the fairies of Fiji.

' When living near the Kauvandra Mountains I often used to hear them sing,' said the old man ; and his eyes brightened as he went on to tell how they would assemble in troops on the tops of the mountains and sing unweariedly. They were all little—' little like children. I have often seen them and listened to their songs.' There are other ' little gods,' children of the waters. These are represented as wild and fearful, and at certain festivals they visit their worshippers, who for several successive weeks assemble morning and evening to allure them by drumming with short bamboos. Little flags are placed at various inland passes to prevent the water-gods from passing through to the forests ; so they halt at an enclosure where offerings have been placed for them, and there the worshippers seat themselves and beat their bamboos, and others dance in most fantastic style while one, called the ' shade-holder,' dances in a circle all round the others, waving a sun-shade which he alone is privileged to carry.

CUMMING, *At Home in Fiji*

Fiji

THE FIRST MAN

WHEN the Earth emerged from Chaos the Male and Female Elements became balanced, the waters subsided into the valleys and the mountains were covered with trees.

One day, shortly after this occurrence, a tree was uprooted on the mountain and was carried down from the heights to the lower levels of the earth. As it fell the tree gave birth to two magic birds, which took refuge in a cave and there made their nest. From the first egg hatched in the cave there emerged a Man, the first of his kind to appear on the Earth, and from whom are descended all who followed after.

DUMOUTIER, *adapted and trans. by E.D.E.*

Indo-China.

FISHING

THE Malay fishermen are certainly of the opinion that fish are gifted with the faculty of hearing, for each canoe is provided with a rattle made of a gourd filled with pebble-stones, which is struck at intervals against the side of the boat for the purpose of attracting the fish. If fish really possessed the disputed sense, this noise which can be heard on a calm day at the distance of several miles, must arrest their attention, were they even at the bottom of the sea ; but one would suppose that it would rather have the effect of frightening them away than of alluring them to the spot. The Malays evidently entertain the contrary opinion, since a fisherman would as soon think of going to sea without his hooks as without his rattle.

EARL

Java

FLORAL CALENDAR

January	. Pine.
February	. Plum.
March .	. Peach and pear.
April .	. Cherry.
May .	. Azalea, peony, wistaria.
June .	. Iris.
July .	. Morning-glory.
August .	. Lotus.
September	. The ' seven grasses ' of Autumn (arrow-root, Chinese agrimony, clover, maiden-flower, pampas, wild carnation, wild morning-glory).
October	. Chrysanthemum.
November	. Maple.
December	. Camellia.

DE GARIS

Japan

FRUITS

OF all the delicious fruits that are produced in the East, perhaps I may venture to say in the whole world, the mangoostan may fairly set up its claim to the preference. The tree on which it grows, though not magnificent, is extremely beautiful, bearing, like the orange, both fruit and flowers at the same time on the extremities of the branches. This fruit is no less fascinating to the eye than it is gratifying to the taste. Its form is round, generally a perfect sphere ; the colour a bright or dark purple, according to the degree of its ripeness ; it rests on a permanent green calyx, and the upper part is surmounted by a corona, which is generally divided into as many rays as the fruit within consists of lobes, which are of a delicate white pulpy substance, covering each a small nut.

The mango is another fruit of exquisite flavour, when of a good sort, but of that peculiar taste which is not relished by every palate. The doorian also grows wild in plenty. Its smell is extremely disgusting, and flavour not unlike what one might suppose the taste to be of a custard flavoured with garlic ; but both the taste and the smell are said not only to lose their offensive qualities by frequent use, but to become extremely fascinating.

BARROW, *Voyage to Cochin China.*

Java

GEOMANCY (FÊNG SHUI)

THE more wealthy often convey their dead a considerable distance, and employ a kind of fortune-teller whose duty it is to find out the most appropriate resting-place. This man goes with the corpse to the place appointed, and of course pretends to be very wise in the selection of the spot as well as in the choice of the soil with which the ashes of the dead are to mingle ; and upon trial, should the particular earth appear unsuitable, he immediately orders the procession off to some other place in the neighbourhood, where he expects to be more successful. A situation on a hill-side is considered of great importance, especially if it commands a beautiful view. But I believe that of all places the one most coveted is where a winding stream, in its course, passes and then returns again to the foot of the hill where the grave is to be made. The director of ceremonies, with a compass in his hand, settles the direction in which the body is to lie, which is another point of great importance.

The fortune-teller is often very eloquent in his description of the future happiness of those who obey his directions. . . . These men are generally great rogues, and it frequently happens that after a corpse has been interred for some time they call upon the relatives and inform them that, for some cause which they effect to explain, it is absolutely necessary to remove and re-inter it. Should the relatives object, the answer is, ' Your children and relations will also be regardless of your remains when you die, and you will be miserable in your graves.'

FORTUNE, *Two Visits* . . .

China

★

The Court is like the sea ; all depends upon the wind.

Chinese Proverb

' A thing like wind, which cannot be comprehended, and like water, which cannot be grasped.'

THE system of *Fêng-shui* (Wind and Water) has four divisions : the general *order* of Nature ; her numerical proportions ; her vital breath and subtle energies ; and her form, or outward aspect. The harmonious blending of these four contribute a perfect *Fêng-shui* ; the contrary will produce calamity.

The three principles laid down by the professors of this art are (1) that heaven rules the earth ; (2) that heaven and earth both influence all living beings, and man has power to turn their influence to his own advantage ; and (3) that the fortunes of the living depend on the good-will and influence of the dead.

The modern system of *Fêng-shui*, formulated in the Sung dynasty (A.D. 1126–1278) takes 10 (or twice 5) as the sacred number for heaven, and 12 (or twice 6) as the number for earth, and from these are constructed the ten heavenly stems and the twelve terrestrial branches. A clever geomancer well versed in the intricate but meaningless array of formulae derived from the combination of these, imposes with ease on his ignorant and superstitious customers.

The Chinese think that the soul of man is two-fold—an animus and an anima ; the first being the breath of heaven and returning thither ; the second being the material or animal element and returning to the earth at death. The common people, modifying this distinction, suppose that the dead are chained to the tomb by the material soul, and that the spiritual soul hovers round the old home ; and therefore, as there must be action and reaction of the two souls on one another, the comfort of the corpse makes the earthly soul complacent ; and flashing complacency to the spiritual soul as well, prosperity to the house of the living is secured by some unseen influence.

And here comes in the art of the geomancer. He is entrusted with the selection of a site for the grave. He must secure for it a right aspect, guarded from noxious northern influences. Trees are planted round and hillocks are raised to ensure this ; there must be water in front, as an emblem of wealth and affluence ; and straight lines in paths and watercourses must be avoided as giving too free access to possible evil influences.

MOULE

China

A GHOSTLY MEETING

ONCE upon a time there were two young men who were devoted friends. Having heard that the entrance to a certain cave was the door to the place of departed spirits, one of them determined to go and see what this land was like. On entering the cave he could see nothing at first but thick darkness, but as he moved forward he saw a speck of light far ahead of him. The further he went, the brighter the light became and the darker the cave behind him. At length he reached a magnificent country, filled with the brightest light. Beautiful forests of trees and mighty plains covered with reeds and grass opened out before him, while rivers of sparkling water divided the lowlands around. After a while he came to a village and saw many people whom he had known in the upper world. He endeavoured to speak to them, but they all looked this way and that in evident perplexity and fear. The dogs, too, set up a grievous howling. Even his own father did not recognise him, and his mother fled away in terror, while everyone cried out that he was a ghost.

After this reception he gave up trying to reveal himself and set out to return to the upper world. On the way he met a man who was carrying a bag on his back and had a weary, haggard look. He thought it was his friend, but as it was dark in the passage he was not sure, so he called out to him by name. But the man rushed by in great alarm and sped swiftly towards the lower world. On reaching the upper air he went at once to his friend's house and, finding him dead, knew that it was the departing spirit of his friend he had met on its way to the lower world.

BATCHELOR, *Ainu* . . . (*adapted*)

Japan

GODDESS OF SAILORS

MA CHU, the goddess of sailors, is extensively worshipped by all who have business connected with the navigation of rivers or the ocean.

This goddess is the daughter of a man who, with his sons, was engaged on the ocean in the pursuit of a living. He was born during the Sung dynasty and lived in Fukien. One day, while the girl was weaving, she fell asleep with her head resting upon her loom. She dreamed that she saw her father and her two brothers on their separate junks in a terrific storm. She exerted herself to rescue them from danger, seizing the junk which contained her father with her mouth, while with her hands she caught a firm hold upon the two junks which contained her brothers. She was dragging them all towards the shore, when she heard her mother calling her and, forgetting that she held her father's junk by her mouth, she hastily opened it, being an obedient girl, to answer the summons. She awoke in great distress, and lo ! it was a dream. But not all a dream, for in a few days the news arrived that the fleet in which the family junks were had encountered a dreadful storm and that the one in which her father was had been wrecked, and he had perished, while those in which her brothers were had been signally rescued.

This girl became, as the result of her dream, one of the most popular objects of worship in China.

DOOLITTLE

China

THE GOOD AND BAD FOXES

PAN'AMBE the fox had a great desire to become rich, so he stretched his tail across the sea to the town of Matsumai. When the Lord of Matsumai saw the tail he said, ' This is a pole sent from the gods. Hang all my best clothes on it to air.' So all the short-sleeved garments and good clothes were hung out. After a while Pan'ambe gently withdrew his tail, and all the silky garments and fine clothing came with it ; so he gained a whole houseful of things and became rich.

Pen'ambe soon heard of his neighbour's good fortune and came to inquire. On hearing the story he was very envious and cried, ' This is just what I meant to do myself. Now you, disgusting Pan'ambe, have forestalled me ! ' So saying, he hurried down to the seashore and stretched *his* tail across the sea to Matsumai. And again the Lord of Matsumai said, ' This is a pole sent by the gods. Hang out all my best clothes to air.' So the clothes were hung upon Pen'ambe's tail.

But Pen'ambe, in a hurry to get rich, began to withdraw his tail too quickly. ' Ah,' said the Lord of Matsumai seeing the tail move ' thus it happened once before. A pole came from the gods just like this one, but when I hung my clothes upon it a thief stole the pole away and we all became poor. Now again the pole has come but this time the thief must not get away with our clothes. Bring a sword and cut the pole in two.' So the officers drew their swords and cut the pole, and thereby salvaged all their clothes, while Pen'ambe was left with only half a tail and nothing in exchange. If Pan'ambe had only listened and not been in too much of a hurry to get rich, he might have obtained what he wanted. But he did not like to take advice from others and so he lost everything.

BATCHELOR, Ainu . . . (adapted)

Japan

THE GOSSIPING GODDESS

THE Island of Hokkaido was created by two gods, a male and a female, who were the deputies of the Supreme Creator. To the female was allotted the west coast, and to the male the east and south. They vied with each other to see who could complete the allotted portion of the island first. But one day as the goddess was working she happened to meet a sister goddess and stopped to have a chat. Whilst they were talking the male god went on with his work and nearly finished his side of the island. Seeing this, the female god became frightened by her own lapse, and in order not to be behind time, finished her task in a hurried and slovenly manner. Hence it is that the west coast of Hokkaido is so rugged and dangerous. If therefore anyone is disposed to grumble on this account he should remember that it is not the Creator who was at fault in the matter, but His deputy.

Ibid.

Japan

THE HARE

THE children in the sky were throwing snowballs at each other, and the snowballs fell into the world of men. As it would have been a pity to waste heaven's snow, the snowballs were turned into hares. But one day the hares were found quarrelling by the god in whose charge they were. To teach them a lesson he seized a fire-brand and beat them with it. This is why hares are white with black ears ; their bodies are made of snow, but their ears are black because they were charred by the firebrand with which the god beat them.

After CHAMBERLAIN

Japan

HOW IT WAS SETTLED WHO SHOULD RULE THE WORLD

WHEN the Creator made the world he left good and bad gods all mixed together in it, and they began to dispute for possession. Finally it was agreed that whoever should first see the sunrise should rule. Thereupon both bad and good gods turned their eyes towards the east whence the sun must rise. The Fox-god alone stood and looked towards the west. After a while he cried out, ' I see the sunrise.' Thereupon all the gods, good and bad, turned round and saw indeed the brilliance of the western mountains tipped with light before the disc of the sun was visible in the east.

After CHAMBERLAIN

Japan

HOW MORTALS OBTAINED THE KAVA OF THE GODS TO DRINK

(*Samoan Folk-Tale*)

IN the Polynesian heaven there is only one god, Tangaloa, a quiescent being who loves peace and tranquillity ; but he has many ways of manifesting himself, according to the nature of the work which he purposes to do. Each of these manifestations is a Tangaloa, with an attribute added to the name to show his special function. Others again are his sons by mortal mothers—not sons of the supreme Tangaloa, who rests in the Ninth Heaven—but begotten by those energising particles of his nature whose duties or inclinations sometimes took them down to earth. All these gods, whether human or divine, had the right to attend the sacred councils in the heavens and were known as the ' family of Tangaloa.'

At every 'council' the first observance was the *kava* cup. The drink was prepared from the heavenly plant, and the cup of ceremony was handed round to the gods in order of rank and dignity. Then, when all had drunk, the 'great consult' began. Such was the order of their doing in heaven above. But on one occasion the 'Miracle-working Tangaloa,' whose seat was in the Eighth Heaven, happened to be on earth, and, desiring some *kava* to drink, he sent his attendants to heaven to fetch the requisite appliances. They brought down not only the bowl, strainer and cup, but the whole of a *kava* plant which they had, in their hurry, torn up by the roots. Of this Tangaloa threw away the greater part, since it is only the 'root-stem' which is chewed to make *kava*. But Pava, a mortal, who saw all that was done, watched his opportunity and gathered up the parts of the plant which the god had rejected, and planted them in the earth where they grew luxuriantly, thus yielding for mortals the drink formerly reserved for the gods.

PRATT (*adapted*)

Polynesia

Constant cutting takes the edge off the knife; constant talking dulls the wits.

Burmese Proverb

JAPANESE ART

THERE are certain pairs of objects which form the main stock of the Japanese artist's designs, and the set of symbols oftenest employed by the poet.

The pine-tree and stork, emblems of longevity, are embroidered on robes presented to newly-born infants.

The willow and swallow, and the bamboo and sparrow, indicative of gentleness, are seen oftenest on screens, fans, and upright objects of household adornment.

The young moon and cuckoo, the bird flying across the crescent, is a poetic reference to a renowned archer who shot a hideous monster. The crescent of the moon represents his bent bow, and the call of the cuckoo was heard while the mikado was presenting him with a famous sword.

The phoenix and the paulownia tree are twin imperial emblems on the mikado's robes, rugs, curtains, etc. This tree, which is very common in Japan, is an emblem of rectitude. Its leaves form the imperial *mon*, or crest.

The peony and the Chinese lion—a beast which never trod this earth—may be seen rampant on temple screens, doors, and panels.

The mulberry and goat are put together by the artist, since this animal has the appetite of a silkworm, and feeds voraciously on mulberry leaves or paper made from mulberry bark.

The hare peeps out from the rushes on many a lacquered box or tray, or is wrought in gold-thread embroidery. Instead of seeing a man in the moon carrying a bundle of sticks, Japanese (and Chinese) fancy beholds the hare scouring the face of the moon with rushes.

The red maple leaves and the stag are painted with fine effect on screens. 'In autumn the maples crimson, and the stag calls the doe.' To send a spray of autumn maple to one formerly loved indicates that the leaf and the heart have both changed.

The cherry-blossom and pheasant are fitly wedded in poetry and art. Most beautiful of all birds is this iridescent queen of the groves, and the cherry-tree is the most beautiful of all trees. ' There are snow-showers which do not descend from the skies.'

The plum-tree, also admired for its blossoms, is joined with the nightingale. The plum is, *par excellence*, the poet's tree, and the nightingale is the poet of birds. ' Send forth your fragrance upon the eastern winds, O flowers of the plum-tree ! and do not forget the spring because of the absence of the sun ! '

It is said that geese flying on long journeys carry rushes in their bills, and drop them before alighting on the water, and then alight upon them. Thus rushes and geese are figured together.

A comical couplet is the baboon and the moon's reflection in water. The long-armed, stump-tailed fool sees the image of the moon in the water and tries in vain to reach it.

The chrysanthemum and fox combination refers to one of the innumerable fox myths. A fox, assuming the form of a lovely woman, bewitched a certain prince. One day, happening to fall asleep on a bed of chrysanthemums, she resumed her proper shape. The prince shot the animal in the forehead. On returning to the house he found that his concubine had a wound in the corresponding part of her head, and thus he discovered her true nature.

The bamboo and tiger are often seen together on large ornaments. The tiger, being afraid of elephants, hides in the bamboo grove.

GRIFFIS, Mikado's Empire

Japan

JAPANESE SUPERSTITIONS

To sweep a room immediately after someone sets out on **a journey** will sweep out all the good luck.

If the medicine is upset the patient will recover.

If the nails are cut before a journey disgrace will be waiting at the end of it.

If a young child looks in a mirror it will live to have twins.

To keep the children free from smallpox fix a notice on the gate to say they are away from home.

A new tooth will replace a lost one only if the old is buried below the foundations of the house, if from the upper jaw ; or thrown on the roof, if from the lower.

If a woman steps over an egg-shell she will lose her reason.

If a man sets his hair on fire he will go mad.

When salt is bought a little must be thrown on the fire to avert quarrelling in the household.

House to Let : If the sign is posted straight the house will not be let promptly.

To speed the parting guest turn a broom upside down and wrap its head in a towel as a wrap is often put round the head on leaving the house ; if the first charm does not work, warm the caller's shoes or get pattens and place them beside the broom ; if this does not have the desired effect, cauterise the visitor's footgear (which will of course have been removed when he first entered the house) with moxa. This third step cannot fail to result in early departure.

To cure diseases of the skin wear a cart-wheel hat and take a dip in the river or the sea, immersing yourself until the hat floats on the water. The disease will remain with the hat.

To win the heart of one who remains indifferent, cause the beloved unwittingly to consume the ashes of a burnt newt.

Bees swarming in the house portend prosperity.

To pick up a fan is a sure sign of good fortune on the way.

It is unlucky to be overtaken by a funeral but lucky to meet one.

White spots on the finger-nails herald an equal number of presents.

If oil is spilt from the lamp in winter the house will be burnt down in summer.

To let rice fall on one's clothes when eating is to risk being **turned** into a cow.

Sneezing once—praised ; twice—cursed ; three times—he has caught cold.

SHIH TÊ TZŬ : 'THE FOUNDLING'

JAVANESE MEDICAL PRACTICE

THEY have both male and female physicians, who have been known to achieve very surprising cures by their knowledge of the medicinal herbs produced in their country. They have sometimes a greater practice among the Europeans at Batavia than those physicians who have been regularly bred, and come from Europe ; but they know nothing of anatomy. Much friction of the affected parts is one of their chief means of cure. This is done with two fingers of the right hand, which are pressed down by the left, and passed continually downwards, after having first annointed the part with water mixed with fine ground wood or oil.

STOCKDALE

JAVANESE MUSIC

MUSIC is probably the art in which the Javanese, compared with most other Asiatic peoples, have made the greatest progress. In common with all the other nations of the Archipelago, they have generally fine musical ears, and are passionate lovers of music. Javanese melodies are wild, plaintive, and beyond all other Asiatic music, pleasing to the European ear. Most of their musical instruments, too, are superior to those of other Asiatic nations. They have wind and stringed instruments, both of them rude and imperfect however. Their best and most frequent are those of percussion. Some of these consist of a single gong (a Javanese word) or a series of them representing different notes, and others of bars of brass or sonorous wood placed over troughs and representing so many keys, after the fashion of the harmonicon. The instruments are all in the same kind of scale as that produced by the black keys of the pianoforte, in which scale so many of the Scots and Irish, all the Chinese and some of the best Indian and North-American airs were composed. Some of the cadences remind us of Scotch music for the bag-pipe. Others in the minor key have the flat seventh, instead of the leading note or sharp seventh, one of the indications of antiquity. In many of the airs the recurrence of the same passages is artful and ingenious. The irregularity of the rhythm or measure, and the reiteration of the same sound, are characteristic of oriental music.

CRAWFURD, Descriptive Dictionary

JU-JUTSU

JU-JUTSU means 'The Art of Suppleness.' It is a mode of self-defence for women as well as men.

The secret of ju-jutsu consists in utilising the strength of an antagonist to one's own advantage, and not in matching strength with strength. There are several methods of overcoming an antagonist : to hurl him down ; to hold him down so that he cannot move ; to strike or push him with the fist and kick him in a vulnerable spot in order to bring him down.

To attain skill in ju-jutsu mental discipline is essential. One must be composed, self-reliant, and, above all, alert to utilise either the mistakes or the strength of one's opponent.

Included in the course of instruction are various ways of causing apparent death by pressure, and of recalling to life from such swoons, also methods of disjointing bones as well as principles connected with moral training.

DE GARIS (adapted)

Japan

JUNKS

THE stern of a Chinese junk rises high and towering, and the deck slopes with a steep ascent to the deck-house, and with a gentler gradient towards the prow. The gunwales are high and strong; and below, in lines round the ship, the province, department and port from which the junk hails are inscribed, and the vessel bears some name or motto at the stern—*The Flying Dragon, The Azure Stork*, or simply the words 'Fair wind and tide.' The sailors are stretching their ochre-red bamboo sails to dry in the wind and sun as we pass; and in a sheltered corner of the deck some of them are

squatting in circles eating their mid-day meal. They gesticulate with their chopsticks, and point at us as we pass; but foreigners are no longer a 'sight' in Shanghai.

We have come down with the very first of the ebb. Many junks have already weighed and are dropping down the river; others are getting up anchor; and as we pass one after another a loud clash and roll of gongs and drums nearly deafens us; crackers are let off at the bows; and paper-money for the use of the spirits is set on fire and cast into the river.

The junk is moving now; and as she drops down the river crackers are discharged till with all sail set and a fair tide they stop their devotions and contentedly smoke their pipes, and hope for a prosperous trip and a quick return.

MOULE

China

JUSTICE

An egg-dealer once had some of his property stolen from a tub of bran in front of his shop. He had his suspicion as to the thief, but only gave the police a hint. The police consulted the judge, who said that unless the merchant could produce definite evidence to convict the person suspected, the police must bring to the court several other persons as well. This was accordingly done. On the day of the trial five women stood before the bar. The judge addressed them and said that they were all accused of stealing eggs, but he

presumed that only one of them was guilty. He assured them that the innocent among them need have no fear, as he could quite easily detect the guilty one because she would have the smell of bran on her hands. He then turned carelessly away and pretended to be adjusting his papers for a moment, but he did not fail to notice that one of the women surreptitiously raised her hands to her nose. Turning back to the group, the judge then smelt the hands of each and accused the culprit, who immediately confessed.

BRYAN (*adapted*)

Japan

THE KINGFISHER

THE sacred character of the kingfisher is remarkable, and the reason of it hard to find. In San Cristoval a kingfisher pecks the head of a lately separated soul which has not yet realised its condition, and it sinks into a ghost. In the Banks' Islands every kingfisher is sacred. They make halcyon days ; it is the name of the kingfisher that carries the power in the charm for sunshine ; they control storms and rain, and the charm calls upon them to eat the rising waves and restore calm. If a man setting out on a journey hears a kingfisher cry he thinks it is angry and would forbid him to go ; so he sings a charm : 'Good luck to me ; let all mischief pass me by and let good fortune be before my face.'

CODRINGTON

Melanesia

★

MAGIC

(1727)

I SAW strange Cures performed by a Malaya Doctor at Malacca. One of them was on an Officer belonging to my Ship. He was going to sleep about Midnight, and lying down on his Bed, was bit in the Calf of the Leg by a *Centipee*, an Insect with many Feet, and very venomous. The Pain that the Bite caused would allow him no Rest. Next Day he expected that the Venom might have

been exhausted, but in that he was mistaken, for it grew first red by Inflammation, and then blue and numbed. I sent for the Doctor aforesaid, who came on the first Summons. I told him of the Accident that had happened, and he said there was no Danger. He saw the inflamed Leg, and kept his Hand moving over it, but did not touch it. He muttered some unintelligible Words, and spit on the Place affected, and in five Minutes he could walk without Pain, tho' before the Cure, he could not stand without something to support him.

HAMILTON

Malacca

THE MALAY LANGUAGE

THE Siamese language cannot compare with the Malay in musical qualities. It has often been insisted that Malay is the Italian of the East, and one never felt the truth of this so much as on such a night as this. The steady pump of the engine aft, the splash of the ripples forward, the occasional clank of the steering chain, and the bursts of shrill piping from the far dark line of jungle, all formed a fitting accompaniment to the long drawling calls of the leadsman in the chains and the low *Lagare* (Steady) of the helmsman peering at the binnacle. And who that has listened to such a nocturne can forget its magic, more lasting than the spells of Chopin or even of Beethoven !

SMYTH

Siam

MANGOSTEENS

IT is impossible to describe the peculiarly grateful taste of this cool and refreshing fruit. It is a mixture of the sweet and acid, blended in the most luscious manner. It is in size somewhat smaller than an apple, and the skin, which is very thick and bitter, of a dark plum colour. The inside, which is nearly white, is divided into four parts, resembling in substance a firm jelly ; and in my opinion, gives one more idea of what nectar was, or ought to be, than anything else which enters into the mouth of man. The Peak of Ternate was the true Mt Olympus, and it was there that the gods were assembled and, in ancient days ate mangosteins, called nectar by the Greeks.

MARRYAT

Borneo

MEDICINE

THERE are said to be two medical schools or systems in Siam contending for the mastery—the Indian and the Chinese—and it would be difficult to say which is the more crowded with superstition. And some *Siamese* remedies seem to combine both, as for instance, the following prescription for a ' morbific fever ' :

Take one part of rhinoceros-horn, one of elephant's tusk, one of tiger's tooth, one of crocodile's, and one of bear's ; one part composed of equal quantities of the bones of vulture, raven and goose ; one part of bison's and one of stag's horn ; and one part of sandal. Mix all these ingredients together on a stone with pure water. Drink one-half of the mixture and rub the body with the remainder.

BOWRING, *Kingdom . . . of Siam*

Siam

THE MOSQUITO

(1762)

THE musketoe is a very small fly, stings smartly, makes a great buzzing, and is much of the nature of our gnats in England. When Europeans come first here, the musketoes are apt to be very troublesome to them ; sometimes their faces and skin are so much swelled by the bites of these animals that a man will find difficulty to know his intimate acquaintance ; but, after we have continued some time here, the effect of their sting is not so great. All the time I was in Batavia, I could get no rest in my bed for them, though I kept my gauze curtains as close as possible.

East Indies

Batavia

THE MAN IN THE MOON

ONCE upon a time there was a boy who refused to obey his parents and hated to fetch water. When ordered to do so he sat still, chopping at the fireplace with a sharp tool. At last he got up and as he went out he struck the door-post, saying : ' You, being only a door-post, do not have to draw water.' Then taking up the bucket and ladle he went down to the river and stood there idly. A little fish swam past, to which he said, ' You, bony creature, being only a fish, do not have to draw water.' Presently, seeing a salmon-trout, he said once more, ' You, being a soft and flabby creature, do not have to draw water.'

Then descending thence, he saw an autumn salmon, to which he said, ' How do you do, Mr. Salmon, how do you do ? ' But the salmon straightway seized him and thrust him into the moon. Thus did the angry gods put into the moon the boy who disliked to draw water. And this they did as a warning to all the world that the commands of parents, whether good or evil, must be obeyed.

BATCHELOR, Ainu . . . (adapted)

Japan

MUSICAL PIGEONS

PEKING, June 14th, 1886.

IT is early morning—the only enjoyable time of the day, before the sun rises high—and I am sitting in the pleasant verandah listening to the pigeons as they fly overhead. There is no dove-like cooing, but a low, melodious whistle like the sighing of an Aeolian harp, or the murmur of telegraph wires thrilled by the night wind. It is produced by the action of cylindrical pipes, like two finger-ends side by side, about an inch and a half in length. These are made of very light wood and fitted with whistles; some are globular in shape and are constructed from a tiny gourd. These little musical-boxes are attached to the tail-feathers of the pigeon in such a manner that as he flies, the air shall blow through the whistle, producing the most plaintive tones, especially as there are often many pigeons flying at once, some near, some distant, some just overhead, some high in the heavens. So the combined effect is really melodious. I believe the Pekingese are the only people who thus provide themselves with a dove orchestra, though the use of pigeons as message-bearers is common in all parts of China. The people of South China have devised another method of producing similar plaintively melodious notes, by inserting several metallic strings in the centre of their kites, so that as these fly in the breeze they emit low silvery notes like the breath of an Aeolian harp.

China   CUMMING, *Wanderings* . . .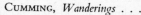

NAVIGATION

THE present system of Chinese navigation is to keep as near the shore as possible ; and never to lose sight of land, unless in voyages that absolutely require it. Knowing the direction of the port intended to be made, let the wind be fair or foul, they endeavour, as nearly as possible, to keep the head of the ship always pointing towards the port by means of the compass. This instrument, as used in China, has every appearance of originality. The Chinese know nothing, from history or tradition, of its first introduction or discovery ; and the use of the magnet, for indicating the poles of the earth, can be traced, from their records, to a period of time when the greatest part of Europe was in a state of barbarism. . . .

Yet even with the assistance of the compass it is surprising how the clumsy and ill-constructed vessels of the Chinese can perform so long and dangerous a voyage as that to Batavia. For besides being thrown out of their course by every contrary wind, their whole construction, and particularly the vast height of their upper works above the water, seems little adapted to oppose those violent typhoons which prevail on the China seas. These hurricanes sometimes blow with such strength that, according to the assertion of an experienced and intelligent commander of one of the East India Company's ships, ' Were it possible to blow ten thousand trumpets and beat as many drums on the forecastle of an Indiaman, in the height of a typhoon, neither the sound of the one nor the other would be heard by a person on the quarter-deck of the same ship.'

BARROW, *Travels* . . .

China

NIGHT-TRAVEL

IN Korea all wanderers abroad at night are required by law to be furnished with lanterns, which, as they swing to and fro by the motion of the men who carry them, look like fireflies flitting about in the darkness. A tallow candle is enclosed in a white paper screen, and this is dangled from the hand by a string. Sometimes the lanterns are given names—an honour which poetry is fond of bestowing upon almost everything in the far-East. By this distinguished attention their lustre has been much diminished ; for the names are painted in large black characters, through which no light can possibly pass. My own lantern was significantly entitled ' The Bright Moon ' ; and never was moon more needed than over that particularly rough road on a cloudy night.

LOWELL, *Chosön*

Korea

ORIGIN OF THE BULIDUPIS

ONE day an old, old woman—of what nation history does not say —ordered her daughter to light a fire. Again and again the young woman tried ; again and again she failed. At length, wearied by her lack of success and by the abuse of her aged mother, who (as far as it is possible to judge of historical personages) seems to have been a woman of violent temper, the young woman exclaimed, ' The Fire Fiend may take me if he will only let me get this fire to burn ! ' No sooner had she spoken than the fire burned up brightly. But at the same instant she disappeared from view.

Time passed, and at length the young woman returned from the lower regions, and, interesting as must have been her adventures (of which, however, history gives us no account) they were not more so than her condition. A few days afterwards she gave birth to a son who was the progenitor of the Buludupi tribe.

GUILLEMARD

Borneo

ORIGIN OF THE RAT AND THE CAT

AFTER the Creator had finished making the world He came down from heaven to see how things looked. As He was viewing His handiwork the Evil One appeared and derided Him saying, 'No doubt you think you have done all for the best. But look at these brambles and thistles. What use can they be?'

The Creator was angry at this criticism, so He put His hand behind His back and created a rat. As soon as the rat was made it rushed into the Evil One's mouth and bit off his tongue. He was so incensed at being left speechless that he caused the rats to multiply until they became a nuisance and a plague to men.

Being more troubled than most by the rats, the Ainu met together one day and called upon the Creator to remedy the evil. So the Creator, being always willing to hear the appeals of men, created cats to keep the rats within bounds.

Yet men should bear a little with rats, for they did a good deed in biting out the tongue of the Evil One. Moreover, it is unwise to speak against anything which the Creator has made, for see how He punished the Evil One for doing so.

BATCHELOR, *Ainu . . . (adapted)*

Japan

★

The best roads don't go far.

Chinese Proverb

PEACOCK AND PEAHEN

ON New-years-day, one of their great Festivals, there was a numerous appearance at Court of gentlemen and ladies, who came thither in their richest apparel, to compliment the Prince on the occasion of the day, and were by him entertain'd at dinner. Among other presents made to him that day, there happened to be a Peacock and Hen. Every one was delighted, and struck with admiration, by the uncommon beauty of these scarce, foreign Birds, whence the Prince took occasion to ask their opinion, which of the two they thought was the cock and which the hen. The gentlemen out of civility to the ladies, unanimously pitch'd upon the most beautiful to be the hen; the ladies on the contrary very modestly apprehended, that the finer of the two was the cock. You are in the right, answer'd thereupon the Prince; Nature itself will have the man best clad, and it seems to me incomprehensible, that the wife should have more pride, and go richer dress'd than her husband, who must be at the expense of maintaining her. An excellent New-year's Sermon from a Heathen Prince.

KAEMPFER

Japan

PLUM-TREES

THE plum-tree is the first to bloom,—not the edible plum, but that species which is known in Japan as *ume*. By the end of January it begins to blossom,—a pretty pinkish-white flower. It is quite beautiful in itself; and then from being the first, it is specially prized.

LOWELL, *Chosön*

Korea

Few of the better houses at this season of the year are without a plum-tree, or at least a branch of one. It blossoms in their gardens ; but this is not close enough companionship for their love. It must be where they can constantly see it ; so it is taken into the house and blossoms in the room in which its owner spends most of his indoor life—for, however many rooms may make up his house there is one which is particularly his dwelling-place by day and by night. Poetry and painting vie with each other in their attempt fittingly to praise the flower. Sonnets innumerable are written in its honour, and have been from dim antiquity.

Ibid.

PREVENTION IS BETTER THAN CURE

Do not overeat.

Breakfast early.

Eat well at noon.

Eat slowly and masticate thoroughly.

Sup betimes and sparingly.

Do not sleep until two hours after eating.

Begin all meals with a little tea.

Avoid smelling at musk and young orange-blossoms, as they contain minute insects which may find the way through the nose to the brain.

Wind is to the air what anger is to the passions, therefore avoid air coming through narrow passages.

DUDGEON

China

★

The dog that runs between two monasteries gets nothing.

Korean Proverb

RAIN

THE Chinese say rain falls because the spirits of earth, trees, and the lower heavens will it, or because the Dragon shows his might by sucking up the sea water, which by his power becomes fresh. They having seen that in the open ocean a wind sometimes sucks up the water transparently into the sky, and that thence arise clouds, believe that the Dragon does it. There is no proof of this. The Brahmins and others who believe in God the Creator, believe that He makes rain to fall, that men may cultivate their fields and live. I cannot say whether God does this or not, for it seems to me that if so, He would of His great love and mercy make it fall equally all over the earth, so that all men might live and eat in security. But this is not the case. Indeed, in some places no rain falls for years together, the people have to drink brackish water, and cannot cultivate their lands, but have to trust to the dew to moisten them ; besides, a very great deal of the rain falls on the seas, the mountains, and the jungles, and does no good to man at all. Sometimes too much falls, flooding towns and villages, and drowning numbers of men and animals ; sometimes too little falls in the plains for rice to be grown, while on the mountain tops rain falls perpetually through seasons wet and dry. How can it be said that God, the Creator of the world, causes rain, when its fall is so irregular ? We now come come to the idea of philosophers, who have some proof of their theory. They say rain falls somewhere every day without fail ; for the earth, the sky, and the sea are like a still, and it is a property of salt water to yield fresh by distillation. The heat of the sun draws up steam from the sea and wherever there is moisture. Do not pools dry up ? The steam is not lost, it flies to cool places above, and collecting in the cold skies, becomes solid like ice, then when the hot season arrives, this ice melts and forms into clouds, floating according to the wind, and when a wind forces a cloud near the earth, the hills and earth act on it like a magnet, draw it down, and there is rain. Hence it arises that rain water is cooler than other water, for it is formed by melting ice, and wherever the sun goes there it is rainy season.

ALABASTER (*from the Siamese*)

Siam

THE ROYAL ELEPHANTS OF SIAM

WHEN we came upon them a Dozen of the King's Elephants were feeding out of their Houses on Sugar Canes fresh gathered and administered by their Keepers. Alighting from our Palenkeens, they loosed one which was Fourteen Feet high. . . . His Body is a Symmetrical Deformity (if I may so say) ; the Hanches and Quarters clapt together seem so many Heaps ; his Neck short, flapping Ears like Scates, little-Eyed, a broad Face, from which drops his *Proboscis* or Trunk, thrusting it out or shriveling it in as he chuses, through its Hollow he sucks his Liquor, and with two Fingers, as it were, reaches the Fodder and brings it under his Mouth. His Tail is curt ; He shuffles at great Pace, moving all the Joints of his legs. When he stands his Legs appear so many Columns scollop'd at bottom, being flat-footed.

FRYER

SEMEIOLOGY

IF the pupil of the eye be of a white colour, the disease lies in the lungs ; if red, then it lies in the heart ; if yellow, in the spleen ; if green, in the gall ; if black, in the kidneys ; but when the whole of the eye is of a yellow colour, that can neither be described nor named, then the cause of the disease lies in the middle of the chest.

SIRR

China

SHINTO

SHINTO is the Japanese conception of the cosmos. It is a combination of the worship of nature and of their own ancestors. But the character of the combination is ethnologically instructive. For a lack of psychic development has enabled these seemingly diverse elements to fuse into a homogeneous whole. Both, of course, are aboriginal instincts. Next to the fear of natural phenomena, in point of primitiveness, comes the fear of one's father, as children and savages show. But races, like individuals, tend to differentiate the two as they develop. Now the suggestive thing about the Japanese is, that they did not do so. Filial respect lasted, and by virtue of not becoming less, became more, till it filled not only the whole sphere of morals, but expanded into the sphere of cosmogony. To the Japanese eye the universe itself took on the paternal look. Awe of their parents, which these people could comprehend, lent explanation to dread of nature, which they could not. Quite cogently, to their minds, the thunder and the typhoon, the sunshine and the earthquake, were the work not only of anthropomorphic beings, but of beings ancestrally related to themselves. In short, Shinto, their explanation of things in general, is simply the patriarchal principle projected without perspective into the past, dilating with distance into deity.

LOWELL, *Occult Japan*

Japan

SHINTOISM is a cult which embraces nature and ancestor-worship. The chief among its 8,000,000 deities is the Sun Goddess, the Great Ancestress of the Japanese Imperial House. Although this vast pantheon includes gods of mountains, seas, rivers, wind and fire, many regard the worship of the Sun Goddess and her relatives and descendants as the chief feature of Shintoism. It is this fact which has held the devotion and loyalty of the Japanese people to the Imperial Throne.

The underlying principle in Shinto services is purification. It is compulsory to wash the mouth and hands before worshipping, and frequent washings of the body are practised by all sincere believers. Externally they must avoid contact with death and human blood ; inwardly they must be cleansed from the evil imaginings of the mind. Divine protection is also sought against natural evils of whatever kind—flood, famine, earthquakes, hurricanes, as well as against great national upheavals.

Shintoism has no system of theology or of ethics. It teaches the innate goodness of the human heart. Its teaching regarding future reckoning for the good and evil done in this present life is not clear ; but it explicitly declares that the spirit lives after the death of the body.

Shintoism knows no asceticism ; its priests may marry and may eat animal food as do the laity. Women serve in the shrines as priestesses or dancers of the sacred dances, but they never become nuns. The offerings to the gods consist of rice, fruit, vegetables, sake, and, on special occasions, the products of the loom.

DE GARIS (*abridged*)

*

In the buzz of the market-place there is money, but under the cherry-tree there is content.

Japanese Proverb

廣成子

KUANG CH'ÊNG TZO

SIAMESE MUSIC

(1828)

IN music the Siamese are entitled to some distinction among Oriental nations—their airs being more agreeable at least to an European ear than those of any Eastern people, with the exception probably of the Turks and Persians. The melodies of the Siamese are sometimes in a wild and plaintive strain ; but more commonly they are in a brisk and lively style, resembling Scotch and Irish music—thus forming to all appearance, a violent contrast with the sluggish and frigid temper of the people themselves.

A full Siamese band ought to consist of not less than ten instruments. The first of these in rank is a kind of staccato, in the form of a semi-circle, within which the player sits striking with two small hammers, the notes, or keys, which consist of inverted vessels of brass. The second is another staccato of the same materials, but less compass, in form of a boat ; the third a violin with three strings ; the fourth a guitar of four strings, played with a bit of wood fastened to the finger ; the fifth a flute ; and the sixth a flageolet. To these are occasionally added an instrument with four strings, in form of a boat, which is said to be borrowed from the Peguans ; and the band is completed by the addition of a drum, cymbals, and castanets.

CRAWFURD, *Journal . . . Siam*

SIAMESE OATH

I, ———, do hereby declare that I am wholly unprejudiced against either of the parties in this case, and uninfluenced by the opinions ,or advice of others ; and that no prospect of pecuniary advantage or of advancement in office has been held out to me : I also declare that I have not received any bribe on this occasion.

If I have not seen, yet shall say I have seen ; if I shall say I know that which I do not know, may I be punished; may I be encompassed wherever I go by dangers from which I cannot escape, whether arising from murderers, robbers, spirits of the earth, of the forest, of the water, of the air, or from the gods of the four elements, and all other spirits ; may blood flow from every pore of my body so that my perjury may be known to all the world ; may any or all of these evils overtake me three days hence ; or may I never stir from the place where I now stand ; or may lightning cut me in twain, so that I may be exposed to derision ; or if I should be walking abroad may I be torn in pieces by one of the preternaturally endowed lions, or destroyed by poisonous herbs or venomous snakes ; or may alligators devour me ; or winds and waves overwhelm me ; or may the dread of such evils keep me a prisoner at home all my life, cut off from every pleasure ; or may cholera cause my death, after which may I be precipitated into hell, there to go through innumerable stages of torture, condemned to carry water over the flaming regions in open wicker-baskets to assuage the heat felt by the King of Hell when he enters the infernal hall of justice ; and thereafter may I fall into the lowest pit of hell.

BOWRING, *Kingdom . . . of Siam* (adapted)

THE SKYLARK

WHEN God created the world he set the skylark among the birds which dwelt in heaven.

One day the Creator sent the lark down with a message to the spirits of Ainu-land, at the same time giving it instructions to return before nightfall. But it found so much to interest it on earth that it was at last overtaken by darkness, and decided to remain where it was till daylight.

Next morning it rose early and flew up several hundred feet, thinking to return to heaven. But at this height from the earth it was stopped by the Creator, who there and then forbade it, on account of its disobedience, ever to rise higher above the earth than it then was.

But the skylark protested strongly : why must it suffer for having found the Creator's handiwork so beautiful that it had forgotten all else ? And every day the skylark rises as high as it is able, voices its protest anew, storming the gates of Heaven ; then tired of the argument, it drops back to earth, where it enjoys itself for a while and then once more flies up to the limit set upon its ascent and tries again by noisy argument to persuade the Creator to let it return to Heaven.

After BATCHELOR

Japan

SMALLPOX

THE Country is fruitful, and the Air so good, that when Strangers come hither in a bad State of Health, they seldom fail of a speedy Recovery ; but the small Pox is dreaded as pestiferous and in the Province of Kirian that Distemper is most dangerous and most infectious, so that if anyone is seized by that Disease, all the Neighbourhood removes to two or three Miles Distance, and builds new Houses, which is easily done with Bambows and Reeds, which they have in great Plenty. They leave with the diseased Person a Jar of Water, a Basket of raw Rice, and some Earthen Pots to boyl it in, then they bid him farewel for twenty-one days. If the Patient has Strength enough to rise and boyl Rice, he may then recover, if not, he must even die alone. And it is observable that, while a Person has that Distemper, the Tiger, for all his Voraciousness, will not touch him. If the Patient dies within the Term of twenty-one Days, then the Smell certifies them on their Approaching the House, and if he live, they carry him to their new built City, and make Him a free Burgess.

HAMILTON

Pegu

SUN FESTIVAL

ON the twenty-fifth day of the eighth month the sun is worshipped. Copies of an address from the sun to the people are gratuitously circulated at the expense of persons who have made a vow to do so on recovery from sickness. The address is as follows :

'When I, the Great Male Luminary, come forth the whole canopy of heaven is tinged with my brightness. Morning and night I weary not, but at all hours steadily pursue my course. My speed is according to my own pleasure. None can urge me on ; none can stay my progress. The dwellings of all men I visit with my light. You, the people, however, do not address me with reverence and respect. Were I, in displeasure, to cease shining, you would all die of starvation, inasmuch as the earth would no longer bring forth its fruits. The salutary vicissitudes of day and night would cease.

'To the gods in general all men pay great devotion, but to me, the Great Male Luminary, homage is seldom paid. The twenty-fifth day of the eighth month is my anniversary, and on this day it is your duty to read this address and to burn tapers and incense to my glory. Families by which these commands are obeyed will be kept from evil. Hell and destruction lie before those who neglect them. Address me as the Great Light which Rules the World and I will stretch forth my golden hands to give you light and to guide you to the Paradise of the Western Heaven.'

GRAY

China

TRIAL BY ORDEAL

For finding out secret Murder, Theft or Perjury, the Trial of Ordeal is much in Custom in Pegu. One Way is to make the Accuser and the Accused take some raw Rice in their Mouths, and chew, and swallow it, but he that is guilty of the Crime alledged, or of false Accusation, cannot swallow his Morsel, but the innocent chews and swallows his easily.

Another Way they have by driving a Stake of Wood into a River, and making the Accuser and Accused take hold of the Stake and keep their Heads and Bodies under Water, and he who stays longest under Water, is the Person to be credited, and whosoever is convicted by this Trial, either for the Crime alledged or for malicious Slander, by Accusation, must lie on his Back three Days and Nights, with his Neck in a Pair of Stocks, without Meat or Drink, and fined to boot. They have also the Custom of dipping the naked Hand in boyling Oyl, or liquid Lead, to clear them from atrocious Crimes, and if the Accuser scalds himself in the Trial, he must undergo the Punishment due to the Crime, which makes People very cautious how they calumniate one another.

HAMILTON

Pegu

'TRIED PRESCRIPTIONS'

Method of extracting Aching Teeth

A tooth ought not to be taken out, as this loosens the remaining teeth. If the pain is acute and interferes with eating and drinking it may be extracted ; otherwise it should be left.

Take a bream about ten ounces in weight, cut it open and insert 1/10th of an ounce of powdered arsenic. Sew up the fish and hang it up in the wind where it is not exposed to the sun or accessible to cats and rats. After seven days a kind of hoar-frost will cover the scales of the fish. Preserve this, using for each tooth about as much as will cover one scale. When required, spread it on a small piece of plaster, press it on the aching place and let it remain for a time. Let the patient then cough and the tooth will fall out by itself.

Another Method

Take a head of garlic and pound to a pulp. Mix it thoroughly with one or two candareens' weight of white dragon's bones and apply to the part affected. After a short time the tooth will fall out.

Recipes for all Occasions

Fires : Take three hen's eggs and write at the big end of each the word ' WARM ' and at the other end ' BEAUTIFUL.' Then throw them one by one into the spot where the fire burns most fiercely, saying, ' Fushefahrun, fushefahrun.' The fire will then be extinguished.

To find the Way : To find the right direction at a cross-roads carry with you a live tortoise, and when you come to a cross-road and do not know which to choose, set the tortoise down and follow it. You cannot go wrong.

To avoid Bogies at Night : With the middle finger of the right hand trace on the palm of the left the words 'I AM A DEVIL,' and close your hand tightly. You may then travel without fear.

Cure for Seasickness : Seasickness may be prevented by drinking the drippings from a bamboo punt-pole mixed with boiling water, or by inserting a lump of burnt mortar from a stove into the hair secretly, or by tracing the character EARTH on the palm of the hand before getting on board the ship.

To clean Ivory : Ivory may be made to look like new by polishing it with the whey of bean-curd.

To preserve Rice : Rice may be kept free of weevils by keeping the shell of a crab in the bin or basket in which it is stored.

To detect foul Air in Wells : The presence of bad air in a well may be detected by dropping a hen's feather into it. If it falls straight the air is pure ; if it circles round and round, it is poisonous. To avert danger, throw in a quantity of hot vinegar before descending.

To keep a Fire in : A fire may be kept alight for three days by putting a walnut among the live ashes.

GILES

China

VULGARITY

WHEN the goddesses first caught sight of the gods they cried out, 'Oh ! what beautiful males !' But the gods were displeased and said, 'We, who are so strong and powerful, should have been the first to speak ; how is it that, on the contrary, these females speak first ? This is indeed vulgar !'

ARNOLD, *Japonica*

Japan

'WALKING THE BRIDGES'

A SINGULAR New Year custom in Seoul is 'Walking the Bridges.'
Up to midnight, men, women and children cross a bridge or bridges
as many times as they are years old. This is believed to prevent
pains in the feet and legs during the year.

BISHOP, Korea . . .

Korea

WATER GARDENS

(1885)

LANDSCAPE gardening in the Far East is carried to a perfection of
beauty quite undreamt of with us.

One variety of what we find in Korea might, without impro-
priety, be called waterscape gardening. It is so pre-eminently
a gardening in which land is second in effect. In Japan a pond,
where possible, is the central attraction ; but in Korea it is the all
in all. The grounds are only settings to the picture.

The garden, then, is a pond, and it is known by the name of the
lotus-pond ; for so universal is the cultivation of the lotus in these
artificial waters that it has given them their distinctive name. Even
where, for some reason, it is not grown, it is assumed to exist ; and
the pond is called the lotus-pond just the same.

The pond may be of any shape, though approximating generally
to the form of a circle. It is of all sizes, from a little basin to a broad
sheet of water. Sometimes its banks are only what still remains of
bordering earth ; sometimes they are encased in stone settings,
layer upon layer, of large granite blocks. But always, if the pond
be of any size at all, there stands in its centre a singular island. This
islet is perfectly circular, and in the middle of it there rises a solitary

tree. The tree is usually a fine old specimen, and is deciduous, not evergreen. Its branches spread out and overhang the water. It is a pretty sight—the lone tree on the round islet ; but this, on the first look, is lost sight of, for the way its singular symmetry piques the curiosity. It has a preternaturally artificial effect. It looks like one of the trees from a child's Noah's ark.

Use, not beauty, is the cause of its being. The idea is no quaint conceit ; and there are good reasons, though not artistic ones, for its having taken precisely the form it has. This is its *raison d'être*.

To those enjoyable qualities, the gift of Nature, which the Korean finds in the little lake, he has added the attraction of fishing. For after the main fact that it exists—its own greatest charm—the chief attribute of the pond is that it is a fish-pond. It is profusely stocked with carp for the pleasure of the noble fisherman to whom the pond belongs—not, indeed, as pets to be fed, but as game to be eaten. Now, to angle for these from the bank is a pastime always possible, of course ; but such is not to Korean ideas the height of enjoyment of the sport. To remain upon the outskirts savours of the stranger, not of the lord and master of the place. To be at the very centre of the whole is the acme of dignified happiness. To afford him, therefore, a spot in the middle where to sit, he made the island ; and to protect him from the sun he planted the tree.

Hither, of a hot, still summer afternoon, the Korean betakes himself, with his rod and books, and seats himself upon the short grass under the friendly shade of the tree. Not without difficulty has a servant forced his skiff through the thick water-growth which in places has seemingly transformed into land the glassy surface of the lake ; for it is the flowering season of the lotus. Where in the spring only the broad dark-green leaves floated lazily upon the surface, now the spot is choked by the wanton luxuriance of vegetation. Other leaves, sturdy, thick, stand erect on their tall stems two feet above the water's level, hustling one another and holding in jealous embrace the stately solitary flowers. Away down among the stems that lie hid in the depths of the water, the lazy carp swim about, rising every now and then, where the plants permit, to snatch with a gurgle some unwary insect that has been thoughtlessly skimming the water's edge. There he sits in quiet contemplation, a mummy in meditation. Nothing breaks in upon his long day-dream save when a fish, after innumerable nibbles too lazy to disturb his reverie, at last insists upon being caught.

LOWELL, *Chosön*

Korea

WHY DOGS CANNOT TALK

IN olden times dogs could talk, but now they cannot. The reason is that long ago a dog fell in love with his mistress, and having inveigled his master into the forest under the pretext of showing him game, caused him to be devoured by a bear. He then went home to his mistress and said, 'My master has been killed by a bear. But before he died he commanded me to tell you that you must marry me.' The widow knew that the dog was lying and refused to listen to him. But he continued to urge her to marry him, so at last, in her grief and rage, she threw a handful of dust into his open mouth, and from that moment neither he nor any other dog was ever heard to speak.

CHAMBERLAIN, *Language of Japan* (*adapted*)

Japan

JAPANESE PROVERBS

Don't rock the cradle and pinch the baby at the same time.

*

Better wash an old kimono than borrow a new one.

*

Better one good deed than three days' fasting.

*

The sparrow flying behind the hawk thinks the hawk is fleeing.

*

Inquire seven times before you believe a report.

*

It takes a clever man to preach a short sermon.

THE TALES THEY TELL AND THE
SONGS THEY SING

CHINESE PROVERBS

The old lady wearing specs—all for show.

★

The old lady in a cart—unsteady.

★

The old lady's tooth—undecided.

★

The old lady at a funeral—coming along behind.

★

The old lady trying to bite—nothing to do it with.

THE ANTS

LONG ago there lived in China a pious man who every day fervently worshipped a certain goddess. One morning, as he was at his prayers a beautiful woman entered his room. Disconcerted by her unannounced arrival, he asked what she wanted. She replied, ' I am the goddess whom you have so long worshipped, and I have come to reward your devotion. Do you understand the language of the ants ? '

Still more surprised by this curious question, the man stammered an apologetic negative, whereupon the goddess produced a small box and, dipping the tip of her finger into its contents, annointed the man's ears, saying as she did so, ' Now go out and find some ants and listen to what they say.'

As soon as he was alone again the man rose and went out to look for some ants. He had not crossed the threshold before he saw two at the foot of a pillar supporting the corner of his house. He stooped over them, and as he did so he heard one say, ' Let us move to some other place ; it is too cold here.' ' Cold ! ' cried the other ant, ' why should it be cold ? I think this would make quite a good home for us.' ' No,' his companion persisted, ' it will be too cold. There are pots of gold below this pillar and gold chills the earth because it absorbs all the sunshine for itself and leaves the earth around without necessary heat.' So together the ants moved off, leaving the delighted eavesdropper to discover a treasure which made him rich for life and the envy of all his neighbours.

ANON.

Japan

WHY ANTS ARE EVERYWHERE

ALL the beasts of the forest came to pay homage to the lion-king. The little ant came with the rest to make its bow to the king of beasts, but it was driven away with scorn. When the king of the ants heard of this uncivil treatment of one of his subjects he sent a worm to creep into the ear of the lion and torment him. The lion roared with pain, and all the animals came running to offer their services to fight the enemy, whoever or whatever he might be. But none of them could do any real good for they could not get at the worm. At last, therefore, the king of the forest was reduced to sending many humble appeals to the king of the ants, who at length dispatched one of his subjects to creep into the lion's ear and pull out the worm.

Ever since that time the ants have enjoyed the privilege of living anywhere they like, while all the other animals have been restricted to the special places assigned to them at the division of the earth.

SHWAY YOE (*adapted*)

Burma

AUTUMN

Can I be dreaming? 'Twas but yesterday
We planted out each tender shoot again;
And now the autumn breeze sighs o'er the plain,
Where fields of yellow rice confess its sway.

Chisato (Trans. Chamberlain I)

★

The dews are all of one pale silv'ry white:
Then tell me if thou canst, oh! tell me why
These silv'ry dews so marvellously dye
The autumn leaves a myriad colours bright?

Toshiuki (Ibid.)

A BEAUTY OF JAVA

(*From a Javanese Poem*)

Her face was fair and bright as the moon, and it expressed all that was lovely.

She shone bright even in the dark, and was without defect or blemish.

So clear and striking was her brightness that it flashed to the sky; the lustre of the sun was even dimmed in her presence, for she seemed to have stolen his refulgence.

Her shape and form were nothing wanting, and her hair when loosened hung down to her feet, waving in dark curls. Her eyebrows were like two leaves of the imbo tree; the ball of the eye full, and the upper eyelashes slightly curling upwards.

Tears seemed to float in her eye, but started not. Her nose was sharp and pointed ; her teeth black as the *kombang* ; her lips the colour of the newly-cut mangostin shell.

Her shoulders even, like the balance of golden scales ; her chest open and full ; her breasts like ivory, perfectly round and inclining to each other. Her arms ductile as a bow ; her fingers long and pliant, and tapering like thorns of the forest. Her nails like pearls ; her skin bright yellow ; her waist like the patram when drawn from its sheath.

Like to the hanging padak flower was the shape of her leg ; her foot flat with the ground ; her gait gentle and majestic like that of the elephant.

RAFFLES

THE BIRTH OF THE BUDDHA

ON the fifteenth day of the eighth month, Suddhodana the king commanded his people to celebrate the festival of the constellation Asanha.

For seven days before the festival the Queen Maia appeared in all the glory and pomp of her high dignity. On the morning of the seventh day, rising from her couch she had sixteen jars of scented water poured over her, and then distributed alms among the sick, the crippled and the destitute.

Having finished her duties, she entered her sleeping-chamber and falling asleep on her couch, she saw a vision.

The four kings of the world bore her on her couch to the top of an immense rock in the Himalayan forest. They then retired ; and their queens bathed her in the Anadot Lake, and having caused her to wash off all human impurities, they annointed her with heavenly scents, robed her in heavenly raiment, and adorned her with heavenly flowers. Then they led her to a golden palace, and prayed her to rest on a couch, whence she saw a golden mountain on which the Royal Being that should be Buddha walked in the form of a white elephant, with a newly expanded lotus flower in his beautiful trunk. Having descended the golden mountain he entered the palace, trumpeting loudly, and having marched round the couch, he appeared to enter the right side of the Queen and pass into her womb.

Next morning the Queen related her vision to the King, who summoned the sixty-four Brahmins that they might show its interpretation. And when they had heard it they said, 'Thy Queen shall bear a son, a Grand Being, of excelling glory and power, of infinite merit, and wisdom beyond estimation. If he devote himself to a wordly life he may rule over all the world, but if he devote himself to religion then he will become a Buddha.'

Then the king rejoiced exceedingly, and gave orders that sleeping or waking, the queen should be surrounded by that which was pure, melodious, harmonious, refined, elegant and simple.

And the forty thousand guardian angels of the ten thousand worlds watched around her, with perfect delicacy. Never were they seen when she desired privacy, but at all other times she saw them guarding her by day and night, and she saw them without fear.

And the Grand Being dwelt in his mother's womb in comfort and happiness, sitting erect and fully aware of the three circumstances of his existence, namely, his conception, his gestation, and his birth.

And Maia felt no pain, nor was her beautiful figure changed. Her body became clear and brilliant, so that she and her child could see each other through it, even as the red thread can be seen through the bright pearls threaded on it.

When Maia had completed a period of ten months, she obtained the king's permission to visit her parents. The king had the road cleared and levelled, and made gay with flags and flowers, and jars of water were placed at intervals along it. A golden litter was provided for the Queen and a thousand noble ladies attended her.

Now in those days there was, between the royal city and the place where the Queen's parents dwelt, a forest of the most splendid trees. It was a lovely spot. Interlacing branches, richly covered with foliage, sheltered the traveller as with a canopy. All over the trees flowers budded, bloomed, and shed their fragrant leaves, and unceasingly budded and bloomed again. Attracted by their sweet pollen, flights of shining beetles buzzed around them, filling the air with a melodious humming like to the music of the heavens. There were pools of lotuses of all colours, whose sweet scent was wafted abroad by gentle breezes.

When the Queen entered this forest all the trees bowed their heads, and the Queen, looking on the great trees, and the forest lovely as the gardens of the angels, ordered her litter to be stayed that she might descend and walk.

Then, standing under one of the majestic trees, she desired to pluck a sprig from the branches, and the branches themselves bent down that she might reach it ; and at that moment her labour came upon her. Her attendants held curtains around her ; the angels brought her garments of the most exquisite softness ; and standing there, holding the branch, with her face turned to the east, she brought forth her son, without pain or any of the circumstances which attend that event in general.

And in that moment there poured from heaven two streams of water, one on the Queen and one upon the Grand Being. And the hands of the Great Bramah received him, and from him he was received by the four guardians of the world, and from them by archangel Indra, and from him by the host of Bramahs, and leaving their hands, he stood erect upon the earth on his own holy feet.

And the ten thousand worlds quaked. The universe was illumined with an exceeding bright light. The moon shone with heavenly radiance. The sun's heat ceased its violence, and gave out but an agreeable warmth. A refreshing shower fell upon the four continents, and all musical instruments gave out harmonious sounds of themselves.

ALABASTER (*adapted*)

Siam

THE BLIND LOVER

My eyes are dead, but my heart is quick ;
I walk eternally in darkest night,
Hearing your laugh, and the sound of your voice,
Like the vibrations of a golden bell,
And I love you.

You told me you had no husband,
No one to make cheerful your room.
Come with me ; I will dress you in beauty,
And entwine you with garlands of golden corn.
Since my eyes cannot behold you
You will allow the touch of my hands.

I hear you not ; are you still near ?
Or have you, displeased with my words,
Deserted me already ?
Nay, let me love you ; you shall go before
To guide me through my living night.

DUMOUTIER (*Trans. from the French by E. E.*)

Indo-China

I

257

BOATMAN'S LOVE SONG

(1852)

A HAPPY and reckless youth I am
As I ply my boat on the deep *Menam*;
My song shall end and my song begin,
In praise of thee, my darling Chin.

Chorus

Begin with the head, and end with the toes;
My praise shall be strong as the tide that flows.

Who that has seen has e'er forgot
Thy pretty hair tied in a sweet knot?
And prettier still than the tuft of hair
Thy brow, unwrinkled by grief or care?
  Chorus : Begin with the head, etc.

The eyebrows black, I'm sure that each
Is as shiny as any fine healthy leech;
No elephant, white, black, short or tall,
Can boast of such eyes, so loving and small.
  Chorus : Begin with the head, etc.

As for thy nose, I'm certain that
None other has one so wide and flat;
And the ebony's bark, in its core beneath,
Was never so black as thy shiny teeth.
  Chorus : Begin at the head, etc.

Complexion of gold, and a high cheek-bone,
Such treasures with pride would a princess own.
Right proud am I to woo and win
Such a lovely bride as my darling Chin.
    Chorus : Begin at the head, etc.

Thy frame is as light as the forest stag,
And as strong and firm as a rocky crag ;
Thy feet and toes (the more good luck)
As pretty and broad as the web-footed duck.
    Chorus : Begin with the head, **etc.**

My life I'd give a prize to him
Who produces a wife like thee can swim ;
Or paddle with skill a heavy canoe,
'Gainst the mightiest wind that ever blew.
    Chorus : Begin at the head, etc.

NEALE

Siam

BORNEO LOVE SONG

COLD is the wind, the rain falls fast ;
I linger, though the hour is past.
Why come you not ? Whence this delay ?
    Have I offended—say ?

My heart is sad and sinking too ;
O, break it not ! it loves but you !
Come, then, and end this long delay,
    Why keep you thus away ?

The wind is cold, fast falls the rain ;
Yet weeping, chiding, I remain.
You come not still—you still delay !
      O, wherefore can you stay ?

BURBIDGE

CHANSONETTE

  SHE hid his coat,
  She plucked his sleeve,
' To-day you cannot go !
To-day, at least, you will not leave
  The heart that loves you so ! '
  The *mado* [1] she undid
  And back the *shoji* [2] slid ;
And clinging, cried, ' Dear Lord, perceive
  The whole white world is snow ! '

ARNOLD, Japonica

Japan

CHILDREN'S SONG

O MOTHER, I would eat rare fruits.
My son, go pick them in the mountain.

O Mother, I would eat shell-fish.
My son, go seek them in the river.

O Mother, I would take a wife.
My son, I too would marry.

DUMOUTIER (Trans. from the French by E. E.)

Indo-China

[1] Window   [2] Sliding wall

CHINESE INVASION OF BURMA

(*From* MAHA RADZA WENG : Chronicles of the Kings of Burma)

WHEN the Emperor of China received the intelligence of the execution of his envoys, he was exceedingly angry, and collecting an army of at least six millions of horse, and twenty millions of foot, sent them down to attack Pugan : the King of which, as soon as he heard of the coming of this force, placed under his generals 400,000 soldiers, and numerous elephants and horses, with orders to attack the Chinese army. The two generals marched to the city of Ngayounggyan, and, after putting it in a proper state of defence, opposed the Chinese army at the mouth of the Bhamo river, killing during three months so many of their army that not even a grass-cutter for their elephants and horses remained. The Emperor of China, however, kept reinforcing his army, sending 200,000 when he heard of the loss of 100,000 men, and 400,000 when he heard of 200,000. Hence the Burman Army was at last overpowered with fatigue and the Chinese crossed the river and destroyed Ngayounggyan.

As the *nats* or spirits attached to either nation were fighting in the air, four of the Pugan *nats* were wounded by arrows. On the

same day one of them returned, wounded, to Pugan and entered the house of the King's tutor, on whom he had been accustomed to wait. The tutor was asleep at the time, but the *nat* wakened him and told him of the loss of the city and the wounding of the guardian *nats*.

The tutor at once sent one of his disciples to the King with the news, explaining how the circumstances came to be known, through the return of the wounded *nat*, on the very day on which they occurred.

The King summoned his council and said, ' The walls of the city of Pugan are low, and enclose too small a space to permit all the soldiers, elephants and horses required for its defence to remain comfortably within them. I propose, therefore, to build a strong wall extending from the upper part of the river straight down to the southward, taking in the village of Yonatha. If we pull down some of the temples and use the bricks we shall be able to complete the wall most expeditously.'

Accordingly 1000 large arched temples, 1000 smaller ones, and 4000 square temples were destroyed. During this operation a sheet of copper, inscribed with a royal prediction, was found in one of the temples. The words were : ' In the city of Pugan, in the time of the father of twins, the Chinese, destroying, will be destroyed.' The King thereupon made enquiries among the royal women, and learnt that a young concubine had just given birth to twins.

His Majesty now being convinced that even if he built the intended fortification he would be unable to defend it, he caused 1000 boats to be made ready and embarked in them all his treasures : in 1000 state boats he embarked his ministers and officers, and in the gilded state boats, his concubines and female attendants. But as these last were so numerous that they could not all be accommodated in the boats the King said, ' The women and servants are too numerous to be all embarked, and if we leave them the Chinese will seize them; tie their hands and feet, therefore, and throw them in the river.'

But the King's tutor observed, ' In the whole circle of animal existence the state of man is the most difficult of attainment. There can be no occasion for your Majesty to commit evil by throwing these people into the river. Such an act would be talked of for ever, even among kings, and would be registered in the annals of the Empire. Let your Majesty grant permission for any person to take such of the royal female attendants as cannot be embarked, and by so doing your Majesty will be said not only to have granted them their lives but to have afforded them protection.' ' Very true,' the

King replied, and set free three hundred of the women of the palace, who were carried away by the inhabitants of the city. The King then embarked in his gilded accommodation boat and retired to the Talaing country.

After remaining five months at Bassein in the Talaing country, the King, hearing that the Chinese had left Pugan, made arrangements to return thither. On his way up the river, his cooks having served him up a dinner of only 150 dishes instead of the 300 to which he had sat down every day of his life, he covered his face with his hands and wept, saying, ' I am indeed become a poor man.' Shortly after, on his arrival at Prome, he was poisoned by the governor of that place, his own son.

FYTCHE (*abridged*)

Burma

CHRONICLES OF THE KING OF BURMA

(Maha Radza Weng)

The Maha Radza Weng commences with describing the self-development of the world and the appearance of men therein. . . .

' Of the world's first inhabitants some were handsome, some not handsome. The handsome ones despised the others, and in consequence of the haughty, evil thoughts thus engendered the ambrosia of the earth disappeared, and they ate of the crust of the earth. Then in process of time, selfishness and desire increasing, the earth's surface crust disappeared. They then ate of a sweet creeping plant ; when that disappeared, the Thalay rice came up which, as they gathered it, was renewed morning and evening. When it was placed in a stone jar, flames issued, and it was then ready to eat. Its flavour was whatever the eater desired. From eating this food human passions were developed, and the beings became men and women. Then, as evil deeds began to prevail, the wise censured and severely treated the others. The latter, wishing to hide their evil deeds, built houses. Then, the lazy among them having stored up the food, the Thalay rice acquired husk, with a coating of coarse and fine bran, and where it had once appeared it did not sprout again. They then said, ' It is good for us to divide among us the Thalay rice plants, and to possess each his own.' Then they distributed the plants. After that, an unprincipled one among them, fearing that his own share would not suffice, stole the share of another. Once and twice he was warned ; on the third offence he was beaten. From that time theft, false-hood and punishment existed.'

McMahon

Burma

THE COMING OF DEATH

QAT and Marawa dwelt in Matan, near to Mount Garat where the volcanic fires still smoulder.

Now the way in which these two made men was thus and thus : First Qat cut the wood of the dracaena tree into shape, forming legs, arms, trunks, and heads complete with ears and eyes. He fitted part to part, taking six days to complete the task, and fixed a period of six days in which they should come to life. Three days he hid them out of sight, and three days he worked on them to give them life. Then he set them before him and danced to them until he saw them begin to move a little ; and he beat the drum for them and slowly they moved more and more. Thus he beguiled them into life until they could stand by themselves, separating them into pairs and calling them husband and wife. Three men he made thus and three women.

But Marawa made his men of another tree. He worked at them six days also, and set them up and beat the drum for them, and gave them life as Qat had done for his. But when he saw that they could move he dug a pit, covered the bottom of it with cocoa-nut fronds and buried his men and women in it for six days. But when he scraped off the earth with his hands to view them after the six days were over he found them all rotten and stinking. And this was the origin of death among men.

CODRINGTON (*adapted*)

Melanesia

*

Every man is a prince on his own sleeping-shelf.

*

Why bother to dye the sea green ?

Malay Proverbs

THE CRANE AND THE BUTTERFLY

A BUTTERFLY challenged a crane to fly to Tonga, tempting him by promising that he would find shrimps there. The butterfly perched himself on the crane's back, where the bird could not see him, and the crane flew on cheerfully thinking the butterfly was far behind. Every now and then the insect would leave his perch and fly along ahead, jeering at the crane, which grew more and more exhausted until at last it fell into the sea and was drowned. The butterfly, having no longer any support, soon perished also.

CUMMING, *At Home in Fiji*

Fiji

THE CRANE AND THE CRAB

THE crane and the crab decided to run a race. The crab said the crane might fly across while he went round by way of the shore. The crane flew off and the crab stayed quietly in its hole, trusting to the multitude of his family to deceive the crane. The crane flew to the first point, and flew down to a crab-hole. He put down his ear and heard a buzzing sound. 'That creature is here before me,' he said to himself, and flew off to the next point. Here the same thing happened, and so on, at point after point, until at last, reaching a point high above the sea, the poor stupid crane fell down exhausted and was drowned.

Ibid.

Fiji

THE ELVES AND THE ENVIOUS NEIGHBOUR

ONCE upon a time a certain Japanese was overtaken by darkness among the mountains and sought shelter in the trunk of a hollow tree. In the middle of the night, a large company of elves assembled at the place ; and the man, peeping out from his hiding-place, was frightened out of his wits. After a while, however, the elves began to feast and drink wine, and to amuse themselves by singing and dancing, until at last the man forgot his fright and crept out of his hollow tree to join in the revels. When the day was about to dawn, the elves said to the man, ' You're a very jolly companion, and must come out and dance with us again. You must give us your promise, and keep it.' And thinking to bind him thus to return, the elves took a large wen that grew on the man's forehead and kept it in pawn. The man then returned to his own house in high glee at having passed a jovial night and got rid of his wen into the bargain. He told the story to all his friends, who congratulated him warmly on being cured of his wen. But a neighbour who was also troubled with a wen of long standing was full of envy at his friend's good luck, and went off to hunt for the hollow tree, in which, when he found it, he passed the night.

Towards midnight the elves came, as he had expected, and began feasting and drinking, with songs and dances as before. As soon as he saw this, he came out of his hollow tree, and began dancing and singing as his neighbour had done. The elves, mistaking him for their former boon-companion, were delighted to see him, and said—

' You're a good fellow to keep your promise, and we'll give you back your pledge.' So one of the elves, pulling the pawned wen out of his pocket, stuck it on to the man's forehead, on the top of the one which he already had. Then the envious neighbour went home weeping, with two wens instead of one.

MITFORD (*abridged*)

Japan

THE ENCHANTED WINE-JUG

(Why the Cat and Dog are Enemies)

In ancient times there lived in Korea an old man whose hut stood on the bank of a river where the ferry-boats landed. He was poor and childless, and being compelled to earn his own food, he kept a little wine-shop, which, small though it was, possessed quite a local reputation, for the aged proprietor would permit no quarrelling on his premises, and sold only one brand of wine of really excellent quality. He did not keep a pot of broth simmering over the coals at his door to tempt the passer-by and thus increase his thirst ; he rather preferred customers who brought their little long-necked bottles, and carried the drink to their homes. There were some peculiarities about this little wine-shop. The old man had apparently always been there, and had never seemed any younger. His wine never gave out, no matter how great the local thirst, yet he was never seen to make or take in a new supply, and he always seemed to pour the wine out of the same old jug, the long, slender neck of which was black and shiny from being so often tipped in his old hand. This had long ceased to be a matter of special interest, however, and only upon the advent of a stranger of an inquiring mind would the subject be re-discussed. The neighbours were assured that the old man was thoroughly good, and that his wine was even better. Furthermore, he sold it as reasonably as other men sold a much inferior article. More than this they did not care to know.

I said the old man had no children. That is true, yet he had two constant companions, the partners of his bed and board. These were a good-natured old dog who was the very impersonation of canine wisdom and good-nature, and a cat who had such a strong vein of humour that age could not subdue his frivolous propensities.

This happy couple lived in the greatest contentment with the old man. They were fair-weather companions up to this time. They had not been with him when a bowl of rice was a luxury. Their days did not antedate the period of the successful wine-shop. The old man, however, often recalled those former days with a shudder, and thought with great complacency of the time when he had befriended a divine being, in the form of a weary traveller, to whom he gave the last drink left in his jug. Afterwards the stranger dropped into the jug a trifling thing that looked like a bit of amber, saying : ' So long as that remains there you will never want for a drink.' He looked at the empty jug, then raised it to his lips, and a most delicious stream of wine poured down his unaccustomed throat.

He lowered the jug and peered into its black depths ; he shook its sides, causing the elf within to dance and laugh aloud ; and shutting his eyes he took another long draught ; then he remembered the stranger, and was about to offer him a drink when he discovered that he was alone. He began to wonder at the strange circumstance, and to think what he was to do. ' I can't sit here and drink all the time, or I will become drunk, and some thief will carry away my jug. I can't live on wine alone, yet I dare not leave this strange thing while I seek for work.'

Like many another to whom fortune has just come, he could not tell at first what to do with his good luck. Finally he hit upon the idea of keeping a wine-shop, the success of which we have seen ; nor should we refuse the old man credit for the wisdom he displayed in maintaining it on a small scale, rather than in exciting unpleasant curiosity and official oppression by attempting to produce and sell wine wholesale. The dog and cat knew the secret, and had always a watchful eye upon the jug, which was never for a moment out of sight of one of the three pairs of eyes.

As the brightest day must end in gloom, however, so was this pleasant state soon to be marred by a most sad and far-reaching accident.

One day the news flashed around the neighbourhood that the old man's supply of wine was exhausted ; not a drop remained in his jug. The old man admitted the statement to be true, but had little to say ; while the dog's ears hung dejectedly over his cheeks, his eyes dropped, and he bore with dignity his portion of the sorrow, sitting upright, but with bowed head.

The cat, on the other hand, seemed to be charged with agitation enough for the whole family. He walked nervously about the floor till he felt that justice to his tail demanded a higher plane, and then betook himself to the beam which supported the roof and made a sort of cats' and rats' attic under the thatch.

All his customers came to condole with the old man, and not one but regretted that his supply of cheap, good wine was exhausted. The old man offered no explanation, though he had about concluded in his own mind that he must have poured the bit of amber into a customer's jug. He talked the matter over carefully to himself at night, while the dog and cat listened attentively.

When at last the old man fell asleep the two began a discussion. ' I am sure,' said the cat, ' that I can detect that thing if I come within smelling distance of it ; but how do we know where to look for it ? ' That was a puzzler, but the dog proposed that they should search every house in the neighbourhood. ' We can go on a " look see," you know, and while you call on the cats indoors, and keep your smellers open, I will chat with the dogs outside, and if you smell anything you can tell me.'

The plan was adopted that very night. They were not cast down because the first search was unsuccessful, and continued their work night after night. Sometimes their calls were not appreciated, and in a few cases they had to clear the field by battle before they could go on with the search. No house was neglected, however, and in due time they had done the whole neighbourhood, but with no success. They then determined that the missing gem must have been carried to the other side of the river, to which place they decided to extend their search as soon as the water was frozen over, so that they could cross on the ice, for they knew they would not be allowed in the crowded ferry-boat ; and while the dog could swim, he knew that the water was already too cold for that. Soon the river froze so solidly that ox-carts, ponies, and men all passed over on the ice, and so it remained for nearly two months, allowing the searching party to return each morning to their poor old master, who seemed completely broken up by his loss, and did not venture away from his door except to buy the few provisions which his little fund of savings would allow.

Time flew by without bringing success to the faithful comrades, and their search took them so much from home that the old man began to think they, like his former customers, were deserting him. It was nearing the time for the spring thaw when one night the cat, chasing over the roof timbers in a house in the settlement across the river, detected an odour that nearly caused him to fall on a man sleeping on the floor below. He carefully traced the odour, and found that it came from a soapstone tobacco-box on the top of a high clothes-press. The box was dusty with neglect, and the cat concluded that the possessor had accidentally turned the coveted gem out into his wine bowl, and, not knowing its nature, had put it into this stone box rather than throw it away. The lid was so securely fastened that the box seemed to be one solid piece, so the cat went out to consult the superior wisdom of the dog. ' I can't get up there,' said the dog, ' nor can you bring me the box, or I might break it open.'

' I cannot move the thing, or I might push it off, and let it fall to the floor and break,' said the cat.

So after they had explained the things they could not do, the dog finally hit upon a plan. ' I'll tell you,' said he. ' You go and see the chief of the rat and mouse guild in this neighbourhood, and tell him that if he will help us we will both let them alone and not hurt even a mouse for ten years.'

' But what good is that going to do ? '

' Why, don't you see, that stone is no harder than some wood, and if they will take turns at it till they gnaw a hole through it, we shall easily get the gem out.'

The cat bowed before the wisdom of the dog, and went off to interview the master rat. The rat was soon found, and being assured of safety, came to the mouth of his hole and listened attentively to the proposition. Needless to say he accepted it, and a contract was made forthwith.

The ice had now broken up and the searchers could not return home, so they waited about the neighbourhood for some months, picking up a scanty living, and making some friends and not a few enemies, for they were a proud pair, and ready to fight on provocation.

It was already warm weather when, one night, the cat almost forgot his compact as he saw a big fat rat approaching. He crouched low and dug his long claws into the earth, every nerve on the jump ; but before he was ready to spring he fortunately remembered his contract. It was just in time, too, for as the rat was none other than the other party to the contract such a mistake at that time would have been fatal to their object.

The rat announced that the hole was completed, but it was so small on the inside that he was at a loss to know how the gem could be got out unless the cat could reach it with his paw. Having acquainted the dog with the good news, the cat hurried off to see for himself. He could introduce his paw, but as the object was at the other end of the box he could not quite reach it, so he went out again to consult with the dog. On his advice a mouse was put into the box, but the hole was too small for the little fellow and his load to get out at the same time, so that much pushing and pulling had to be done before the gem was safely out and handed over to the dog for safe-keeping. Then, with much purring and wagging of tails, the contract of fellowship was again renewed, and the party broke up ; the rats to go and jubilate over their prospective decade of safety, the dog and the cat to carry the good news to their unhappy master.

Canine wisdom was again called into play to devise a means of crossing the river. The now happy dog was quite equal to this, however, and instructed the cat to hold the gem firmly between his teeth, mount on his partner's neck, and hold on to the long hair on his neck while he swam across the river. All went well until a party of school-children on the opposite bank chanced to notice them and burst into uproarious laughter. They clapped their hands and danced with glee, while some fell on the ground and rolled about in an exhaustion of merriment at seeing a cat astride a dog's back being ferried across the river.

The dog was too weary to see much fun in it, but the cat shook his sides till his agitation caused the dog to swallow great gulps of water. This but increased the cat's merriment, till he broke out in a laugh so hearty that he dropped the precious gem into the water. The dog dived at once, regardless of the cat, who could not let go in time and was dragged under the water. In his agony of suffocation he stuck his claws into the dog and caused him so much pain that he missed the object of his search, and came to the surface without it.

The cat got ashore as best he could, greatly angered at the dog's rude conduct. The latter, however, cared little for that, and as soon as he had shaken the water from his hide, he made a lunge at his unlucky companion, who had lost the result of a half-year's faithful work by one moment of foolishness. The cat, however, could still climb a tree, and there he stayed till the sun had dried his fur and he had ejected the water from his inwards in the constant spitting he kept up with his new enemy, barking ferociously below.

The dog did not give up his efforts even now. He dived many times and spent his days sitting on the river bank, apparently lost in thought. Thus the winter found him—his chief two aims being to find the gem and to kill the cat. The latter kept well out of his way, and ice now covered the place where the former lay hidden. One day he espied a man spearing fish through a hole in the ice according to custom. Having a natural desire to be around where anything eatable was being displayed, and feeling a sort of proprietorship in the particular part of the river where the man was fishing, he went down and looked on. As a fish came up, something natural seemed to greet his nostrils, and as soon as the man laid down his catch, the dog grabbed it and rushed off in haste to his master, who, poor man, was now at the end of his string of cash and almost reduced to begging. He was therefore delighted with a present of a fresh fish, and at once commenced to clean it. But when he slit it open to his infinite joy his long-lost gem fell out of the fish's belly. The dog was almost delirious with joy, jumping upon his master, licking him with his tongue, and striking him with his paws, barking meanwhile as though he had again treed the cat.

As soon as their joy had somewhat moderated, the old man carefully placed the gem in his trunk, from which he took the last of his money and some fine clothes—relics of his more fortunate days which he had already shown to the pawn-brokers. Leaving the fish baking on the coals, he donned his fine clothes, and taking the money, he went out and purchased wine for his feast, and for a beginning ; for he knew that once he placed the gem back in the jug, the supply of wine would not cease. On his return he and the dog made a happy feast of the fish, and the old man completely recovered his spirits when he had quaffed deeply of the familiar liquid to which his mouth had so long been a stranger. Going to his trunk, he found to his amazement that it contained another suit of clothes exactly like the ones he had removed, and beside them a string of cash of just the amount which he had previously taken out.

The whole truth then dawned upon him, and he saw how he had failed to make full use of his privilege before in being content to use his talisman simply to run a wine-shop while he might have

had money and everything else in abundance by simply giving the charm a chance to work.

Acting upon this principle, the old man became immensely wealthy, for he could duplicate anything with his piece of amber. He carefully tended his faithful dog, who never again to the end of his days molested a rat, and never lost an opportunity to attack every cat he saw.

ALLEN (*adapted*)

Korea

*

Don't take a sabre to kill a mosquito.

*

A poor horse may have a bushy tail.

Korean Proverbs

275

THE FEARSOME HARE

PRESENCE of mind can make heroes of cowards, but rashness is generally fatal.

In the midst of a thick and virgin forest, where everything seemed to slumber, an elephant began to utter doleful cries, and a tiger replied by others still more dreadful, which froze all the other animals with terror, monkeys, stags, and all the inhabitants of trees or dens. The elephant himself panicked and was running away with all speed when he met a hare, who called out, ' Why do you run thus without aim and without reason ? ' The elephant paused in his flight. ' Did you not hear the frightful roaring of the tiger ? ' he asked. ' Would you have me stay and be devoured ? ' ' Stay here, and have no fear ; I will see that no harm comes to you,' said the hare ; ' only crouch down, that I may jump up on your back.' Somewhat reassured, the elephant approached and the hare popped a piece of betel into his mouth and mounted on the elephant's back.

' Now, get up again,' said he, ' and you will see that all will go well.' He then gave the elephant further counsel, and afterwards let out along his back a long stream of saliva, reddened by betel. Soon the tiger came up and stopped to look at them. ' What are you wanting here ? ' demanded the hare brusquely. ' Can't you see that this elephant is not too much for me alone. Do you think I mean to share it with you ? ' The tiger drew back and slunk behind a tree to see what passed. The hare then seized hold of the elephant's ear, made him roar, and seemed perfectly master of his prey, and busy at his work. ' Heavens ! how strong he is ! ' said the tiger ; but still he drew near. ' Wait a minute, and I will come down to you,' cried the hare in threatening tones and making as though to spring ; and the tiger, struck with terror, turned and ran away. A chimpanzee, seeing him running in obvious alarm, burst out laughing. 'What! you laugh at my misfortune?' cried the tiger. 'I have just escaped death, but you have no pity for me.' 'How so?' said the chimpanzee. 'I should like to see the beast who frightened you; take me to him.'

'What! to be devoured? That will I not,' the tiger retorted. 'Don't be afraid; I will get on your back, and will not leave you: we will fasten our tails together if you like; and thus united we shall run no risk!' The tiger was persuaded and they both returned to where the elephant was. The hare still seemed busy at his work: he had chewed his piece of betel, and had made another stream, red as blood, on the elephant's back. 'You dare to come back again!' he cried in an angry tone to the tiger. 'You knew I had only enough meat here for myself, and yet you want to snatch my prey from me; you deserve to be punished.'

At this point the elephant uttered a piercing cry; the hare had made an enormous bound on his back; and the tiger, struck with terror, rushed precipitately away at full speed, saying to the chimpanzee, 'Now you see; you laughed at my fears, and we have both narrowly escaped death.' But the chimpanzee did not hear; for in the tiger's precipitate retreat he had fallen off his back, struck his head against a tree, and died, cursing his rashness with his last sigh.

MOUHOT

Indo-China

FIGHTING WATER

A YOUNG man from one of the inland provinces went down for some purpose to the south coast of Java, where a heavy sea is always tumbling in upon the land from the Indian Ocean. On arriving at the sea-shore he was amazed at the sight which presented itself, for the waves came rolling in, apparently endeavouring to jump on each other's backs, and dashing with the greatest fury against the beach. This state of affairs being so different from the quiet inland waters which had hitherto been the object of his contemplation, he concluded that there must be a battle-royal going on among the billows, and with some trepidation filled his bottle with the fighting water to show his friends at home. When he returned to his native village, the inhabitants crowded about him to hear an account of his adventures. After relating the perils he had encountered on his journey to the coast, he proceeded to describe the appearance of the ocean.

' When I approached the great sea,' said he, ' I heard a noise like the roaring of bulls, and I saw that there was a great battle of the waters. They were not quiet and peaceable like those of our lake, but were tearing and fighting, aye, fighting like tigers and buffaloes.' The audience gaped with astonishment. The Jaxa, who was the oldest, and therefore the wisest, man in the village, at last found speech. ' Beware, young man,' said he, ' how you endeavour to impose upon us. Waters fight ! Are we goats, or buffalo-calves, that you tell us such a tale ? What is there to make the waters of the great sea fight, any more than those of our lake ? I have seen the sea myself, when I went to eat the wind (take the air) on the top of Taggal Mountain, and it was as smooth as a paddy-field.'

The traveller looked around him with a triumphant glance, and requested one of the women to bring him the bottle she would find in his bag. ' Now,' said he, ' I expected that the extraordinary fact which I have just related would be doubted, and I therefore procured a bottle of the water ; bring me a basin and you may judge for yourselves.' The listeners crowded about him, all eager to obtain a near view of the proceedings. With a sneer at the ignorance of his fellow-villagers, the man who had seen the world drew the stopper from the bottle and, after a moment's hesitation, poured the water into the basin. To his utter amazement and dis-.

comfiture, the water 'wouldn't fight;' but lay quite still, as if it had never in its life felt pugnacious. The Jaxa, who from the confidence displayed by the traveller had begun to fear that he had been premature in his doubts, and that his consequence as the village oracle would therefore be lowered, now denounced the poor man as an impostor, and pushed his vantage so strongly that the luckless experimentalist was glad to shut himself up in his house to avoid the reproaches of his neighbours.

EARL

Java

GENJI LEAVES THE TEMPLE

THE night passed away and dawn appeared. The sky was again hazy, and here and there melodious birds were singing among the mountain shrubs and flowers that blossomed around. The deer, too, added to the beauty of the picture. Gazing around at these, Genji once more proceeded to the temple. The hermit, though too infirm to walk, again contrived to offer up his prayers on Genji's behalf. The tremulous accents of the old man imparted a greater reverence to his prayers.

Genji's attendants now arrived from the capital, and congratulated him on the improvement in his health. A messenger came from the Imperial Palace for the same purpose. The priest collected wild and rare fruits not to be met with in the town and, with all respect, presented them to Genji, saying : ' The term of my vow has not yet expired ; I am therefore unable to descend the mountain with you on your departure.' He then offered to him the parting cup of saké.

' This mountain, with its waters, fills me with admiration,' said Genji, ' and I regret that the anxiety of my father, the Emperor, obliges me to quit the charming scene ; but before the season is past I will revisit it ; and—

> ' The city folk from me shall hear
> How mountain cherries blossom fair,
> And ere the Spring has passed away,
> I'll bid them view the prospect gay.

To this the priest replied :

> ' Your noble presence seems to be
> Like the rare flowers of Udon tree,
> Nor does the mountain cherry white,
> Attract my gaze while you're in sight.'

Genji smiled slightly and said : ' That is a very great compliment ; but the Udon tree does not blossom so easily.'

The priest also presented a rosary of precious stones obtained from Korea, enclosed in the case in which it had been sent from that country ; some medicine of rare virtue in a small emerald jar ; and several other objects, with a spray of wistaria and a branch of cherry blossom.

Just as the party was on the point of starting, some one observed that it was a pity to leave so lovely a spot without resting a while among the flowers. This was immediately agreed to, and they took their seats on a moss-grown rock, a short distance from which a little streamlet descended in a murmuring cascade. There they began to drink saké, and one of the company, taking his flute, evoked from it a rich and melodious strain ; while another, tapping his fan in concert, sang *The Temple of Toyora*. Genji, leaning against a rock, presented a picturesque appearance, though he was still pale and thin. The priest brought a *koto* and begged him to play on it. Genji said that he was no master of music, but, nevertheless, he played, with fair ability, a pleasing air. Then they all rose up and departed.

Japan   SUYEMATSU (*adapted*)

GENJI VISITS HIS WIFE

AFTER he had quitted the mountain Genji went first of all to the Palace, where he had an interview with his father, the Emperor. Then his father-in-law entered and entreated him to accompany him to his mansion. Genji did not feel very anxious to accept this invitation, but was persuaded to do so.

They arrived ; but, as usual, his bride did not appear, and only presented herself at the earnest request of her father. She was one of those model princesses whom one may see in a picture, very formal and very sedate. It was difficult to draw her into conversation, and she was very uninteresting to Genji. Turning to her, he said with some reproach in his accents, ' Surely you should sometimes show me a little of the ordinary affection of people in our position.'

She made no reply ; but glancing coolly upon him, murmured with modest yet dignified tone :

> ' When you cease to care for me,
> What can I then do for thee ? '

' Your words are few, but they have a sting in them. You say I cease to care for you ; but you do me wrong in saying so. May the time come when you will no longer pain me thus,' said Genji ; and he made every effort to conciliate her. But she was not easily appeased. He was unsuccessful in his efforts, and soon retired to his apartment, where he fell asleep at once.

Ibid.

Japan

THE HAPPY MAN

THE sky is vast and clear,
The moon sheds her bright rays ;
The bamboos wave in the breeze,
The air is fragrant and fresh ;
The family is happy and gay.

The parents sit in the garden
Sipping tea and humming tunes ;
The house is full of the sound of voices,
The voices of children at their lessons,
And the youngest, calling for his nurse.

He who lives thus with his family
Is the happiest man on earth ;
Riches and glory mean nothing to him ;
His life slips smoothly by
To the thought that he will survive in his children.

DUMOUTIER (*Trans. from the French by E. E.*)

Indo-China

THE HARE AND THE ALLIGATOR

(KAREN FOLK-TALE)

SOME crows conceived a spite against an alligator, and contrived a plan to kill him and feast on his flesh. They went to the alligator and told him they had found a mountain pool which was alive with fish, and promised to guide him to it if he would agree to throw them out an occasional fish in payment of their services. The alligator agreed and set out after the crows, who led him farther and farther away from any water until he was almost exhausted. When he refused to go any farther on his little short legs, they lured him on by saying that the wind murmuring among the pines was the dashing of the waves on the sides of the pool, now near at hand.

At last, worn out and nearly dead, the alligator met a carter, who told him there was no pool in that neighbourhood, and finally agreed to carry him back to his original pool in his ox-cart.

To make sure that the alligator would not fall from the cart, the carter lashed him firmly like a log and set out. The jolting of the cart made the ropes cut deeply into the alligator's flesh, and he was in a sorry state by the time they reached the pool.

When they arrived the carter drove his oxen into water deep enough for the alligator to swim in, as he protested that he was too weak to walk even a step on dry land. No sooner was he released from the ropes and back once more in his own element than the ungrateful creature seized one of the oxen and was about to devour it. The carter pleaded for his ox, and protested against this unworthy return for saving his life.

The alligator, however, pleaded necessity, saying he was too weak to find his food in the normal way and must eat the ox or starve.

While the discussion continued the hare came along and the case was referred to him for decision. After examining the cuts made by the ropes the hare said, ' You have certainly been wronged by someone, but you haven't proved that it was the carter who injured you. Before I can give judgment I ought to see you both re-enact the affair.'

So the alligator climbed again on to the cart and the carter began to tie him again with the ropes. ' Tighter, tighter,' cried the alligator, anxious to make a good case against the carter.

When the carter could strain the ropes no tighter the hare said, ' Now take your club and pay him off.'

The carter then beat the alligator until he burst his bonds and escaped more dead than alive into the pool. He vowed vengeance on the hare and laid in wait for him and at last caught him as he was stooping to drink from the pool.

' Um-m-m-m-m,' chuckled the alligator, holding the hare fast with his horny lips.

' That's a woman's noise,' said the hare scornfully ; ' a *man* would cry " Ha-a-a-a " when he had gained a victory.'

The alligator, anxious to vindicate his sex, opened his mouth to shout ' Ha-a-a-a.' The hare jumped out, pulling the alligator's tongue out as he went, so that from that day alligators have had no tongues.

SMEATON (*adapted*)

Burma

THE HARE AND THE SNAIL

ACCORDING to the Siamese, hares originally had thick ears ; but one day one of the family having more legs than memory, met a snail dragging himself painfully along the ground, and in a moment of pride sought to humiliate him. 'Why, little one, where are you going at this pace ? ' said he. ' To the beautiful rice-fields of the next village.' ' But, my poor fellow, you will be a long time reaching them. Why did not Nature furnish you with legs like mine ? Confess you envy me. How long, now, do you think it would take me to get there ? '

' Perhaps longer than it would take me, though you pity me so much,' replied the snail coldly.

' You jest, do you not ? '

' No.'

' Well, will you bet on it ? '

' Whatever you like.'

' Well, then, if you win you shall nibble my ears since you cannot eat me ; and if you lose I will eat you : will that suit you ? '

' Perfectly.'

' Then set off ; for I will give you a start.'

While the hare began to browse the snail set off at his slow pace, and went to his brother, who was a little way off, and to him he communicated a pass-word, which he in turn told to another, and so on along the whole road which the rivals had to travel, so that it quickly reached the end.

Soon the hare, having satisfied his hunger, set off and simply flew over the ground, calling to the snail, whom he believed to be close by. ' Ohé ! ' came the answer from a long way ahead. ' Oh, he is already well on the way,' cried the hare, and set off again like an arrow. In a few minutes he stopped and called again. ' Ohé,' answered a voice still farther on. ' Really, he goes very quickly,' thought the hare, and off he set again. A quarter of an hour later he stopped, quite out of breath. 'Now,' said he, 'I may rest; I must be far in advance; but I will call and see. Ohé! snail.' 'Ohé!' replied a voice a long way on. 'Oh! I must hurry or I shall lose my bet,' muttered the hare. He ran, and ran, and at last stopped, quite exhausted, only a few yards from the goal. There, coming towards him was a snail. 'Oh, snail,' cried he faintly; 'have you been and come back again? Unfortunate that I am, I have lost my bet!' He made a feeble effort to get up and escape, but, alas! his strength failed him, and the snail pitilessly gnawed his ears.

Since that day the hare has always avoided damp places for fear of meeting one of the creatures who punished him for his pride.

Mouhot

Siam

THE HISTORY OF A NOSE

In the city of Chulla lived a politician who was in debt to the government to the amount of ten thousand strings of cash, and being unable to pay, was condemned to death. Cast into prison, he awaited only the King's order to carry out the sentence. After thinking hard without discovering any means of getting out of his difficulty, he bethought himself of a strategem. Addressing the jailer, he said:

'Helloa! you there, you'll do well to let me go free a little while.'

'Helloa!' answered the jailer, 'what stupid talk is this! After I have set free a man who is likely to be put to death to-morrow, what shall *I* do?'

The prisoner replied, 'Are we not friends? If you will not let me out, who can save my life? Think! My wife, my children, my house, all I have, all my relations and friends being here in the city, whither shall I fly? If you set me at liberty for a while not only will I not run away, but I shall be able to take steps to save my life, so please release me.'

After much persuasion the jailer, being not altogether without compassion, allowed him to go.

At midnight the condemned man presented himself before the door of the governor's room.

'Are you asleep?' he called. 'Is Your Excellency sleeping?'

Hearing and recognizing the voice of the officer who was soon to be executed, the governor asked in surprise,

'Who are you?'

'Your servant,' answered the officer.

'A scoundrel on the eve of execution,' retorted the governor dryly. 'What are you doing here?'

'If I may come in and salute you,' said the officer, 'I have something particular to say to you.'

'Oh, well, come in and speak.'

The officer entered, took a seat, and said, 'I pray Your Excellency to consider my case. If you put me to death there will be simply one man less in the world, and the money I owe will be lost to the government. If, on the other hand, you preserve my life there will be one man more in the world, and I shall repay the whole of my debt to the government. Let me live then.'

'If it ought to be so, I wish you no harm,' replied the governor.

'Your servant will come again, then, to-morrow night to see you.'

'As you will.'

The next night the officer presented himself again at the yamen and this time was introduced. After making the customary prostrations, he drew from his sleeve a sketch representing a human nose and begged the governor to put his seal upon the sketch, which was immediately done.

The officer then went with three companions who were in the plot to the coast of the Eastern Sea, where they found a populous village, in the midst of which stood a lofty mansion. Taking their drink of spirits at an inn in the suburbs of the village beyond the house, they prepared to sup. Addressing their host they put this question :

'What is the name of the village just behind us ? Whose is the big house ? '

' That is the house of a very rich noble,' the inn-keeper replied. ' Last year he was awarded the doctor's degree and he will soon obtain a high position under the government.'

After supper the officer took one of his comrades, and repaired to the mansion where everything showed abundant means, and asked to see the son of the house in private.

' See here,' said he, when they were alone, ' the king is very ill, and physicians have been called in from all the eight provinces for consultation. They have declared that the only cure is to find a nose like the one sketched on this paper and to concoct a remedy from it. For this reason we two have been commissioned by the Court officials to find, " without distinction of place or persons," a nose similar to this and to take it to the palace. We have sought all over the kingdom without finding a nose conforming to the sketch, but now it appears that your honourable father's nose resembles it exactly. We must therefore see him, and we shall not dare to leave without cutting it off.'

The son sat in horrified silence and reflected : ' This is an affair of state. It is a matter which we cannot avoid but must try to circumvent.' Then aloud he said, ' We will give you half our fortune if you will go away without taking my father's nose.'

The officer replied, ' We had made up our minds not to depart without it, but as you seem to be a son devoted to his father, and as we are taught not to hinder filial piety in others, we will reconsider our decision. If you will give us the sum you mentioned we will go elsewhere to procure a nose for the King's physicians.'

Then, with money in his pocket equal to many times ten thousand strings of cash, the officer added :

'You will be wise to say nothing of this affair. If it leaks out, and the government comes to know that having found a suitable nose we were bribed not to cut it off, we shall be arrested and put to death, and they will certainly cut off your father's nose and take the rest of your fortune too. Pray then be careful not to divulge this secret.' Thereupon the conspirators took their leave.

GRIFFIS, *Corea . . . (adapted)*

Korea

THE JAPANESE WIFE

ACT III

SCENE 2

Garden of ADZUMA'S *house, with Pavilion opening upon it.* ADZUMA
is sitting upon the mats there with her maids, O YOSHI *and* O TAMA.

ADZUMA: Our bravest garments, Girls ! We'll not be shamed
Even by maple-leaves. To-morrow falls
The great feast in the groves of *momiji*
Where all the city flocks to see the year

K   289

Put on its autumn dress, golden and green,
Scarlet and purple, saffron, russet, rose :
No ? maidens mine ! This earth were good as Heaven
If all men lived as those should live who own
A house to dwell in, so embellished.

O TAMA : *Okusâma !* What robe shall we lay for you ?

ADZUMA : The pearl-grey one with obi of pink silk
Sewn with white stars, because my Lord likes that ;
But you, my Tama ! You, my Yoshi San !
Be splendid like the autumn butterflies,
Like Autumn's self, though 'tis your time of Spring ;
Fetch forth such silks, such crapes, such girdle-cloths
Jiban, and *kanzashi,* the maple-leaves
Shall flutter out of jealousy. My girls,
We will be glad and gay. Wataru comes.
Be sure you take my writing-box and reeds ;
I shall make poetry.

O YOSHI : Madam, you can
With any that are best. That last you wrote—
The *uta* of the moon—everyone sings.

ADZUMA : How went it, Yoshi ? Play it if you know.

                              [O YOSHI *sings to her samisen.*
           ' Moon of the autumn sky !
             Sentinel, silver and still,
             Where are the dear ones that die ?
             Is it well ? Is it ill ? '

ADZUMA : Ah, Yoshi ! that was in the sombre mood
Which sometimes comes upon my dreaming string ;
Now all's for lightness—since my Lord returns
On honoured errand of the Emperor,
And we'll make sunshine for him in the house
And sunshine out of doors, if it be scant ;

But, sure, I think a day all blue and gold
Will paint Takawo for us. Give me here
The *samisen* : I'll strike a happier strain.

[ADZUMA *sings to her own accompaniment.*

'I would hide my soul, as the *Asajiu*
  In the reeds of Ono's moorlands do ;
    And none should know me, or see :
  But the *Asajiu* gleam, by their blooms revealed ;
  And the gladness of love in my bosom concealed
    Shines forth in despite of me !'

Think you my Lord took strength enough with him ?
There's an ill league to travel in those woods.

O TAMA : Dear Mistress ! He is safe. What wicked men
Would stand to see Wataru's sword flash forth ?

ADZUMA : I think so, Tama ! though he had but two.
Besides, I still remember what he said :
There comes no evil to the man that's good ;
So is he safe, plated against all harm
By that which cannot fear, a soul serene
Doing no wrong, and dreading none, But I
Count the slow minutes when he is not nigh.

[*Exeunt.*

Japan

ARNOLD, *Adzuma*

JAVANESE LOVE SONG

LET a thousand countries be travelled, another like you, my love, will not be found.

Your face is as the moon ; your forehead is alabaster.

The hair on your temples resembles a string of coins.

Your eyebrows are the leaf of the Imba.

Your soft eyelashes look upwards.

Your long jet hair falls undulating.

Your eyes, sharp-angled, are becoming ; your cheek is a section of the Durien ; your mouth the fissure of a ripe Mangostin ; your slender nose is beautiful.

The lock behind your cheek is as the blossom of the Turi tree.

Your chin is as the angle of an adze, with its handle.

Your neck bends like the tendril of a weeper.

Your wide bosom is becoming ; your breasts are as the ivory coco-nut, leaving nothing to desire.

The breasts of my princess are like two young coco-nuts, bound in a vest of red, full and smooth, intoxicating to madness. Her shoulders are polished and slender ; her arms are like an unstrung bow ; her waist is as if it would break by an effort.

The tips of her fingers are as thorns, her nails long and becoming ; her legs are shaped as the flower of the Pudac ; the soles of her feet are arched.

My fair one looks as if she would perish at the breath of love.

Were all her perfections to be enumerated, how little room, how much to write. A year's search will not produce her equal.

CRAWFURD, *History of the Indian Archipelago*

KOREAN LOVE SONG

Farewell's a fire that burns one's heart,
    And tears are rains that quench in part,
But then the winds blow in one's sighs,
    And cause the flames again to rise.

My soul I've mixed up with the wine,
    And now my love is drinking,
Into his orifices nine
    Deep down its spirit's sinking.
To keep him true to me and mine
    A potent mixture is the wine.

Silvery moon and frosty air,
    Eve and dawn are meeting ;
Widowed wild goose flying there,
    Hear my words of greeting !
On your journey should you see
    Him I love so broken-hearted,
Kindly say this word for me,
    That it's death when we are parted.
Flapping off the wild goose clambers,
    Says she will if she remembers.

Fill the ink-stone, bring the water,
    To my love I'll write a letter ;
Ink and paper soon will see
    The one that's all the world to me,
While the pen and I together,
    Left behind, console each other.

Bishop, Korea . . .

LAW OF DEATH

A CERTAIN woman had a little son of whom she was very fond, and when he died suddenly she took him in her arms and went round to all her neighbours begging them to restore him. But the neighbours protested, saying : ' Art thou mad, to carry thy dead child about thus ? ' and sent her away.

But one, wiser than the rest, and pitying her want of understanding, said to himself : ' It is because she knows not the law of death ; I will help her to find the truth.' So when the woman appealed to him, instead of sending her away directly, he said : ' I cannot cure thy son, but the Lord can.'

So she sought the Lord and made obeisance and begged his aid to bring her child back to health. ' Do you know what medicine can restore my son ? ' she queried anxiously.

' I know,' answered the Lord. ' What you need is a handful of mustard-seed from one in whose house no son, no husband, no parent, no servant, has died.'

So the woman took her child on her hip and went from house to house making her request. But to her inquiry she received always the same answer, ' Oh, woman ! What do you say ? The living are few but the dead are many. Go to some other place.'

So finding no house which death had not entered, she could not obtain the mustard-seed, and at last came enlightenment. ' I have erred greatly,' she reflected. ' I am not the only one who has lost a son ; everywhere, throughout the land, sons and parents die.' So, having laid the body of her son in the jungle, she returned to the Lord and told him all that had befallen her, and how she had at last found enlightenment.

Then the Lord said unto her : ' The law of death is, that there is no permanence in being.'

FORBES

Burma.

LIFE IS A DREAM [1]

(A Lyric Drama)

Dramatis Personae :

THE PILGRIM ROSEI
AN ENVOY
A MINISTER
CHORUS

SCENE : *Inn at the village of Kantamu in China.*

TIME : *Early in the eighth century.*

ROSEI. Lost in this pathless world of woe,
    Where nothing is, but only seems,
    How may the weary pilgrim know
    His waking moments from his dreams ?

    My name is Rosei, and I dwell in the land of Shu. . . . I
have hitherto idled my life away without so much as seeking
to tread the Buddhist path. But they tell me that on Mt Yauhi
there dwells a learned and venerable priest, and thither do I
now turn my steps to search after the one great thing needful.

CHORUS. On hill and moor the setting sun
    Full oft has left him desolate ;
    But half his course at length is run
    What time he sees Kantamu's gate.

               [*He arrives at the village of Kantamu.*

ROSEI. What is this ? Is it the celebrated pillow of which I have
heard ? Heaven must have placed it here to bestow . . . a
dream on me. . . .

[1] For the original Chinese version of this tale see E. D. Edwards, *Chinese Prose Literature*, Vol. ii, p. 212.

CHORUS. 'Tis but a wayside inn to spend the hour
    Of burning noon or wait the passing shower ;
    But he would fain thro' some strange dream be led,
    And on the magic pillow lays his head.

ENVOY. I have a message for thee, Rosei.

ROSEI. Who art thou then ?

ENVOY. An ambassador from the emperor, who wishes to relinquish
    the throne in thy favour.

ROSEI. Incredible ! Why should I be raised to the supreme
    dignity ?

ENVOY. It must be because thou possessest the capacity to rule the
    world. But hasten ! hasten ! Enter the palanquin sent to
    carry thee to the capital.

CHORUS. Onward the palanquin they bear
    In jewelled flowery radiance fair ;
    And he (unwitting that his power
    Forms but the dream of one short hour)
    Outsoars the clouds to find a throne
    'Mid scenes of beauty past comparison.

ROSEI. And in the east (to please the monarch's will),
    Full thirty fathoms high,

CHORUS. There rose a silvern hill,
    O'er which a golden sun hung in the sky.

ROSEI. And on the western side,
    O'er a golden mountain thirty fathoms high,

CHORUS. A silver moon did ride. . . .

MINISTER [*to* ROSEI]. How shall I venture to address Your Majesty ?
    . . . It is already fifty years since Your Majesty ascended the
    throne, but if Your Majesty will deign to partake of this nectar
    your imperial life may be prolonged to a millenium.

ROSEI. What then may nectar be ?

MINISTER. It is the drink of the Immortals.

[ROSEI *drinks, and the dance commences and continues until he awakens from his dream.*

. . . .

SCENE III

CHORUS. So speed the hours, and now the time is o'er ;
   His fifty years of splendour are no more :
   'Twas all a dream, whose every shadowed grace
   Must in a moment vanish into space,
   Naught, as he wakes, bequeathing in their stead
   Save the famed pillow where he laid his head.
   . . . His eyelids ope, and all the grandeur fades :
   Astonished he sits up.

ROSEI. But those sweet maids,

CHORUS. In queenly garb, singing soft melodies ?

ROSEI. 'Twas but the zephyr rustling through the trees.

CHORUS. And those vast halls of royal wealth and pride ?

ROSEI. Nought but this inn where I did turn aside.

CHORUS. Thy reign of fifty years ?

ROSEI.   One hour of dreams,
   While in the pot a mess of millet steams.

CHORUS. Strange ! Passing strange !

ROSEI.   But he that ponders well

CHORUS. Will find all life the self-same story tell,—
   That, when death comes, a century of bliss
   Fades like a dream ; that 'tis in nought but this
   Must end the monarch's fifty years of state,
   Age long drawn out, th' ambition to be great,
   And all that brilliant, all that joyful seems,
   For there is nought on earth but fading dreams.

ROSEI. Save, Precious Triad [1] ! save a suppliant soul !

---

[1] *i.e.*, the Buddha, the Law and the Priesthood.

CHORUS. Kantamu's pillow leads him to his goal,
  Through insight to renounce all earthly things.
  Thrice-bless'd the dream which such salvation brings !
  LIFE IS A DREAM is what the pilgrim learns,
  Nor asks for more, but straightway home returns.
              CHAMBERLAIN, *Classical Poetry* . . .

Japan

HSÜAN CHÊN TZŬ

LOVE

Upon the causeway through the land of dreams
Surely the dews must plentifully light ;
For when I've wandered up and down all night,
My sleeve's so wet that nought will dry its streams.

Tsurayuki (Trans. Chamberlain)

Japan

LOVE AT FIRST SIGHT

The night was advancing, and he was surprised when sounds from a distant draught-board met his ear. ' Who, at this late hour, can be so busy at play ? ' With the softest tread, he approached the eastern side, and saw in the distance a tub of peonies. Half shaded by the trees, he perceived a lighted lamp, and under the trees several persons were seated. He heard bursts of laughter, with which the voices of girls mingled. The air was burthened with the scent of fragrant flowers. He stole stealthily to a spot whence unobserved he might spy what was going on. The moon was overclouded, so that, even if discovered, the female servants would take him for the son of the house and nothing would be reported to their mistresses, He returned to the balustrade, and saw two lovely, graceful ladies laughing together and playing at draughts.

The long hair of the lady who sat on the western side was hanging loosely over her shoulders. At the first glance Liang's heart was overwhelmed. . . . His presumption broke all bounds, and he sprang forward to salute the ladies. Little dreamed he of the fright he caused. They closed their glittering eyes. They let the draught-board fall, and fled. But while they fled he took emphatic note of their persons. The expression of their countenances was that of the hibiscus; their eyebrows, long willow-leaves; their red lips, most charming and alluring—in a word their form and features were perfect, enough to transpierce the heart of any man. He heard their silken garments fluttering in the wind; he saw their noiseless feet, like golden lilies not two inches long, disappear. Once they looked round, and he perceived a smile upon their cheeks.

'Under these trees,' cried Liang, 'here and now, under these trees, will I lie down and die!'

BOWRING, *Flowery Scroll*

China

THE LOVE LETTER (RECITATIVE)

I TAKE up my brush to inform my beloved of the state of my heart.

In the night watches, full of thought and disquietude, I sought for words ; but what words are there to describe what I feel ?

The letter is written and lying before me, but I cannot make up my mind to fold and seal it.

Looking at my reflection in the mirror, I see the charms of my youth at the full, and I am disturbed, mortified even, by the thought that I am still unmarried.

A year is made up of twelve months, and a whole year is a long time to wait—think of it, my dear Lover !

As the day draws near when the Herd-Boy and the Spinning-Maid Stars meet I grow ever sadder.

On these autumn nights, sitting outside the door under the awning, I listen to the night sounds and in imagination am transported to you in the royal city.

Watching the bright moon, I think of the approaching winter and wonder if you have warm clothes to keep out the cold.

The bamboos quiver in the breeze as my heart quivers under its sad thoughts. What can I do to lift this depression and recover my serenity ?

I can sing no more.

DUMOUTIER (*Trans. from the French by E. E.*)

Indo-China

LULLABY

SLEEP, sleep, little brother,
Sleep and cry no more.
Mother is gone to the market at Set
To buy her some lime with her betel to eat ;
Soon, soon, she'll come home.

DUMOUTIER (*Trans. from the French by E. E.*)

Indo-China

MACASSAR LOVE SONG

LET the world disapprove of thee, I love thee still. When two suns appear together in the sky my love for thee may alter.

Sink into the earth or pass through the fire, and I will follow thee. I love thee, and our love is mutual, but fate keeps us asunder.

May the gods bring us together, or to me this love will prove fatal.

I should count the moment of meeting thee more precious than that of entering the fields of bliss.

Be angry with me, or cast me aside, still my love shall not change.

Nothing but thy image meets the eye of my fancy, whether I sleep or wake.

Visions alone are propitious to my passion ; in these only I see thee and converse with thee.

When I expire let it not be said that I died by the ordinary decrees of fate, but say I died through love of thee.

What is comparable to the delightful visions which paint my love so fresh to my fancy ?

Let me be separated from my native country, and at a distance from thee, still is my heart not far from thee.

In my sleep, how often am I found wandering about in search of thee, hoping that perchance I may find thee ?

CRAWFURD, *History of the Indian Archipelago*

Celebes

MALAY LOVE SONG

WHEN my mistress looks forth from her window, her eyes sparkling like a star, its brilliant rays glancing and glittering, her elder brother (*i.e.*, lover) cannot support its lustre.

Like a red mango is the hue of her cheek, becoming her tapering neck, traversed with shadows whenever she swallows.

Her features are those of a shadow figure—her forehead like the new moon at its first appearing ; her eyebrows so fair I could devour her.

Long has she been chosen to be my mistress—wearing a ring with gems of Sailan—her long nails shining like lightning ; transparent as a string of pearls.

Her waist is slender, and extremely elegant ; her neck turned like a polished statue.

Eloquent is the enunciation of her words. Her parting words are like the crimson red-wood.

Not by dress, but by herself is she adorned. Black are her teeth, stained with Baja powder. Graceful, slender, appearing like a queen.

Her locks are adorned with Saraja flowers ; her features beautiful, with no defect of symmetry.

My soul is often fluttering, ready to depart, glancing eagerly forth from my eyes and quite unable to return to its station.

Asiatic Researches

THE MISER

MISER. Alas ! how long are the days to one who suffers as I do !
It is nearly twenty years since I adopted this young hare-brain
. . . and he still knows nothing of the value of money. If he
only knew the pain it gives me to lay out even the tenth part
of a tael.

BOY. Father, don't you want something to eat ?

MISER. No. I am sick, and my sickness is caused by a fit of anger.
I went to buy a roast duck in the market. They were just
roasting one from which there flowed the richest gravy, so
under the pretence of bargaining for it I picked it up and held
it till my fingers were all covered with gravy. Then, without
buying the duck, I came home and ordered a dish of rice.
With each spoonful of rice I licked a finger ; but after about
four spoonfuls I fell asleep, and while I slept a dog came and
licked my last finger clean. When I discovered the theft I
was so enraged that I became ill, and my sickness will soon be the
death of me. Well, I will spend something just for once ; go
and get me some bean gruel.

BOY. I will take a few farthings and buy some.

MISER. One farthing will suffice.

BOY. One farthing ! Who would sell me a farthing's worth ?

[The boy takes ten coppers and brings gruel.

MISER. I saw you take ten pieces—was there ever such extravagance !

BOY. He will give me back five in change another day.

MISER. You should not have trusted him without inquiring his
name and those of his neighbours on the right and left.

BOY. Why such precautions for a trifle ?

MISER. If he decamps with my five farthings who will repay me ?
. . . I feel my end approaching. Tell me, son, what kind of
coffin will you bury me in ?

BOY. The handsomest coffin of fir [1] that I can find.

MISER. Don't be foolish—fir costs too much, and when one is dead there is no difference between fir and willow. You can make me an excellent coffin out of that old stable-trough in the yard behind the house.

BOY. But it will be too broad and too short ; we should never get you into it ; you are too long.

MISER. If the trough isn't long enough you will have to shorten my corpse. Take a hatchet and cut me in two and put one

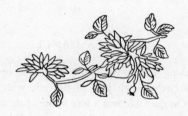

piece in on top of the other. But don't use our good hatchet for the purpose ; borrow one from next door.

BOY. But with one of our own why borrow a neighbour's ?

MISER. You don't realise how hard my bones are. If the edge of the hatchet is turned it will cost something to sharpen it.

BOY. As you will. And now give me some money and I will go to the temple and burn incense for you.

MISER. It is useless ; burn no incense for me.

BOY. I must ; I made the vow long ago.

MISER. Well, here is a farthing.

BOY. Too little.

MISER. Two farthings.

BOY. Too little.

MISER. Well then, three ; that's enough—too much ! too much !

[1] To keep off evil spirits fir is the most efficacious of all woods.

My last hour is come. Don't forget, when I am gone, to go
and demand the five farthings that are due. [*Dies.*]

DAVIS

China

PARTING

MINE oft-reiterated prayers in vain
The parting guest would stay : Oh, cherry-flowers !
Pour down your petals, that from out these bowers
He ne'er may find the homeward path again !

Anon (Trans. CHAMBERLAIN)

Japan

THE PLEASUANCE

LIANG saw nothing but books ; row over row upon the shelves.
The room was circled with pots of flowers, which filled it with
their odours. On the table was a lute upon a jade stand, and clouds
of fragrant smoke rose from a golden chafing-dish. A silver harp-
sichord and a flute of jasper hung upon the walls. In a corner were
two draught-boards, and, on both sides, scrolls of ancient poetry
and fanciful paintings, representing lakes and woods, bridges and
pagodas.

He stood up to feel the fresh air from the window, looking upon
a winding balustrade which hung over a white lotus that was
swimming on the lake below. A stork crept slowly and stealthily
along in the moonlight ; the wind shook down the willow-catkins
upon the water, over which a vermilion painted bridge led to the
inner garden. He admired the stripes of wavelets, broken by the
light of the moon. On both banks the branches of mournful
willows were trembling, under one of which a boat was fastened,
to enable the gardener to tend the lotus flowers. . . .

Liang crossed the bridge and entered a pavilion on the farther
side. From the balustrade he stretched his hand to gather a rose ;

the branch broke and the frightened birds flew away. A cuckoo cried as if it were the waning of the moon.

The piping of the goldfinches troubled his spirits; their flight interfered with the moonbeams. Drops of dew hung upon the flowers. He passed another small bridge and came upon a slippery path on which unripe plums were lying. Two peacocks strutted away, and a cockatoo screamed from a golden cage.[1] Before him was a park, wrapt in shadow. Two lines of peach trees formed a charming alley. 'Surely this is a fit abode for spirits,' whispered Liang to himself.

Proceeding westward, he crossed a garden of red apricot trees: he admired their bloom, and passed on over luxurious and sweet-smelling grass, from which climbing rose trees sprang to intertwine themselves in mulberry branches. He did not linger long among these attractive scenes, but returned with slow steps to the study.

BOWRING, *Flowery Scroll*

China

A POOR SCHOLAR

A MAN lately deceased appeared for trial before the King of the Infernal Regions. The King adjudged that as he had in his previous existence lived in excessive luxury, he must return to life on Earth in the character of a Scholar. A demon lawyer remonstrated, saying, ' This man has been a great transgressor and does not deserve such kind treatment.' The King laughed and replied, ' His having been a great transgressor is the very reason why I decree that he shall return to life to be a poor scholar. With a large family of small children raising their disturbing cries in his ears all day, he will have punishment enough.'

Canton Register, 1828

China

[1] Evil omens all, presaging sorrow and disappointment.

PRAYER FOR THE USE OF THOSE ON
EVIL DEEDS INTENT

HERE is our sure helper.
Arise on our behalf;
Stand at the door of this house,
O thou divine spirit !

We are on a thieving expedition—
Be close to our left side to give aid.
Let all be wrapped in sleep.
Be as a lofty cocoanut tree to support us.
O house, thou art doomed by our god.
Cause all things to sleep.

Let deep sleep overspread this dwelling.
Owner of the house, sleep on !
Threshold of this house, sleep on !
Ye tiny insects inhabiting this house, sleep on !
Ye beetles inhabiting this house, sleep on !
Ye earwigs inhabiting this house, sleep on !
Ye ants, inhabiting this house, sleep on !
Dry grass spread over the house, sleep on !
Thou central post of the house, sleep on !
Thou ridge-pole of the house, sleep on !
Ye main rafters of the house, sleep on !
Ye cross-beams of the house, sleep on !
Ye little rafters of the house, sleep on !
Ye minor posts of the house, sleep on !
Thou covering of the ridge-pole, sleep on !
Ye reed sides of the house, sleep on !
Thatch of the house, sleep on !

The first of its inmates unluckily awaking,
Put soundly to sleep again.
If the divinity so please, man's spirit must yield,
O Rongo, grant thou complete success !

GILL

Polynesia

THE PREMATURE BIRTH OF THE MOON

A LONG time ago a certain man in New Guinea, whose name has now been forgotten, was digging a new garden. He was not content to turn the surface of the earth but decided to dig down to a great depth. After some weeks he grew tired of his self-imposed task and he had just made up his mind to stop when he saw in one corner of his excavations the edge of a smooth, silvery, shining object. His curiosity was aroused and he continued to dig until at length he disclosed to view a shining circular object which he had no difficulty in lifting up in his hands. He was much gratified by his find and held it up for all to see. But as he held it, it grew rapidly larger, though it did not seem to become heavier. This astonished him, but being unusually quick-witted he was delighted instead of terrified and cried out :

' This thing which I have found is alive. It is a spirit, but from time to time it will take the form of a woman, and I shall marry her.'

On the advice of his friends he carried his treasure to the sea and washed it. By this time it had become much larger, and it was so brilliant that the people could hardly bear to look at it. As it was still rather misty he tried to wash it again, but he could feel it growing lighter, and rising into the air, and when it almost lifted him off his feet he hurriedly let it go.

309

No sooner had he released it than it floated away to a short distance, shining very brightly, and surrounded by a silvery cloud. It did not go far, however, but poised itself above the heads of the people who were now watching it with fear, and from the cloud which enveloped it a beautiful, clear voice was heard speaking in angry tones :

'Why did you disturb me?' it said. 'Many years have still to pass before the appointed time of my birth. Now I am like a child born prematurely, small, and with little strength. Had I been brought forth by my mother earth at the appointed time I should have cast a perpetual light on her, but now I shall be compelled to change in brilliance from day to day. Although in ignorance you disturbed me you have committed sacrilege and must die ere long.'

The voice became fainter and fainter, and the object began to recede to the horizon and finally it sank into the sea. The people watched till it had vanished and when it had disappeared the young man who was responsible for these strange happenings was the only one who was not throughly frightened and perplexed.

'Did I not tell you,' said he, 'that the jewel I found was alive, and that it was a woman? I shall go and search for her, and when I find her I will marry her, for though she is angry now she will be grateful to me by-and-by for releasing her from a dark hole in the ground and giving her power to float through space. When she sees that what I have done was for the best she will relent and reveal herself to me and we will be married. Now I will collect my dogs and my weapons and travel over the country until I find her.'

His people did not try to dissuade him, though the undertaking seemed both foolish and dangerous. The next day he left the village, and for many weeks he wandered about, living on the game he hunted and never sleeping twice in the same place.

After a time he came one day to the banks of a river, and there he determined to settle for a while. The place was lonely, although, in fact, he was not very far from his own village, his wanderings having taken him almost in a circle.

Every afternoon after he finished hunting, he would go to a beautiful pool in the river to bathe and refresh himself after the work and heat of the chase. One day his dogs, which always accompanied him to the pool, set up a great barking, and on reaching the river-bank he saw the most beautiful woman he had ever beheld bathing in the river. On the bank was her grass petticoat, lying where she had cast it off. Her skin was fair and her hair was yellow, and in beauty of face and form she was far superior to any woman he had ever dreamed of.

' This must be she,' he meditated, ' the woman for whom I have been searching,' and he remained quietly waiting for her to come out. Attracted by the dogs, which were now lapping the water at the river's edge but not daring to enter, she raised her eyes and saw him sitting on her petticoat.

' What are you ? ' she asked, ' are you a man ? '

' Yes,' he replied, ' I am a man and I have been looking for you for a long time because I want you to marry me and live with me for the rest of our lives.'

' For the rest of our lives ! ' she cried. ' I am a spirit and do not die ; you are only a man, and man's life is short at best. And as for you, you must die within these two days, for you have touched my clothes and are even now sitting on them.' With that she looked at him earnestly and added, ' I have seen you before ; you are the man who dug me up from my mother earth. I could not see you very clearly then as I saw and spoke through a cloud, but now I see that you are the same man.'

' Yes,' he replied, ' I am the man, and I have come to ask you to be my wife.'

' If I marry you,' she said, ' you must die ; but as you must in any case die because you have touched my garments I will be your wife for one day, and afterwards you must return to your village and prepare for death.'

So they were married for a day, and then, warning him again that he must die on the morrow, she soon disappeared from sight. But before she left him she told him that it was her fate to be married to the sun, and that the sun would be very angry because she had been married, even for a day, to a man.

The young man went home, prepared a great feast, took a last farewell of his relations and friends, and about an hour before sunset retired to his house and shut the door. As the sun declined on the horizon he became weaker and weaker, and finally, as it dipped into the sea his spirit departed with it.

Meanwhile the moon had returned to her lawful husband the sun. But in appearance she did not quite come up to his expectations on account of the accident at her birth, of which perhaps he was ignorant, He did not like the fact that half her deeds were done in darkness, owing to her inability at all times to illumine her mother earth. He complained too that she pursued a different track from the one in which he moved, and he entertained the most injurious suspicions of her motives in so doing. He accused her of flirting, and of being eccentric in her orbit. In particular he complained that she never appeared at her best in his presence, and maintained that the motive for this line of conduct could not be one that would redound to her credit.

The moon replied peaceably that his fears were groundless. She assured him that the only person she cared to please was her mother earth, and that her brilliance, incomplete as it was, was for her benefit alone.

The sun retorted that she was afraid to shine whilst he was present in the sky, and that she added insult to constant injury by appearing once every month in her greatest splendour at the precise moment when he had gone to bed for the night.

The domestic argument continued. The sun could not induce

the moon to alter her course; and the moon wanted to know what the sun did with his time during the several days during each month when they were actually out of sight of each other, hinting that for her part she took the dimmest possible view of the probabilities.

This widened the breach between them to such an extent that they agreed for the future to be seen as little as possible in each other's society. For the sake of appearances they would show themselves together a few times each month, but for the rest, they agreed, they would walk in their own paths without prejudice to the actions of the other party, and to this day, so far as is known, their difference of opinion has not been adjusted, nor does there appear any immediate probability of that desirable event coming to pass.

ROMILLY (*adapted*)

New Guinea

Find yourself a thrifty wife, though you wear out your shoes seeking her.

Japanese Proverb

QAT

QAT was not without beginnings but had as a mother a stone which burst asunder and brought him forth. He was born on the road and he had no father. As soon as he was born he grew up and talked, and finding that he had no father or maternal uncle to name him, he called himself Qat. He had as brothers Tangaro the Wise, who understood all things and could instruct others ; Tangaro the Foolish, who was ignorant of everything and stupid ; and nine others whose names are the names of leaves and plants. These all grew up, like Qat himself, as soon as they were born, and lived in the village where their mother, a stone, may still be seen. There Qat began to make things—men, pigs, trees, rocks—as the fancy took him. But even after he had made many things he had not found out how to make night, and it was always daylight.

Then his brothers complained and said, ' This is not at all pleasant. We have nothing but daylight and we grow weary of it ; can you not do something about it for us ? '

So Qat enquired, and heard that there was night to be had at Vava, in the Torres Islands. Taking with him a pig, he therefore sailed in his canoe till he came to Vava, and with his pig he bought night from I Qong, who dwelt there. And when he had also learned how to make dawn he returned to his brothers, taking back with him some birds and a cock to give notice of the time for the return of light.

And coming to his brothers he bade them prepare themselves bed-places from cocoa-nut fronds plaited together. Then for the first time they saw that the sun was moving and sinking into the west, and they called out to Qat in fear, that the sun was crawling away. 'Yes,' answered Qat, 'it will soon be gone out of sight, and when you see a change coming over the face of the earth you will know that that is night.' Then he let loose the night.

'What is this coming up out of the sea?' they all cried, 'and covering the sky?'

'Nay,' answered Qat, 'that is night. Sit down in the house, and when you feel something press upon your eyelids lie down and be quiet.'

Presently it was dark, and their eyes began to blink.

'Qat! what is it? Shall we die?'

'Shut your eyes,' Qat urged, 'for this is it. And now go to sleep.'

When night had lasted long enough the cock began to crow and the birds to twitter. Then Qat took a piece of red obsidian and cut through the night; and the light over which the night had spread itself shone forth again, and Qat's brothers awoke, and lo! it was day.

CODRINGTON (adapted)

Melanesia

THE RABBIT AND THE FISHES

ONE day the king of the fishes got a hook in his nose while snapping at a worm. He managed to break the line and so escaped having his bones picked by hungry mortals, but he was in great pain and no one could think of a way to relieve him.

As His Majesty grew worse the council was summoned, and from the turtle to the whale they all did their best to think of a remedy. At last the turtle had an idea. He announced that a poultice made from the fresh eye of a rabbit would relieve the king at once. He was listened to attentively, but his plan was voted down since there were no fresh rabbit eyes available. But the turtle was not to be silenced. He declared that he had a passing acquaintance with a rabbit and offered to bring him to the palace if the doctors would then take over the responsibility, as the sight of blood did not agree with him. He was thanked for his offer and went off quickly, realising that his career was made if he succeeded, and that it would be very much unmade if he failed.

It was a very hot day when the turtle came out of the water and dragged himself up the bank, but he had not gone far when he spied the rabbit sunning himself. The latter jumped out of the way, cocked his ears and looked over his shoulder to see who the intruder was. Seeing it was only the turtle, he asked : ' What are you doing up here out of the water on such a hot day, Sir ? '

' Oh,' replied the turtle, ' I just came up for the view. But I have seen enough. It is all very poor compared with the view under water. There we have beautiful forests of waving green trees, mountains of cool stones, valleys and caves, royal processions from our palaces, and none of this walking about, for the water bears you up and you go everywhere without exertion.' Without looking at the rabbit he turned to go, but the rabbit followed, longing, for he was a most curious animal, to see all the lovely sights under the water.

' Don't you have any difficulty in the water ? ' he asked. ' Doesn't it get into your eyes and mouth ? '

' Oh, no ! it is just the same as air when once you get used to it,' the turtle replied.

' I should like to see the place very much,' said the rabbit, rather to himself than to the turtle, ' but it's no use ; I couldn't live in the water like a fish.'

' No, of course not by yourself,' said the turtle, in a voice that sounded calm though he felt very excited at the success of his plan ; ' you couldn't get along by yourself, but if you would really like to see something that will surprise you get on my back and I will take you.'

The rabbit hesitated for a little longer, but his curiosity was too strong and at last he allowed himself to be persuaded. Down he went on the back of the turtle, who held him firmly by the fore-paws, and after a little while he did not much mind the discomfort of the water getting into his eyes and his mouth and his ears, for he was charmed and bewildered by everything he saw.

When they reached the palace the council of learned doctors welcomed him warmly, but while sitting in an elegant chair and admiring the magnificence of everything, he happened to overhear a discussion as to the best way to secure his eyes while he was still alive.

He was so shocked at this treachery that he opened his mouth to gasp and was nearly choked by the water he swallowed. Then he quickly pulled himself together and thought of a way of escape. He explained politely to the council that he possessed two pairs of eyes, his real ones and a pair made of mountain crystals, which, unfortunately, were the ones he happened to be wearing. He declared that he would be most willing to spare them one of his real eyes, and would feel honoured to assist in the king's recovery if the turtle would take him to land so that he could dig up his real eyes without delay and send one back to the palace by the turtle so that his majesty's recovery might not be further delayed.

Marvelling at the rabbit's courtesy, the fishes felt ashamed of the rude way he had been kidnapped when a simple request would so obviously have accomplished their purpose. The turtle was rather brusquely ordered to carry him back to land, and somewhat shame-facedly did so.

As soon as he was set down by the turtle to dig for the eyes in the sand, the rabbit shook the water from his coat, told the turtle to do his own digging, and tore away up the mountain side. Since that time the rabbit has been careful to give the turtle a wide berth.

ALLEN

Korea

THE RAT AND THE CUTTLE-FISH

ONE day a rat fell out of a canoe into the sea and landed on the head of a cuttle-fish, to the great alarm of both. The cuttle-fish was about to shake off the rat, when the latter begged him to carry him to a place where his grandfather and grandmother were waiting for him. The kind cuttle-fish agreed, and swam, and swam, and swam, till he was all weary and out of breath ; but the rat, who was enjoying this new form of transport, urged him on farther and farther. At last they came near to a grassy bank where the rat decided to land : but being a suspicious person, he feared that the cuttle-fish would play some trick on him, so he begged not to be put ashore there. But the cuttle-fish was by this time quite tired of his passenger and swam straight to the bank, whereupon the rat jumped on shore and made off, and instead of thanking his rescuer he ran away jeering at him. So now the cuttle-fish hates the rat and is always on the watch to catch and punish him. And this is why the Fijians make little rats out of cowrie shells and use them as bait to catch cuttle-fish.

CUMMING, *At Home in Fiji*

Fiji

318

REMARKABLE EFFECTS OF A MIRROR

A YOUNG Korean was going on a journey to Seoul. As he was leaving home his wife called him back.

'Hé,' she said. 'Listen a moment. I have heard Mr. Kim's mother speak of a very lovely thing made of glass and metal. She says that when you look into it you see very curious things. I want you to buy one for me in the city.'

'Is it expensive?' asked the husband.

'No,' replied his wife, 'you will have to pay something for it, but not really very much.'

When he had finished his own business in Seoul the husband set out to fulfil his wife's commission. He made enquiries among his acquaintance in the city, discovered that the object in question was called a mirror, and bought one without any difficulty. In his eagerness to get home he put it into his wallet without even looking at it properly.

When he reached home his wife almost snatched the mirror from him in her impatience. But when she looked into it and saw the face of a woman in it, she burst into tears and began to scold:

'Oh, the villain! Not content with disporting himself in the city, he brings home a concubine! Who is this woman you have brought to insult me?'

The husband, taken aback by this unwarranted attack, looked into the mirror over his wife's shoulder, and seeing a man's face there, became violently angry.

'What sort of conduct is this for the wife of a respectable man?' he cried, almost black in the face with anger. 'How dare you bring a libertine like that into the house?'

So incensed was he that he would probably have murdered his wife had not his old mother hurried in to find out why they were fighting. Each began to accuse the other. The weeping daughter-in-law raved about a concubine; the angry son of a paramour, and both pointed to the mirror.

The old woman tried to pacify them. 'Don't be vexed,' she began quietly. Then, looking into the mirror she saw the face of an old woman looking at her and broke into a laugh.

'Is it this old woman the argument is all about?' she asked. 'It is only the widow Pak from next door come to borrow some fire.' So saying she went out to speak to her.

But not finding anyone, she went in again to her husband, and said in puzzled tones, 'There is something very odd in the children's room. You can see all kinds of queer things in it and they are quarrelling over it. You had better come and see what it is.'

The old man rose and went into the room where his son and daughter-in-law were still abusing each other. His wife handed him the mirror, and in it he saw the face of an old man.

'Ai-ya!' he exclaimed, 'here's that old dog of a teacher come to collect his fees and I haven't a penny for him. This is not too good!'

One by one and two by two, the villagers looked into the mirror, and with every new arrival the uproar grew. At last they decided to take it to the magistrate, who might know more about such things than country-folk like themselves. So the village repaired as one man to the yamen.

But the magistrate was more astonished than anyone by what he saw in the mirror. Hastily summoning his officers, he bade them prepare horses and pack his baggage at once. 'For,' said he, 'a new magistrate has come to take over my office, though I have no idea what I have done to lose my place.'

Really believing that he had been cashiered, he was so busy making preparations for a hurried departure that it was some time before he could be dissuaded by a junior officer who, after a careful examination, pointed out how the mirror reflected the face of each individual in turn.

GRIFFIS, *Corea . . . (adapted)*

Korea

張
果

CHANG KUO

THE RETURN

(Extract from the *Tosa Diary*)

The moon was shining brightly when I reached my house and entered the gate, so that its condition was plainly to be seen. It was decayed and ruined beyond all description—worse even than I had been told. The heart of the man in whose charge I had left it was in an equally dilapidated condition. The fence between the two houses had been broken down, so that both seemed but one, and he appeared to have fulfilled his charge by looking in through the gaps. And yet I had supplied him by every opportunity with the means of keeping it in repair. To-night, however, I would not allow him to be told this in an angry tone, but in spite of my vexation I offered him an acknowledgment for his trouble. There was in one place something like a pond where water had collected in a hollow, by the side of which grew a fir-tree. It had lost half its branches, and looked as if a thousand years had passed during the five or six years of my absence. Younger trees had grown up round it, and the whole place was in a most neglected condition, so that everyone said it was pitiful to see. Among other sad thoughts that rose spontaneously to my mind was the memory—ah, how sorrowful !—of one who was born in this house, but who did not return here along with me. . . . I cannot write down all my regrets and memories ; be it for good or evil, here I will fling away my pen.

Reed

Japan

*

Don't look for blossom on a dead cherry tree.

Japanese Proverb

322

ROYAL SOLICITUDE

THERE was in Chosen (Korea) a king called Cheng-chong, who was celebrated throughout the kingdom for his goodness of heart.

One night, disguised as a countryman and accompanied only by a single servant, he set out to make a circuit of his capital in order to inform himself of the temper of his subjects, and to become better acquainted with the details of their lives.

After some time he came upon an isolated and miserable hut, so dilapidated outside that he suspected a state of things within difficult to imagine. Wishing to know more, he poked a peep-hole in the paper window and saw inside an old man weeping, a man in mourning singing, and a nun or a widow—he could not tell which—dancing. Quite unable to explain the meaning of this curious scene, he ordered his servant to call forth the master of the house.

Hearing a voice, the man in mourning made his appearance. His Majesty saluted him and said :

' I think we have not met before ? '

' True,' replied the mourner, ' but how is it that you come to seek me out at midnight ? To what family do you belong ? '

The king answered, ' I am Mr. Ni, from Tong-ku-an. As I was passing I heard strange sounds issuing from this house, so I made a hole in the window and saw within an old man weeping, a nun dancing, and a gentleman in mourning singing. As, naturally, I wished to know *why* the old man wept and the nun danced and the man in mourning sang, I made my friend here call the house-holder so that I could enquire.'

The man in mourning rejoined, ' Why should you be interested in other people's affairs ? Why interfere in what concerns you not at all ? The night is nearly over, so take my advice and go home.'

' Not at all,' protested the king, ' I admit that it is not very becoming to pry into the affairs of other people, but this is such a very unusual case that I beg you will throw some light on it.'

' Well,' answered the man, ' since you are so urgent, I cannot refuse to tell you. My family has always been poor. There has never been enough food in the house, and I have hardly enough land to afford squatting-room to a flea. In short, I cannot support my old father by my own exertions, and so my wife has from time to time sold a tress of her hair to eke out our resources. This evening she parted with the last lock to buy a cup of bean soup for the old man and came home looking like a nun. Then he, seeing his daughter-in-law turned into a nun for his sake, burst into tears and cried, " Why have I lived to see this day and to disgrace my daughter-in-law and my son thus ? "

' To cheer him my wife began to dance, and although I am in mourning, I too tried to help. She danced, and I sang, and so my father smiled a little and perhaps was comforted. And now, sir, you have heard my story, and I must ask you to leave me.'

The king, much impressed by the devotion of both son and daughter-in-law, replied, ' This is a most extraordinary affair, and one which shows a very able mind. I suppose, sir, you will be among the candidates at the Literary Examination to-morrow ? '

' An examination to-morrow ? ' exclaimed the man in mourning. ' What examination ? '

' Why certainly,' said the stranger, ' to-morrow there is to be an examination, and you must not on any account fail to be present.'

' But,' protested the other, ' I have not heard of any examination to-morrow.'

' Whether you have heard of it or not,' replied the king, ' you must be prepared to compete. I shall be there and I will see that you are admitted.'

With that the king took his leave and returned to the palace to await the stroke of the great clock-bell announcing the dawn. As soon as its mighty vibrations ceased His Majesty issued an order for an immediate examination. The news quickly spread through the city and beyond the walls. The scholars were very surprised and said to one another, ' As late as last night there was no mention of an examination. What can it mean ? ' But all the candidates among them who were sufficiently prepared, and some who were not, began without delay to flock to the examination halls.

Even the poor householder, who had been told to present himself, went with the others. ' For,' he said to his wife, ' though I knew nothing about it, the stranger evidently did, so I had better go as he advised.'

On the road he fell in with a crowd of other candidates all hurrying towards the halls, and he had no difficulty in gaining entrance to the enclosure.

The subject of the examination essay, chosen as usual by His Majesty, was announced as soon as all were seated. The theme ran, ' The song of a man in mourning, the dancing of a nun, the tears of an old man.'

Of all the candidates present none could conceive how this mysterious subject should be treated save one who, from bitter experience, expounded the theme clearly and submitted a paper without a mistake in it. He was therefore awarded the doctorate and received a summons to appear at the palace to receive it in person from the king.

When they were alone in the audience chamber the king at once made himself known. The new graduate would have manifested his gratitude with all the appropriate kneelings and bowings, but the king cut short his prostrations.

' Go quickly,' he said graciously, ' and tell your Honourable Father and your Devoted Wife of your success.'

Thus was filial piety recompensed by appointment to high office joined with royal munificence.

GRIFFIS, Corea . . . (adapted)

Korea

PRESENTATION AT COURT IN OLD JAPAN

(ELEVENTH CENTURY)

MOUNT FUJI is in this province far to the west. It towers up painted with deep blue, and covered with eternal snow. It seems that it wears a dress of deep violet and a white veil over its shoulders. From the little level place on the top smoke was going up. In the evening we even saw fires burning there. The Fuji River comes tumbling down from the mountain. . . . I think the gods assemble there on that mountain to settle the affairs of each new year.

While I lived in the country I had gone to the temple from time to time, but even then I could never pray like others, with a pure heart. In those days people learned to recite sutras and practise austerities of religious observance after the age of seventeen or eighteen, but I could scarcely even think of such matters. The only thing I could think of was the Shining Prince who would some day come to me, as noble and beautiful as in the romance of Genji. If he came only once a year I, being hidden in a mountain villa like Lady Ukifuné, would be content. I could live as *heart-dwindlingly* as that lady, looking at flowers, or moonlit snowy landscape, occasionally receiving long-expected lovely letters from my Lord.

> On the moon-birth of the Rice-Sprout month I saw
> The white petals of the Tachibana [1] tree
> Near the house, covering the ground.
> Scarce had my mind received with wonder
> The thought of newly fallen snow—
> Seeing the ground lie white—
> When the scent of Tachibana flowers
> Arose from fallen blossoms.

---

[1] A species of orange.

In our garden trees grew as thick as in the dark forest of Ashigara, and in the Gods-absent month [1] the red leaves were more beautiful than those of the surrounding mountains. A visitor said, ' On my way here I passed a place where red leaves were beautiful.' I improvised thus :

> ' No sight can be more autumnal
> than that of my garden
> tenanted by an autumnal person
> weary of the world ! '

The Princess Yuko, who had heard about me through a distant relative, said it would be better for me to be with her than passing idle, lonely days.

My old-fashioned parents thought the Court life would be very unpleasant . . . but others said, ' People now-a-days go out as ladies-in-waiting at the Court, and then fortunate opportunities of marriage are naturally numerous ; why not try it ? ' So, at the age of twenty-six I was sent to the Court against my will.

. . . As I have said before, my mind was absorbed in romances, and I had no important relatives from whom I could learn distinguished manners or court customs, so except from the romances I could not know them. I had always been in the shadow of my antiquated parents, and had been accustomed not to go out but to see moon and flowers. So when I left home I felt as if I were not I, nor was it the real world. . . . I had often fancied in my countrified mind that I should hear more interesting things for my heart's consolation than were to be found living fixed in my parents' house.

I felt awkward in Court in everything I did, and I thought it sad, but there was no use in complaining. . . . After ten days or so I got leave to go out. Father and mother were waiting for me with a comfortable fire in a brazier.

OMORI *and* DOI

[1] October, when all the local gods go to the province of Idzumo to confer with the oldest god of all.

THE SNAKE-KING AND THE EAGLE'S WIFE

A LONG time ago there lived a few miles inland from the coast of New Guinea a large eagle. He did not often come down to the sea, but sometimes people saw him and were afraid of him on account of his great age and enormous size. He had been well known to their fathers and grandfathers, and there was no bird in all the country which could compare with him. His home was in the dense bush inland where the people feared to go. The same sort of birds, beasts, and reptiles which frequented the coast lived there, but they practised magic, could speak all human languages, and were of terrific size.

Now, the eagle was regarded as king of this country, and there was no such tree to be seen in the whole land as the one in which his nest was built. But he had no one to mate with, as no other eagle could compare with him in strength or wisdom. As he flew over the hills he used to ponder on this and one day, as he was circling high above the coast town, he discerned a young woman more beautiful than any he had ever seen. She was tall and of a good figure. Her five grass petticoats were each of a different colour ; sweet smelling flowers were arranged in her hair, and she was decked with ornaments. As soon as the eagle saw her he decided that she, and she alone, must be his wife ; but he had to wait for an opportunity to catch her, for she was sitting among her relations on the platform of the house.

At last, after a long time, as it seemed to the eagle, she took a water-pot on her shoulder and stepped down to the ground. The eagle saw his chance, swooped down suddenly and carried her away quite easily, without hurting her in any way. Her father and mother ran out and followed for many miles, till they reached the border of the enchanted country. Here they stopped, for they were afraid to go farther. Soon the sun went down, and in the darkness they lost sight, as they supposed for ever, of their daughter. Sadly they returned home, and told the story to their friends, while the eagle flew on, holding the girl gently so as not to hurt her. When he reached his nest he put her in it and sat down by her side. She reproached him sharply, but he said :

'Have I hurt you? I am the king of this country, but until I saw you I could find no one fit to wed with me. Now you must marry me and share my kingdom.'

The girl understood that she could not refuse ; moreover by this time she admired the eagle on account of his great strength, so she consented to remain. Every day the eagle brought in food which she cooked, and they lived very happily. In course of time a son was born, and the years passed pleasantly as the child grew big and strong.

But one day the boy saw smoke rising in the direction of the sea, and asked his mother what it meant.

His mother replied, ' That is the smoke from my village, where my father and mother live.'

' Let us go and visit our relations,' the boy cried, but his mother said, ' No, they think I am dead.'

But the boy cried so much that at last his father said, ' You shall go together to visit the old people as soon as I have caught some fish for your journey.'

So the next day, with plenty of cooked fish in a bag, mother and son were carried by the eagle to the ground. Before he left them he gave them careful instructions :

' Follow the path you are now on,' he said, ' till the sun is above your heads, and you will come to a place where two paths meet. You must be sure then to take the left-hand path. If you take the other you will get into the country of the big snake and he will try to take you from me.'

His wife promised to obey orders and agreed to be back at the same place in five days' time.

At noon mother and son came to the place where two paths met. The boy set off along the left-hand one, but his mother insisted on taking the road leading to the right.

They walked for some time without seeing anything unusual, but when they turned a corner they both stopped, for a monstrous snake lay coiled in the path. The mother now wanted to turn back, but the boy laughed and said, ' No, let us go on ; I should like a snake like that to play with.'

As he spoke he ran towards it. His mother called to him not to touch it, but it was too late. The snake rose on its tail with a great hiss and said :

' Now that your son has touched me you must remain with me. You are my wife and he is my son, and where I go you must follow.' With that he uncoiled himself and set off along the path with his new family behind him.

After a while the woman began to think of escaping.

She waited till they were near to her village, then she began to drop some of the fish out of her bag, and when they were only a short distance from her home, she persuaded the snake to go back to collect them.

As soon as he had gone she made a dash for the village. Her parents recognised her at once and in a few moments her story was told. Some of the young men hastily launched a canoe and rowed mother and son to a house on an island in the sea and there hid them.

But it was no use. Guided by his sense of smell, the snake tracked them to their hiding-place and said he would live there with them.

The next day the woman begged her two sisters to invite the snake to go hunting with them in a distant part of the bush, and as soon as they had gone she took her son and went into the bush towards the place where her rightful husband, the eagle, lived.

At the appointed time they reached the place where he had agreed to meet them, and without further adventures they reached the eagle's nest in the great tree in the enchanted country, where they told all the story of their journey. The eagle blamed the woman's foolishness, but he was not angry, for he knew very well what women were like.

When the snake returned from hunting and found his 'wife' gone, he knew where to look for her, and very soon he reached the foot of the eagle's tree and demanded that she should return to him, for the fact that the boy had touched him, he insisted, made him the rightful husband and father. When the eagle laughed and refused to hand over his family the snake began to coil himself around the great tree to destroy it. But as soon as he had exerted his strength sufficiently to threaten the safety of the tree, the eagle spat at him and the damage was made good.

The snake grew tired of wasting his strength in this way and challenged the eagle to mortal combat. Thereupon the eagle swooped down, seized the snake-king in his talons, and flew with him high in the air. Higher and higher he rose, until the snake grew frightened.

'Do not go higher,' he cried in a voice made shaky with alarm, 'I will give up the contest and the woman and the boy shall be yours.'

"They belong to me already,' said the eagle-king, and flew up and up, until, in spite of his great size, he could no longer be seen from the earth. Then he let go his hold and the snake fell to the earth and was broken to pieces.

Romilly (adapted)

New Guinea

SNUB-NOSE

THERE once lived in a small town in China a husband noted for his stupidity and a wife remarkable for her cunning. ' Always remember,' she used to say to her husband when he went out, ' that all people with long beaked noses are good-for-nothings, beggars, cheats, bad payers, coiners of false money, false-swearers, and will go to hell ; while people with small turned-up noses are good, and will go straight to heaven. Therefore, that you may not lose, sell only to these last ; for, I repeat, the others are bad.'

Every day the husband went out, and passed from street to street, examining the passers-by, but never addressing any but those who had their heads raised to look at something, so that he very seldom sold anything.

One day, when he was observing noses as usual, he saw a man reading a placard which was placed very high. ' That man will go straight to heaven,' thought he ; ' his nose is so much turned up. Will you buy some clothes, good man ? ' said he.

' Clothes ! you see I have some."

' But you appear to me the most honest man I ever saw.' (I never saw such a nose,' he added to himself) ; ' and I should like to sell you a whole suit ; my wife makes them herself.'

' Well, what is the price ? '

' Of my wife ? '

' No ; of the clothes.'

' Two koou ' (about ten francs).

' But why do you come to this retired place to sell your clothes, when there are so many people elsewhere ? '

' Oh ! I have been there ; but all the people had long beaky noses, you see ! and I only sell to snub-nosed people.'

' I do not understand ; why will you not sell to people with long noses ? '

' My wife, who is a very clever woman, tells me that all people with long, beaked noses are knaves.'

' Really, your wife is very sharp, and I understand you now. Well, my friend, I will buy your clothes ; but as I have no money with me, I will pay you to-morrow. You have only to come to my house ; I live near here. You will see a hurdle covered with eggs, a flag at the end of a mast, and a little plantation of betel.'

' Very well ; that will do.'

The merchant went home to his wife and told her he had sold a suit of clothes to a man with a snub nose.

' Where is the money ? ' said she.

' I have not got it yet, but I shall be sure to get it to-morrow. I am to go to a place where there are a hurdle covered with eggs, a flag on a mast, and a little betel plantation.'

The next day the wife said, ' Go for your money.'

The man went off, but could not find the house, and after a long search he came home again.

' Did you get the money ? ' asked his wife.

' No, I could not find the house.'

' Well, I will go and look for it myself. If I am not back in an hour you will know that I am drowned.'

After an hour, as his wife did not return, the man set off to the river with the sieve with which he sifted rice, and with this he began to empty the water out. A passer-by asked what he was doing.

' I am emptying the river,' replied he ; ' for my wife is drowned, and she had on her best yellow bonnet.'

' Nonsense,' said the other ; ' I met her just now running away with a man with a snub-nose.'

MOUHOT

Indo-China

333

*

HE who is fond of asking questions will have plenty; he who depends only on himself will have little.

Chinese Proverb

SONG OF SPRING

THE night is still and deep,
The sound of *dan* and drum
Breaks through the silence.
My heart is dull and sad ;
I hear girls' voices singing,
The clear, sharp sound of bells,
And sadness overwhelms me.

Dawn comes, and the risen sun ;
His rays light up and warm the earth ;
Many-tinted clouds float above our heads.
Memory awakes ; the heart revives ;
Love warms it with the sun,
And soon the mind is thronged
With sweet words seeking vent.

The sound of *dan* and drum,
Voices of singers and noise of bells
No longer grieve the heart
As we watch, above the trees,
Lovely dragon-shaped clouds.

Let us take our guitars and sing,
Make the best of spring nights and days ;
Let us haste to enjoy their beauties
Ere the autumn winds blow down
The leaves from Ngo Dong.
Youth passes in a flash.

DUMOUTIER (*Trans. from the French by E. E.*)

Indo-China

SPRING-SONG

THE Korean, prisoned during the winter in his small, dark, dirty and malodorous rooms, with neither a glowing fire nor a brilliant lamp to mitigate the gloom, welcomes spring with lively excitement, and demands music and song as its natural accompaniment— song that shall express the emancipation, breathing-space, and unalloyed physical pleasure which have no counterpart in our English feelings.   Thus a classical song runs :

> The willow-catkin bears the vernal flush of summer's dawn
> When winter's night is done ;
> The oriole, who preens herself aloft on a swaying bough,
> Is summer's harbinger ;
> The butterfly, with noiseless *ful-ful* of her pulsing wing,
> Marks off the summer hour.
> Quick, boy ! Thy zither ! Do its strings accord ? 'Tis well.
> Strike up ! *I must have song.*
>
> BISHOP, *Korea* . . .

Korea

SPRING

SPRING, spring has come, while yet the landscape bears
Its fleecy burden of unmelted snow !
Now may the zephyr gently 'gin to blow,
To melt the nightingale's sweet frozen tears.

Anon (Trans. CHAMBERLAIN)

★

Amid the branches of the silv'ry bowers
The nightingale doth sing : perchance he knows
That spring hath come, and takes the later snows
For the white petals of the plum's sweet flowers.

SOSEI (*Ibid.*)

No man so callous but he heaves a sigh
    When o'er his head the withered cherry-flowers
Come flutt'ring down.—Who knows? the spring's soft show'rs
May be but tears shed by the sorrowing sky.

Kuronushi (Ibid.)

SUMMER

In blossoms the wisteria tree to-day
    Breaks forth, that sweep the wavelets of my lake:
When will the mountain cuckoo come and make
    The garden vocal with his first sweet lay?

Attributed to Hitomaro (Ibid.)

Japan

THE TAMING OF THE HARP

Once in the hoary ages in the Dragon Gorge in Honan stood a Kiri tree, a veritable king of the forest. It reared its head to talk to the stars; its roots struck deep into the earth, mingling their bronzed coils with those of the silver dragon that slept beneath. And it came to pass that a mighty wizard made of this tree a wondrous harp, whose stubborn spirit should be tamed only by the greatest of musicians. For long the instrument was treasured by the Emperor of China, but vain were the efforts of those who in turn tried to draw melody from its strings. In response to their utmost strivings there came from the harp only harsh notes of disdain, ill-according with the songs they fain would have sung. The harp refused to recognise a master.

At last came Peiwoh, the prince of harpists. With tender hand he caressed the harp as one might seek to soothe an unruly horse,

337

and softly touched the chords. He sang of nature and the seasons, of high mountains and flowing waters, and all the memories of the tree awoke. Once more the sweet breath of spring played amidst its branches. The young cataracts as they danced down the ravine laughed to the budding flowers. Anon were heard the dreamy voices of summer with its myriad insects, the gentle pattering of rain, the call of the cuckoo. Hark ! a tiger roars—the valley answers again. It is autumn ; in the desert night, sharp like a sword gleams the moon upon the frosted grass. Now winter reigns, and through the snow-filled air swirl flocks of swans, and rattling hailstones beat upon the boughs with fierce delight.

Then Peiwoh changed the key and sang of love. The forest swayed like an ardent swain deep lost in thought. On high, like a haughty maiden, swept a cloud bright and fair ; but passing, trailed long shadows on the ground, black like despair. Again the mode was changed ; Peiwoh sang of war, of clashing steel and trampling steeds. And in the harp arose the tempest of the Dragon Gorge ; the dragon rode the lightning ; the thundering avalanche crashed through the hills. In ecstasy the Celestial monarch asked Peiwoh wherein lay the secret of his victory. ' Sire,' replied he, ' others have failed because they sang but of themselves. I left the harp to choose its themes, and knew not truly whether the harp was Peiwoh or Peiwoh were the harp.'

OKAKURA, *Book of Tea* (*abridged*)

Japan

THOU SHALT NOT COVET

An old, lame priest was so renowned for his self-denying liberality that the Emperor Ch'ien Lung himself paid him a visit. After some conversation the Emperor presented him with a valuable pearl which the old man immediately bestowed on a beggar in the crowd. His Majesty was somewhat taken aback at this act of rudeness and asked if it was his habit to give everything away in the same manner. On receiving a reply in the affirmative, the Emperor added, ' Even down to the crutch you lean upon ? '

' Ah,' said the priest, ' it is written that the superior man does not covet what his friend cannot spare.'

' But supposing,' said the Emperor, ' he was not a superior man ? '

' In that case,' answered the priest, ' you could not expect me to be his friend.'

GILES

China

THRIFT

A thrifty old scholar once took lodgings next to a shop to which all the epicures of the town resorted to enjoy the speciality of the shop—eels fried in soy-sauce. The appetising smell penetrated into his room and the scholar daily enjoyed his bowl of plain rice and the delicious smell of fried eels that always accompanied it. In this way he saved himself the expense of fish and vegetables.

The eel-merchant decided to charge his stingy neighbour for the smell of his eels and presented his bill. The scholar brought out his cash-box, opened it, jingled his money and locked it up again.

' Are you not going to pay me ? ' the eel-man asked indignantly.

' Why, no,' replied the scholar, ' You have brought me a bill

339

for the smell of your eels and I have paid it with the sound of my money.'

GRIFFIS, *Mikado's Empire*

Japan

THE THREE WISHES

THERE once lived a poor elderly couple with no children to care for them. One winter evening as they sat gazing into the heart of the brazier after supper the good man suddenly spoke :

' For the rich the winter is an excellent season,' he said. ' Their food is prepared in advance, and they have nothing to do but take their ease. But for the poor, without sufficient food or fuel, it is a hard time.'

The good dame replied : ' They say that Heaven is just. Why then does it permit such things ? They say, besides, that if you pray to Heaven, you will surely get what you need. Suppose we pray to become rich——? " said she hesitatingly.

' You are right,' replied her husband, ' let us do so.'

And both prostrating themselves, they gave themselves to fervent prayer. Suddenly an angel appeared.

' In spite of your sin of murmuring, Heaven pities you, and will grant you three requests, after which you may ask no more. Reflect well, choose, and ask.' Saying this he disappeared.

The old man made the first suggestion. ' Shall we ask for riches, health and long life ? '

' No,' said his wife, ' we could not enjoy any of those things if we had no child. What pleasure would they give us ? '

' Well ! I have not asked yet. What shall we do ? If only he had promised *four* things at the good moment ! Why did he say only *three* ? Since we wish for a child, must we forego freedom from sickness, or renounce riches, or give up long life ? It is hard to decide. Let us think it over seriously to-night and decide to-morrow.'

Both sat plunged in reverie for a while, then as they lay down to sleep the old woman stirred the fire and commented, 'If we could have three or four feet of sausage to toast on the brazier it would be nice.'

As she spoke three feet of sausage appeared beside her.

The husband, beside himself with rage, screamed out :

'Oh ! what a woman ! By one stroke you have destroyed all our hopes. To punish you I wish the sausage would hang itself on the point of your nose.'

Immediately the sausage made a leap and attached itself to the old dame's nose.

At this the husband cried out, 'Alas ! In my anger I too have wasted a wish.' Seizing the sausage they pulled, first one way and then another, almost dislocating the nose ; but the sausage held on.

'Alas !' wailed the woman in tears, 'if this is to remain hanging here, how can I live ?'

The husband, not at all disturbed, replied, 'If we wish for a fortune and get it, we could make a tube of gold to hide the sausage. But his wife, quite unconsoled by this suggestion, cried out, 'Oh wretched me ! Whether you become rich or live long, as for me, I shall go and commit suicide.'

Saying this she took a cord and prepared to hang herself from a beam. The husband in alarm rushed to prevent her. 'Stop,' said he, 'there still remains one wish. I give it to you. You shall wish what you like.'

'In that case,' said the old woman, 'I wish that what hangs to my nose may come loose.'

As she spoke the sausage fell to the ground, and out of the air came a voice speaking in anger :

'You have obtained the three things which you wished for, but have you gained any advantage ? If you wish to enjoy true blessing in this world be content with what Heaven gives you, and do not foster vain desires.'

There being nothing to say, the two old folks spitted the sausage, toasted it, ate it, and went to bed.

But on the morrow their supreme ambition, which was to have a son, was fulfilled, for they found an orphan at their door, and, having adopted him, they gave him a good education and lived happily with him to extreme old age.

GRIFFIS, *Corea* . . . (*adapted*)

Korea

THE THUNDERBOLT

THERE lived in a Chinese village an old couple who were childless. One day the husband worked himself into a passion and beat his wife for never having given him a son. The poor old woman rushed out of the house, crying, and ran a long way. A Buddhist met her and asked what was the matter.

' My husband was angry to-day, and beat me because we have no children,' she replied.

' Listen to me,' said the priest, ' and I will make you happy ! Dig up a handful of this clay and knead it.' The woman obeyed, and the priest then sat down and moulded nine little clay figures.

' These,' said he, ' will be your children. The first will have long ears and very quick hearing ; the second, piercing sight ; the third, a skin so thick that he will not feel any blow ; the fourth will withstand fire without being hurt ; the fifth will have an enormous head, as hard as iron ; the sixth, legs long enough to wade through the deepest streams ; the seventh, feet as large as those of an elephant, for walking in the mire ; the eighth, an immense stomach ; and the ninth, a nose as long as a pipe, from which jets of water will issue at command. Now,' he continued, ' go home, and every year eat one of these figures.' The old woman bowed low several times, professing her gratitude and happiness, and returned home ; but in her excitement, instead of contenting herself with eating one figure, she ate up all nine at once. Soon her husband was beside himself with joy at the prospect of a son and became very kind and attentive.

At last the day arrived. The father received the first child, and ran to wash him in the stream ; but there came a second. ' Another ! ' cried the father, and ran again to the river. Returning, he found a third, then a fourth. He opened his eyes and cried, ' Really this is quite enough : what can we give them to eat ? ' But the whole nine made their appearance on the same day.

All were prodigies : they grew rapidly ; never cried ; ate enormously, and began to run about in two months. The old man did not know what to call them all, and complaining to his wife that he could not distinguish one from another, he got into a passion again and beat her. The old woman ran away, crying, and went to find the priest who had helped her before. ' Why are you crying now ? ' said he. ' My husband says we have so many children now that he does not know what to call them.' ' It is very foolish of him,' replied the priest, ' not to be able to distinguish them by their special characteristics. Tell him to call one " Quick-ear," another " Hard-head," and so on.'

The old man had calmed down when his wife returned ; but

debts accumulated as the children grew up, strong, fearless, and always hungry.

One day a creditor came and asked to be paid. 'I have no money,' replied the old man, and turned the creditor out of the house. A few days later this man collected some of his friends, and went again to demand his money, declaring that unless he was paid he would seize one of the children and whip him. 'Quick-ear' heard all, and 'Piercing-eye,' sitting in a tree, saw all, that went on. They decided that 'Thick-skin' had better go, and the creditor succeeded in binding him and taking him away. After every cane had broken on his back without hurting him they took an immense cudgel, which broke in the same way; and seeing that it was lost time to beat him, they let him go home.

But a few days later the creditor came back, determined to kill one of the children with boiling water. 'Quick-ear' heard the project and went off with all his brothers except 'Invulnerable,' who was left at home, and was consequently carried off. He was thrown into a boiler full of water and a large fire was lighted underneath. But the next day, when all the available firewood was exhausted, he was allowed to go free. 'This is too bad,' said the creditor; 'I cannot get my money this way. I will write a letter to Heaven, and ask that fire may burn the house of my debtor.' This he did, but 'Quick-ear,' who heard the threat, warned 'Fountain-nose,' who thereupon took care to water the roof. A thunderbolt fell, but glided from the roof to the ground. Using their combined strength the children lifted it, chained it up, and placed it in the house.

'Is it possible,' cried the creditor, 'that they are not all dead? I must throw one of them into the sea.' This time it was 'Stilt-legs'' turn. The boat in which they carried him out to sea had not gone far from the shore when a storm arose and upset it, and all in it were drowned, except 'Stilt-legs' who, thanks to his long legs, escaped. However, his brothers feared for him, and sent

' Big-head ' to look for him. He found him fishing on the shore surrounded by so many fish that he did not know how to carry them home. Luckily ' Big-head ' had his hat, so they filled it and returned with their immense catch. ' Large-feet ' hurried out and cut wood to fry it ; but ' Great-stomach ' ate it all up before his brothers had time to begin. ' Weeping-eyes ' began to cry, and an inundation ensued in which many of the neighbours perished.

Thereafter all the children went out to seek for food, and the mother was left at home alone. Seeing the thunderbolt chained in a corner she unfastened it. Immediately it rose in the air, then, falling again, struck the poor woman, and killed her.

MOUHOT (*adapted*)

Indo-China

THE TIGER AND THE FOREST

A TIGER and a forest had made a pact of close friendship and mutual protection. When men wanted to take wood or leaves from the forest they were dissuaded by their fear of the tiger ; and when they would take the tiger he was concealed by the forest. After a long time the forest was rendered foul by the presence of the tiger and began to be estranged from him. The tiger thereupon quitted the forest, and men, finding that it was no longer guarded, came in numbers and cut down the trees and stole the leaves, so that in a short time the forest was destroyed and became a bare place. The tiger, on leaving the forest, was soon seen, and although he tried to hide himself in clefts and valleys, men were able to attack and kill him. Thus, through their disagreement, the forest was exterminated and the tiger lost his life.

CRAWFURD, *History of the Indian Archipelago*

Java

THE TIGER AND THE MAN

A POOR cultivator left his breakfast every morning in his hut in the field, and every day a tiger came and stole it. The man in his anger set a trap of huge logs so arranged as to fall on any animal that touched the bait. The tiger was caught and was badly crushed by the logs, but was still alive. When the man came in on hearing the roars, the tiger pleaded hard for his life. He admitted the daily theft, but urged that theft was not a capital crime, and that he had been so severely punished already by the fall of the logs that he ought in justice to be released from the trap.

The man refused, saying he feared the tiger would eat him if released. The tiger swore most solemnly never to attempt revenge, and was released.

As soon, however, as he was out of the trap he seized the man and was about to devour him. The man pleaded the sanctity of the oath just taken. The tiger replied that necessity knew no law, and that crippled as he was, he could no longer catch game for his daily food, but *must* eat the man or starve.

The hare happened to be passing, and the case was referred to him for decision.

The hare, with a wise look, said, ' I can't understand this matter clearly. Now you both act out just what each did.'

The man told him how he hid his breakfast every day, and how he set the trap. The hare said he could not understand the trap, and made the man set it to show how it was done. The tiger was then ordered to show what he did, and accordingly entered the trap, but walked round gingerly, carefully avoiding the spring of the trap.

' I don't see that anything happened to you that you can justly complain of,' said the hare. ' How could you have received these terrible bruises ? "

The Tales they Tell and the Songs they Sing

The tiger, eager to make out his case, edged nearer and nearer, till at last he touched the spring and the trap fell again.

'Take your knife and dispatch him,' the hare advised the man, 'and learn not to restore the advantage to an enemy too strong for you.'

SMEATON

Burma

THE TRUE ENJOYMENT OF SPLENDOUR

A Chinese Apologue

DOUBTLESS, saith the illustrious Me, he that gaineth much possession hath need of the wrists of Hong and the seriousness of Shan-Fee, since palaces are not built with a teaspoon, nor are to be kept by one who runneth after butterflies. But above all it is necessary that he who carrieth a great burden, whether of gold or silver, should hold his head as lowly as is necessary, lest in lifting it on high he bring his treasure to naught, and lose with the spectators the glory of true gravity, which is meekness.

Quo, who was the son of Quee, who was the son of Quee-Fong, who was the five hundred and fiftieth in lineal descent from the ever-to-be-remembered Fing, chief minister of the Emperor Yau, one day walked out into the streets of Pekin in all the lustre of his rank. Quo, besides the greatness of his birth and the multitude of his accomplishments, was a courtier of the first order. . . . Ten huge and sparkling rings, which encrusted his hands with diamonds, and almost rivalled the sun that struck on them, led the ravished eyes of the beholders to the more precious enormity of his nails, which were each an inch long, and by proper nibbing might have taught the barbarians of the West to look with just scorn on their many writing machines. But even these were nothing to the precious stones which covered him from head to foot. His bonnet, in which a peacock's feather was stuck in a most engaging manner, was surmounted by a sapphire at least the size of a pigeon's egg ; his shoulders and sides sustained a real burden of treasure ; and as he was one of the handsomest men at Court, being exceedingly corpulent, and indeed, as his flatterers gave out, hardly able to walk, it may be imagined that he proceeded at no undignified pace. He would have ridden in his sedan had he been lighter of body ; but so much unaffected corpulence was not to be concealed, and he went on foot that nobody might suspect him of pretending to a dignity he did not possess. Behind him three servants attended, clad in most gorgeous silks ; the middle one held his umbrella over his head ; he on the right bore a fan of ivory ; and he on the left sustained a purple bag on each arm, one containing opium and areca-nut and the other the ravishing preparation of Gin-Seng, which possesses the Five Relishes. All the servants looked the same way as their master—that is to say, straight forward, with their eyes majestically half-shut, only they cried every now and then with a loud voice, ' Vanish before the illustrious Quo, favourite of the mighty Brother of the Sun and Moon.'

Though the favourite looked neither to the right nor to the left he could not but perceive the great homage that was paid him as well by the faces as the voices of the multitude. But one person, a Bonze, seemed transported beyond all the rest with an enthusiasm of admiration, and followed at a respectful distance from his side, bowing to the earth at every ten paces, and exclaiming, ' Thanks to my lord for his jewels.' After repeating this for about six times, he increased the expression of his gratitude, and said, ' Thanks to my illustrious lord from his poor servant for his glorious jewels,'—and then again, ' Thanks to my illustrious lord, whose eye knoweth not degradation, from his poor servant who is not fit to exist before him, for his jewels that make the rays of the sun like ink.' In short, the man's gratitude was so great, and its language delivered in phrases so choice, that Quo could contain his curiosity no longer and demanded to know his meaning. ' I have not given you the jewels,' said the favourite, ' and why should you thank me for them ? '

' Refulgent Quo,' answered the Bonze, again bowing to the earth, ' what you say is as true as the five maxims of Fo, who was born without a father ; but your slave repeats his thanks, and is indeed infinitely obliged. You must know, O dazzling son of Quee, that of all my sect I have perhaps the greatest taste for enjoying myself. Seeing my lord therefore go by, I could not but be transported at having so great a pleasure, and said to myself, " The great Quo is very kind to me and my fellow-citizens ; he has taken infinite labour to acquire his magnificence ; he takes still greater pains to preserve it, and all the while I, who am lying under a shed, enjoy it for nothing." '

A hundred years after, when the Emperor Whang heard this story, he diminished the expenditure of his household one-half, and ordered the dead Bonze to be raised to the rank of a Colao.

Leigh Hunt

THE TWO COUSINS

In a Chinese village lived two cousins, both orphans : the elder, who was called Mou, was cunning and egotistical ; the other, whose name was A-lo-Sine, was all goodness and simplicity. The time for ploughing came. A-lo-Sine possessed a buffalo, so Mou, who had only a dog, went to his cousin and said, ' Here is my dog ; give me your buffalo : my dog will plough your field, which is not very large, and you will have a very fine crop of rice.'

A-lo-Sine agreed, and worked so well with the dog that his rice crop was first-rate, while the field ploughed by the buffalo produced hardly anything.

Full of spite, Mou then went by night into his cousin's field and set fire to it. A-lo-Sine saw the flames, and, unable to repress his despair, uttered piercing cries, and rolled about in the field.

Some apes, marauding in a neighbouring field, witnessed this spectacle, and said to each other, ' That must be a god, since the fire does not hurt him.' So they took him by the feet and arms, and carried him to the top of a mountain, where they laid him down, plunged in deep sleep. The monkeys then piled rice and delicious fruits in bowls of gold and silver, and went back to the fields.

When A-lo-Sine awoke, and saw around him so many treasures, he thought no more of his misfortune, but gathered them up and returned to his hut full of joy.

Mou, seeing him so happy, followed him, and, at the sight of the gold, ' Heavens ! ' cried he ; ' you are as rich as a prince, cousin ; give me something.'

' No,' replied A-lo-Sine, ' I will not ; for you are wicked, and you set fire to my field.'

Mou then went out to his own field, and set fire to it, and imitated all that his cousin had done ; he wept, cried, and, like him, threw himself into the flames. Five monkeys, one of them a young one, who were feasting close by, drew near, curious to see what he was about. ' He is a god,' said they, ' the flames have spared him. Let us carry him away.' No sooner said than done. Each seized an arm or a leg and they set off.

They reached a neighbouring wood ; but there the little monkey began to cry, ' I want to carry him too.' ' But there is nothing to hold by,' said his mother. The little monkey, however, seized Mou's long tress of hair and put himself at the head of the procession.

But this hurt Mou, and he tried to disengage his hair, making the little monkey cry again. ' Ah, now you are angry ; stay there, then ! ' said the others, and they threw their burden into a prickly bush.

Mou had great trouble in extricating himself from his disagreeable position, and it was nearly evening when he reached home, all covered with blood.

'Well, cousin, have you found any gold and silver?' asked A-lo-Sine. 'Alas!' said Mou, 'I am well punished for the harm I did you. I have brought back nothing but thorns; call the women to take them out of me.'

MOUHOT (adapted)

Indo-China

UBAZAKURA

THREE hundred years ago there lived a good man named Tokubei, who was the richest man in this district as well as the headman of the village. In all things save one Tokubei was fortunate; but he reached the age of forty without ever having any family. Both he and his wife offered up many earnest prayers about their childless state and at last a daughter was born to whom they gave the name of Tsuyu, and for whom, according to custom, they called in a foster-mother called O-Sodé.

O-Tsuyu grew up charming and beautiful, but at the age of fifteen she suddenly fell ill and the doctors could do nothing to save her. O-Sodé therefore hurried to the temple and prayed fervently for the life of her beloved foster-child. Every day she went, and after twenty-one days O-Tsuyu recovered, suddenly and completely.

Great was the rejoicing in the home of Tokubei, and a feast was prepared to celebrate the recovery of his daughter. On the night of the feast O-Sodé was suddenly taken ill, and in the morning the doctor announced that she must die.

All the family, deeply grieved, gathered round the bed to take a last farewell.

'Before I die,' the foster-mother said faintly to her master, 'I must tell you that I am dying because I promised my life in exchange

for that of O-Tsuyu, and the gods heard my prayer and granted me this favour. You must not, therefore, grieve for me. But one promise I made remains to be fulfilled. I vowed to plant a cherry-tree in the temple garden for a thank-offering and remembrance. I shall not have time to keep my vow and I beg that you will plant the tree for me. And now good-bye; do not forget that I die happy because I die for O-Tsuyu.'

After the funeral of O-Sodé the most beautiful cherry-tree that could be found was planted in accordance with her vow. And every year for two hundred and fifty-four years, upon the anniversary of the death of O-Sodé, the tree blossomed; and its flowers, all delicate pink and white, were like a woman's breasts bedewed with milk. And people called the tree *Ubazakura*, the Cherry-tree of the Foster-mother.

HEARN, *Kwaidan* (*adapted*)

Japan

WINTER

WHEN from the skies, which wintry gloom enshrouds,
The blossoms fall and flutter round my head,
Methinks the spring e'en now his light must shed
O'er heavenly lands that lie beyond the clouds.

FUKAYABU (*Trans.* CHAMBERLAIN)

Japan

WONDERS OF THE WEST

From the Autobiography of Abdulla Munshi

IN this year also we first heard of steam vessels about to come out
to Singapore. We had heard a rumour about such things previously,
but to most of the people it was like the news given in history—
the news had the appearance of nothingness. On this account I did
not believe it, nor did anyone else receive it in his understanding.
As the Malays say, to hear it is not to receive it. But now a picture
of a steamship came to Singapore, and there were also in the place
men of trust who had sailed in them, and they told me. On this
account I now believed true enough, but it was the belief of mind
only—I had not seen them, nor could I conceive their actual appear-

ance. It is also true that I dilated to my neighbours on the skill and ingenuity of Europeans in all things, that I had seen or heard from Englishmen of standing ; but when I came to the steamship they fell in a rage at me, and wrangled with me so as to knock me over. Others accused me of always foisting up the English and telling lies. Others found fault with me for speaking so much about it. If I had ventured to speak to them of gas burning without a wick or oil in thousands and thousands of houses in England, and waggons that ran by steam at a rate of twenties of miles to the hour, or of a road under the earth nine hundred feet long in London, over which a river flowed with twenties of ships sailing thereon, and under which horse-carriages and men went and came, . . . or of a species of bird which can carry up people into the air, besides many other miracles which I have heard of, they would certainly shut their ears and turn away their faces, calling me a big bear. But let this subject alone—there are those that will not believe that there are lions in the world, and so they wrangle at what I tell them. But when the lions are brought from other countries they will be forced to admit that I am right and that they are wrong.

Again, I have had to bear a great deal of opposition from these people regarding things that I have learnt from scientific men, who have competent knowledge of the geography of the world, which they say is truly round, and which I have repeated to them ; and I have specially been answered that such a fact could not be believed, for such a thing was never heard of before, nor have our ancestors informed us of it. I showed them numbers of signs and proofs that the world was round, yet they would not believe me. Each and every one talked about it as they liked, some saying it was four-cornered, others seven. To this I replied, 'Have not the white men's ships gone round the world numbers of times ?' But this also they would not believe ; adding, 'How could they do this ? For is not the hill of Kaf in the way, and various kinds of mountains and dark seas ?' Then again, about the obscuring of the sun and the moon I had constant arguments, for they spoke as they liked. Some said the eclipse of the moon was owing to a snake eating it ; others that because of the great sins of mankind God darkened the world to make us reflect. Others again said that the moon was sick. Others say that the moon had fallen into a sea of mud and other such absurdities. . . . I tried to explain to them that the cause of an eclipse of the sun was in the moon being in a direct line between the earth and the sun . . . but my explanations were like a pot of fresh water poured into the sea, it also became salt, and my instruction had no result.

HIHAYAT ABDULLA (Trans. THOMSON, J. T.)

Malaya

CONCLUSION

(1847)

EVERYONE at all acquainted with the Malay character will agree . . . that it is just from those Malay nations, who are now most dreaded as pirates and robbers, that, under proper treatment the largest results may be expected in commerce and civilisation.

One of the great defects of the Malay character in general, as among the Javanese for instance, is a want of enterprise and hardihood. Where those qualities exist, however they may have been

misdirected hitherto, we have far more valuable materials to work upon, than where they are absent. What European nations were of old the greatest pirates and freebooters? Those, our own included, who have afterwards attained the highest pitch of civilisation.

Europe has hitherto brought little but ruin and rapine, and commercial restriction into this, the fairest and most fertile region of the earth. Surely, she owes it a tardy reparation. For any nation wishing to diffuse among these peoples the blessings of commerce, of enlightenment and civilisation, I do not think territorial acquisitions advisable, beyond a few small posts or stations, for its naval and mercantile marine. A strong feeling exists on the part of many of the inhabitants of the Archipelago in favour of England, which our manufacturing and commercial necessities would urge us to take advantage of. Our policy would be, I believe, to keep the seas from outrage, to make them everywhere safe for all those ' passing upon them on their lawful occasions,' whether natives or Europeans ; to break up the strongholds of piracy, and eradicate the disposition to it, by rendering its practice unsafe or impossible. Having done that, we may safely trust to the gradual, though slow, operation of commerce, or to individual enterprise and philanthropy for the enlightenment and civilisation of the nations of the islands, and look forward to an ultimate reward in the markets that will be opened for our trade and manufactures.

. . . There is one obstacle in the way it may be said, namely, the Dutch and their possessions. But why should our old allies, and very good friends at home, be our natural enemies in the East? Let them join with us in assuming the policing of the seas, and encouraging the civilisation and commerce of the natives. Let certain places, conveniently situated for posts and stations, either be assigned to each, or held in common, or occupied merely under the native governments. Why, I ask again, should we quarrel when our friendship and co-operation would be so mutually beneficial?

The old national prejudices are now fast wearing out of all our hearts, why not look forward to a time when they shall be altogether effaced ?

Whether, however, we act jointly with others, or alone, the time is surely now come when so large, so fair, and so accessible a portion of the earth should be no longer ignorantly or carelessly abandoned to barbarism ; when it is almost our duty, if it were not our interest, to spread through it what we can, whether of physical comfort or of moral and intellectual enlightenment. Happy, perhaps, is it for those nations that they have hitherto lived even so far undisturbed as they have, down to an age when it becomes possible for the European to have close intercourse with them, without carrying death and ruin in his train, when with a more humane because a wiser and more far-seeing policy than of old, it is acknowledged that we cannot hope ultimately to benefit and enrich ourselves unless we act so that our customers and allies be likewise enriched and benefited.

JUKES

*

(1848)

It is essential to the good government of the natives to treat them on a footing of equality. On this point most Europeans are grievously wanting ; they always adhere to their own customs, feelings, and manners, and in a way force the natives to conform to them, and never give themselves the trouble of ascertaining how far these manners or habits are repugnant to the prejudices of Eastern people. I have seen so much of this want of consideration for native customs that, had I power, I should be careful in the selection of persons to govern a new native country, and very severe on any display of harshness or severity. When we desire to improve and elevate a people, how ignorant of the first impulse of the human mind to treat them as an inferior race : and yet this is too generally the nature of European rule in Asiatic countries.

MUNDY

*

It is contended, and always will be contended, that the location of a just and liberal European people amid uncivilised or demi-civilised races, is calculated to advance the best interests of those races by the diffusion of knowledge, the impartial administration of justice, the liberal principles of government and the increase of commerce ; . . . but taking it in the most favourable point of view, granting that a government is all that it ought to be, let it be asked, have any people ever been so civilised, especially where the difference of colour stamps a mark of inextinguishable distinction between the governing and the governed ? Is it not as necessary for states as for individuals to form a distinctive character ? The vassalage of the mass, like the dependence of a single mind, may form a yielding, pliant, and even able character ; but, like wax, it retains one impression only, to be succeeded by the next that shall be given. The struggles of a nation, its internal contests, its dear-bought experience, its hard-earned rights, its gradual progress, are absolutely necessary to the development of freedom. Any other mode, any patent means is but reducing a people from a bad state to a worse, and whilst offering protection and food, depriving them of *all that stimulus* which leads to the independence of communities. Has any European nation ever been civilised by this process ? I know of none. The downfall of Rome was the first dawn of liberty to her conquered provinces ; and what struggles, what bloodshed, what civil wars, what alternate advancement and retrogression, have marked the strife of liberty in our own country ! How slow has been its pace ! How severe the training which has impregnated the mass with the desire as well as with the knowledge of freedom ! Could this otherwise have been ? Can it ever be ? Is not dependence, however slight, an insuperable bar ? I should answer, Yes. National independence is essential to the first dawn of political institutions, and that can only be affected in two ways : first, by the amalgamation of two races, the governing and the governed ; or secondly, by the expulsion of the former. In the case of the dark races, the latter is the only alternative ; and anybody who may not like this philosophy, must go the Penny Cyclopedia and look for one to suit his taste.

Ibid.

GUIDE TO SUBJECT-MATTER

INDEX OF PROPER NAMES ETC.

Most of the proper names mentioned in the text but not included in this list will be found on page 96.

Index of Proper Names

Index of Proper Names

INDEX OF SOURCES

Abraham, J. J., *The Surgeon's Log*, Impressions of the Far East (Chapman & Hall, 1911), 77, 87, 168, 186.

Adams, Arthur, F.L.S., *Travels of a Naturalist in Japan and Manchuria* (Hurst & Blackett, 1870), 33, 83, 84, 116.

Alabaster, Hy., *The Wheel of the Law* (Routledge, Kegan Paul, 1871), 174, 233.

Alcock, Sir R., *Art and Art Industries in Japan* (1878), 161.

— — *The Capital of the Tycoon* : a Narrative of a Three Years' Residence in Japan, 2 vols. (Longmans Green, 1863), 160.

Allen, H. N., M.D., *Korean Tales* (G. P. Putnam's Sons, New York, 1889), 268, 315.

Anon, 69, 251, 306, 336.

Arnold, Sir Edwin, K.C.I.E., C.S.I., *Adzuma, or the Japanese Wife* (Longmans Green, 1893), 289.

— — *Japonica* (J. R. Osgood, 1891), 162, 244, 260.

Asiatic Researches (London, 1820), 303.

Baber, E. Colborne, *Travels and Researches in Western China*, R.G.S. Supplementary Papers, Vol. I, Part 1 (John Murray, 1882), 39.

Ball, J. Dyer, *Things Chinese* (Sampson Low, 1893), 196.

Barrow, Sir John, *Travels in China* (Cadell & Davis, 1804), 134, 228.

— — *A Voyage to Cochin China–China in the Years 1792 and 1793* (London, 1806), 14, 205.

Batchelor, Ven. Dr. J., *The Ainu of Japan* (R.T.S. 1892), 125–6, 193, 208, 210, 211, 226, 230.

— — *Uwepekere, or Ainu Fireside Stories* (Tokyo, 1924), 239.

Beechey, Capt. F. W., *Narrative of a Voyage to the Pacific and Beering's Strait in 1825–6–7–8* (Colburn & Bentley, 1831), 3.

Bevan, T. F., *Toil, Travel and Discovery in British New Guinea* (Routledge, Kegan Paul, 1890), 88, 104.

Bishop, Mrs. I., *Korea and her Neighbours*, 2 vols. (John Murray, 1898), 245, 293, 336.

Bock, Carl, *The Headhunters of Borneo* (Sampson Low, 1881), 23, 26.

— — *Temples and Elephants* : the Narrative of a Journey of Exploration through Upper Siam and Lao (Sampson Low, 1881), 108.

Bowring, Sir John, *The Flowery Scroll* (Allen & Co., 1868), 299, 306.

— — *The Kingdom and People of Siam*, 2 vols. (John Parker, 1857), 225, 239.

Bridgeman, E. C., *Chinese Chrestomathy* (Macao, 1851), 134.

Bryan, J. Ingram, M.A., M.Litt., Ph.D., *Japanese All* (Methuen, 1928), 221.

Burbidge, F. W., *The Gardens of the Sun* (John Murray, 1880), 22, 200, 259.

Canton. *Description of the City of Canton* (Canton, 2nd ed., 1839), 32.

— *Canton Register*, 1828, 307.

Carles, W. R. F.R.G.S., *Life in Korea* (Macmillan, 1888), 72.

Chamberlain, B. H., *The Classical Poetry of the Japanese* (Routledge, Kegan Paul, 1880), 253, 295–8, 299, 306, 336, 337, 354.
— — *The Language, Mythology and Geographical Nomenclature of the Japanese* (Tokyo, Imperial University, 1887), 247 (*After* Chamberlain, 195, 211, 212).
Chinese Gleaner, Vol. I (1851), 136.
Codrington, R. H., D.D., *The Melanesians. Studies in their Anthropology and Folklore* (Oxford, Clarendon Press, 1891), 222, 265, 314.
Coleridge, H. J., S.J., *The Life and Letters of St. Francis Xavier* (Burns & Oates 1890), 82.
Crawfurd, John, F.R.S., *A Descriptive Dictionary of the Indian Islands and the Adjacent Countries* (London, 1856), 166, 181, 218.
— — *History of the Indian Archipelago*, 3 vols. (Edinburgh, 1820), 292, 302, 345.
— — *Journal of an Embassy . . . to the Court of Siam and Cochin-China* (Hy. Colburn, 1828), 99, 146, 238.
Cumming, C. F. Gordon, *At Home in Fiji* (Blackwood, 1882), 2, 203, 266 318.
— — *Wanderings in China* (Edinburgh, Blackwood, 1886), 34, 192, 226.

Davis, Sir J. F., *The Chinese*, 3 vols. (London, 1851), 136, 186, 304.
De Garis, F., *We Japanese* (Japan, n.d.,), 189, 240, 219, 236.
Dennys, N. B., Ph.D., *A Descriptive Dictionary of British Malaya* (London, 1894), 183.
Dickson, W., *Japan*, being a sketch of the history . . . of the Empire (London, 1869), 49.
Doolittle, Rev. J., *Social Life of the Chinese*, 2 vols. (Sampson Low, 1866), 209.
Drake, Sir Francis, *The World Encompassed*. Ed. W. S. W. Faux, M.A. (Hakluyt Society, 1854), 115.
Dudgeon, John, M.D., *The Diseases of China* (Glasgow, 1877), 232.
Dumoutier, G., *Les Chants et les Traditions Populaires des Annamites* (Paris, E. Leroux, 1890), 196, 203, 257, 260, 282, 301.

Earl, Geo. Windsor, *The Eastern Seas* or Voyages and Adventures in the Indian Archipelago in 1832–3–4 (London, 1837), 17, 111, 126, 203, 277.
East Indies, *A Voyage to the East Indies in 1747 and 1748* (London, 1762), 13, 31, 225.

Finlayson, Geo., *The Mission to Siam and Hué . . . in 1821–2* (John Murray, 1826), 101, 105.
Forbes, F. E., *Five Years in China from 1842–7*, with an account of the occupation of Labuan and Borneo (Rd. Bentley, 1848), 294.
Fortune, R., *Two Visits to the Tea Countries of China. . . .* 2 vols. (John Murray, 3rd ed., 1853), 41, 55, 145, 206.
— — *Yedo and Peking*, a Narrative of a Journey to . . . Japan and China (London, 1863), 61, 200.
Foster-Fraser, Sir John, *Round the World on a Wheel* (Methuen, 1899), 28, 30, 117.
Fryer, John, *A New Account of East Indies* (London, 1698), 234.
Fytche, Lt.-Gen. A., C.S.I., *Burma, Past and Present* (Routledge, Kegan Paul, 1878), 261.

Index of Sources

Giles, H. A., *Chinese Sketches* (London, Trübner, Shanghai, Kelly & Walsh, 1876), 242, 339.

Gill, W. W., *Myths and Songs from the South Pacific* (H. S. King, 1876), 308.

Goldsmith, *Citizen of the World* (1762), 142.

Golownin, Admiral V. M., *Recollections of Japan* (1819), 158.

Gray, John Henry, M.A., LL.D., *China*, a History of the Laws, Manners and Customs of the People, 2 vols. (Macmillan, 1878), 141, 184, 241.

Griffis, W. E., *Corea, the Hermit Nation* (W. H. Allen, 1882), 286, 319, 323, 340.

—— *The Mikado's Empire* (New York, Harper Brothers, 1876), 214, 339.

Guillemard, F. H. H., M.A., M.D., F.L.S., *The Cruise of the Marechesa to Kamschatka* (John Murray, 1886), 25, 26, 63, 76, 112, 229.

Guppy, H. H., *The Solomon Islands and their Natives* (Kegan Paul, 1887), 109, 110.

Gutzlaff, Chas., *Journal of Three Voyages along the Coast of China in 1831-2-3* (London, 1834), 134.

Hadfield, E., *Among the Natives of the Loyalty Group* (Macmillan, 1920), 182.

Hamilton, Alexander, *A New Account of the East Indies . . .* (Edinburgh, 1727), 240, 242, 254.

Han Yu (*d.* A.D. 874), scholar and official, 181.

Hearn, Lafcadio, *Glimpses of Unfamiliar Japan*, 2 vols. (Osgood; McIlvaine, 1894), 64, 65, 162.

—— *In Ghostly Japan* (Sampson Low, 1899), 66.

—— *Kokoro* (Osgood; McIlvaine, 1896), 63, 67.

—— *Kottō* (New York, The Macmillan Co., 1902), 66.

—— *Kwaidan* (Jonathan Cape, 1907), 190, 352.

—— *Out of the East* (Osgood; McIlvaine, 1895), 52.

Hübner, Baron de, *A Ramble Round the World*, 1871. Trans. by Lady Herbert, 2 vols. (Macmillan, 1874), 50, 65, 160.

Huc, E. R., *The Chinese Empire*, 2 vols. (London, 1855), 137-40.

Hunt, Leigh. *Selected Essays*, 348.

Jukes, J. Beete, M.A., F.G.S., *Narrative of the Voyage of H.M.S. Fly. . . .* 2 vols. (London, 1847), 36, 81, 167, 356-9.

Kaempfer, E., M.D., *The History of Japan*, 2 vols. (London, 1728), 57, 58, 73, 89, 152-7, 231.

Kartini, Raden Adjeng, *Letters of a Javanese Princess*. Trans. from the Dutch by Agnes L. Symmers (Duckworth, 1921), 68.

Lowell, P., *Chosön, the Land of Morning Calm* (Routledge, Kegan Paul, 1885), 72, 169-72, 228, 231, 245-7.

—— *Occult Japan* (Boston and New York, Houghton Mifflin & Co., 1895), 163, 235.

Lyne, Chas., *New Guinea* (Sampson Low, 1885), 118.

Man, E. H., *On the Aboriginal Inhabitants of the Andaman Islands* (Routledge, Kegan Paul, 1883), 12.

Mandeville, *The Voyage and Travaile of . . .* (London, 1727), 37-9.

375

Marryat, F. S., *Borneo and the Indian Archipelago* (Longmans, Brown, Green & Longmans, 1848), 19–21, 54, 73, 106, 147, 224.

Marsden, Wm., F.R.S., *The History of Sumatra* (London, 2nd ed., 1784), 176.
— — *The Travels of Marco Polo* (London, 1818), 120.

M‘Leod, John, *Narrative of a Voyage . . . to the Yellow Sea and . . . to the Island of Lewchew* (Murray, 1817), 74–5.

McMahon, Lt.-Col. A. R., F.R.G.S., *The Karens of the Golden Chersonese* (Harrison, 1876), 27, 51, 264.

McNair, Major J. F. A., R.A., C.M.G., *Perak and the Malays* (Tinsley Bros., 1878), 103, 198.

Melville, H., *Moby Dick*, 5.
— — *Typee*, 4.

Mendoza, Juan C. de., *The History of the . . . Kingdom of China* (Hakluyt Society, 1853–4), 130.

Milburn, Wm. (Compiler), *Oriental Commerce* (Ed. Thos. Thornton, M.R.A.S.), London, 1825, 32, 58.

Mitford, A. B., *Tales of Old Japan* (Macmillan, 1871), 267.

Moresby, Capt. J., *Discoveries and Surveys in New Guinea* (John Murray, 1876), 44–6, 69.

Mouat, F. J., M.D., F.R.C.S., *Adventures and Researches among the Andaman Islanders* (Hurst & Blackett, 1863), 11.

Mouhot, Henri, *Travels in the Central Parts of Indo-China (Siam), Cambodia and Laos in 1858–59–60*, 2 vols. (John Murray, 1864), 13, 276, 285, 332, 342, 350.

Moule, A. E., *New China and Old* (Seeley & Co., 1891), 90, 207, 220.

Mundy, Capt. Rodney, *Narrative of Events in Borneo and Celebes . . . from the Journals of the . . . the Rajah of Sarawak* (John Murray, 1848), 22, 359–361.

Neale, F. A., *Narrative of a Residence at the Capital of the Kingdom of Siam* (Office of the National Illustrated Library, 1852), 258.

Newbold, T. J., *Political and Statistical Account of . . . the Straits of Malacca*, 2 vols. (John Murray, 1839), 172.

Okakura, K., *The Book of Tea* (London and New York, G. P. Putnam's Sons, 1906), 337.
— Y., *The Japanese Spirit* (Constable, 1905), 48, 164.

Omori, Annie S., and Doi, Kochi, *Diaries of Court Ladies of Old Japan* (New York, 1920), 326.

Osbeck, Peter, *A Voyage to China and the East Indies, 1751. . . .* 2 vols. (London, 1771), 131.

Paske, C. D., Deputy Surgeon-General, *Life and Travel in Lower Burma* (W. H. Allen, 1892), 29.

Penny, A., *Ten Years in Melanesia* (Wells Gardner, n.d.), 46, 92, 108.

Pinto, Fernand Mendez, *The Voyages and Adventures of Fernand Mendez Pinto* (London, 1653), 95.

Polo, Marco, *The Travels of Marco Polo* (New York, n.d.), 11, 89, 113.

Pratt, G. (Translator), *Some Folk Songs and Myths from Samoa* (Sydney, The Royal Society of New South Wales, 1891), 212.

Index of Sources

Raffles, Sir T. S., *The History of Java*, 2 vols. (John Murray, 2nd ed., 1830), 165, 166, 253.

Reed, Sir E. J., K.C.B., *Japan, its History, Traditions and Religions.* . . . 2 vols. (John Murray, 1880), 60, 322.

Rennie, D. F., M.D., *Peking and the Pekingese*, 2 vols. (London, 1865), 98.

Romilly, H. H., C.M.G., *From My Verandah in New Guinea.* . . . (David Nutt, 1889), 309, 328.

Rundall, Thos. (Editor), *Memorials of the Empire of Japon in the XVIth and XVIIth Centuries* (Hakluyt Society, 1850), 149, 150, 159.

Ryley, J. H., *Ralph Fitch, England's Pioneer to India and Burma* (Fisher Unwin, 1899), 94.

Satow, Sir E. M., K.C.M.G. (Editor), *The Voyage of Captain John Saris to Japan, 1613* (Hakluyt Society, 1900), 2.

Seeman, B., Ph.D., F.L.S., F.R.G.S., *Viti: An Account of a Government Mission to the Vitian or Fijian Islands in 1860–61* (Macmillan, 1862), 114.

Shuay Yoe (Scott), *The Burman, his Life and Notions*, 2 vols. (Macmillan, 1882), 252.

Sirr, Hy. Chas., M.A., *China and the Chinese*, 2 vols. (W. S. Orr, 1849), 234.

Smeaton, D. M., *The Loyal Karens of Burma* (Routledge, Kegan Paul, 1887), 283, 346.

Smyth, H. Warington, M.A., LL.B., F.G.S., F.R.G.S., *Five Years in Siam from 1891–6*, 2 vols. (John Murray, 1898), 174, 224.

Stockdale, J. J., *Sketches, Civil and Military, of the Island of Java and its immediate Dependencies* (London, 1811), 16, 195, 218.

Suyematsu, K., *Genji Monogatori* (Routledge, Kegan Paul, 1882), 280–82.

Swettenham, Sir F. A., *About Perak* (Straits Times, 1893), 1, 103, 173.

Taw Sein Ko, K.I.H., I.S.O., *Burmese Sketches* (British Burma Press, 1913), 188.

Thomas, Pascoe, *A True . . . Journal of a Voyage to the South Seas, 1740–1744* (1745), 130.

Thomson, J., *The Straits of Malacca, Indo-China and China* (Sampson Low, 1875), 107.

Thomson, J. T. (Translator), *Hakayat Abdulla, c. 1840* (King, 1874), 354.

Thunberg, C. P., M.D., *Travels in Europe, Africa and Asia between the Years 1770 and 1779*, 4 vols. (W. Richardson, n.d.), 58, 157–8.

Vincent, Frank, *The Land of the White Elephant* (Sampson Low, 1873), 128.

Wallace, Alfred Russell, *The Malay Archipelago*, 2 vols. (Macmillan, 1869), 197.

Wang Ta-Hai, *A Desultory Account of the Malayan Archipelago* (Chinese Miscellany, Part. II, 1791). Translated into English, 1849, 17.

Williams, Thos., *Fiji and the Fijians*, Vol. I. *The Islands and their Inhabitants* (Alexander Heylin, 2nd ed., revised 1860), 148, 190.

Winston, W. R., *Four Years in Upper Burma* (Epworth Press, 1892), 127.

Woodard, David, *The Narrative of Captain David Woodard and four Seamen . . . in the Island of Celebes* (1791). London, 1804, 128–9.

Younghusband, Capt. Francis, *Among the Celestials* (John Murray, 1898), 85.